The
Garland
CLASSICS OF
FILM LITERATURE

REPRINTED IN PHOTO-FACSIMILE
IN 32 VOLUMES

MAKING A FILM

Lindsay Anderson

GARLAND PUBLISHING, INC. ● NEW YORK & LONDON ● 1977

This edition published by arrangement
with George Allen & Unwin Ltd.

Library of Congress Cataloging in Publication Data

Anderson, Lindsay, 1923-
 Making a film.

 (The Garland classics of film literature ; 1)
 Reprint of the 1952 ed. published by Allen
and Unwin, London.
 1. Secret people. [1. Motion picture]
I. Title. II. Series.
PN1997.S32 1977 791.43'7 76-52087
ISBN 0-8240-2863-5

Printed in the United States of America

Making a Film

Prod. 741. 28th March, '51. Night Int. VIEUX CHAPEAU
Script scene. B53. Slate 47
Camera. Mitchell A7. Lens, 35 mm. 3.2
Focus, 4'-7'

PLAYBACK FOXTROT, TANGO.
C.S. Panning and Tracking and finishing in M.C.S.
MARIA, LOUIS, ANSELMO
FRENCH GIRL, NORA, RODD
STEENIE, DANCERS, CROWD
FIVE-PIECE BAND
WAITERS, CIGARETTE GIRL

Camera shoots on to DANCING COUPLE
in C.S. They dance out l. and MARIA
AND LOUIS dance into shot and then
continue dancing left round the floor
CAMERA PANS WITH THEM
AND TRACKS BACK
They talk as they dance

LOUIS. *I've forgotten how to dance*

Making a Film

THE STORY OF 'SECRET PEOPLE'

Chronicled and Edited by
LINDSAY ANDERSON

Together with the Shooting Script of the Film
by Thorold Dickinson and
Wolfgang Wilhelm

> This is how things are really put
> together. And to re-experience this as
> it takes place, and to participate in
> it oneself, seems to me a most useful
> and productive process for a student.
> SERGEI EISENSTEIN in *Film Form*

London
GEORGE ALLEN AND UNWIN LTD.
Ruskin House Museum Street

PRINTED IN GREAT BRITAIN
in Georgian type
BY THE BLACKFRIARS PRESS LTD
LEICESTER

Introduction

The intention of this book is to give to the interested reader an impression of what it is like to make a feature film in a British studio to-day. By 'the interested reader' I mean the reader who finds himself already intrigued by this powerful and still comparatively novel method of communication. This is not one of those books which seeks to go out among the literate unconverted and persuade them that the cinema is an *art*, and that it is their moral, social, æsthetic duty to cultivate a response to it. That ground has already been sufficiently covered.

Nor do I claim that this book will tell you how a film is made. It sets out to give you a day-to-day account of how a film *was* made, which is a different thing. 'To generalise is to be an idiot.' Of course, in spite of Blake, we all draw generalisations from the particular; but he was right to the extent that all generalisations except the platitudinous will sooner or later be falsified. Circumstances alter cases. So do personalities. The many attempts which have already been made to describe the film-making process by detailed analysis of the various functions involved are usually limited in their rewards (it seems to me) precisely because they omit these considerations— which are not merely intriguing or amusing in a gossipy way, but also relevant and influential creative factors.

Certainly the aim of this book, to cover something of the circumstantial as well as the technical side of the business, is exposed to its own hazards. Temperamentally I am with Mr. Mybug in believing in 'utter frankness about these things,' but readers will appreciate that no such account as this can either tell the whole truth, or even be quite all true. (A comment on maliciousness and stupidity in human nature rather than a hint at dark or disgraceful secrets behind the making of this film). There is anyway enough of the truth in the pages that follow for me not to be afraid to admit a civilised percentage of omission.

Inevitably, the arrangement of this book to a certain extent reflects the complexity of the process it describes. Readers will probably prefer to find their own way about it; but I would recommend that instead of proceeding strictly in the order in which it is assembled, they acquaint themselves with the story of the film, and its scope, by reading the script before starting on the account of its preparation. Ideally, one would like to have reproduced the full 'treatment' of the subject after the section entitled 'Beginnings,' for comparison with the final shooting script, but lack of space made this impossible. Also regretfully curtailed is the account of processes which the film goes through between the end of shooting and its full completion. This, I hope, will be found the fault of a virtue. It was judged that the interest of the book as a whole would be considerably greater if its appearance could coincide with, or even precede, the first public distribution of the film. As a result, parts of it had to go to the press before the whole was completed, and the rest followed almost immediately on the end of shooting.

I am grateful to very many people who have helped me. First of all to Thorold Dickinson, who had the original idea for this book, and without whose constant interest and extraordinary indulgence—at a time when he was fully occupied with matters of much greater importance—the thing could never have been done at all. To Denis Forman, Ernest Lindgren and the Governors of the British Film Institute, who helped to make the scheme practicable; to Sir Michael Balcon and the Directors of Ealing Studios, who so readily allowed me the necessary facilities; to Sidney Cole, producer of the picture. I thank also my friends Christopher Barry, who most kindly assisted me in the tiresome business of proof-reading, and Gavin Lambert, who read most of the typescript and made valuable suggestions.

Which brings me to Ealing. Looking back over the months, I am amazed at the toleration—often even welcome—extended towards me by every department in the studio, and in particular by the technicians and actors on the picture. If amongst all these I mention by name Ralph Hogg and Spike Priggen, and the ladies and gentlemen of Mr. Dooley's stills department, it is only because I think I subjected them to even greater strain than most. But to all, my thanks. I hope that the dedication of this book will not seem any the less personal or sincere because it has had unavoidably to be collective: in my mind it includes everyone, named and unnamed, who helped to make *Secret People*.

LINDSAY ANDERSON

To the Unit

CONTENTS

Introduction   page v

BEGINNINGS   11

PREPARATION   16

Unit List   53

Schedules   56

THE DIARY   58

THE SCRIPT   131

Appendices
    I   *Treatment into Script*   202
    II   *Script into Film*   206
    III *Music*   215
    IV *Steps after Shooting*   216
    V   *Studio Plan*   217
    VI *Full Credit Titles*   218
    VII *Biographical Notes*   222

ILLUSTRATIONS
between pages 128-129

Beginnings

The true beginnings of *Secret People* go back a long way before 1951, its year of production—ten years back, in fact, to a morning in December, 1940, when the film producer, Michael Balcon, and the film director, Thorold Dickinson, reported at the War Office to discuss the making of a film which might discourage the prevalent wartime vice of careless talk. This meeting renewed a broken acquaintanceship: although Dickinson had edited a picture for Balcon some years back, he had left Ealing—where he had been in charge of the Cutting Rooms—shortly before Balcon arrived in 1938 to take charge of production. As a result of their discussion that morning, a film was commissioned, to be made by Ealing Studios for the armed forces: almost immediately Dickinson (who was to be responsible for the story basis of the film as well as its direction) left for a Northern seaport, to investigate the background of his subject.

Those of his researches which led directly to *The Next of Kin* do not concern us here. In making them, however, and working in the closest co-operation with the political police—more properly known as the Special Branch—Dickinson was made free of a number of facts of a kind not usually revealed to the layman. One of these, an example of the effect of public violence on the private conscience of a worker for an illegal political organisation, lingered in his mind with particular obstinacy. Its potentialities as a film subject impressed him immediately; and besides its quality simply as a *story*, it carried implications which seemed as useful as they were sympathetic. Here was the true conception of our film.

The delivery was to be protracted. First there was *The Next of Kin* to be made, and after that a series of training films for the Army: the idea had to wait. But it was far from forgotten, and in 1945, when Dickinson came at last to the end of two exhausting years' work on his African subject, *Men of Two Worlds*, he brought it into the air and discussed possible approaches to the subject with Joyce Cary (responsible for the script of *Men of Two Worlds*). Progress was soon checked, though, by an abortive visit to India, undertaken at the request of the India Office. Returning, Dickinson was invalided into hospital. It was only after his recovery some months later that the subject could be tackled in earnest. By the end of 1946 there was in existence, the property of Two Cities Films, Ltd., a full treatment of *Secret People*, by Joyce Cary and Thorold Dickinson.

It is interesting to consider this treatment in comparison with later versions of the story. Written in terms of action and dialogue (very few specifically cinematic directions), it is composed of 54 scenes varying in length from a half to three or four pages each. It is the story of Maria Brent, a widow in her late thirties, living in pre-war London with her father-in-law and her daughter,

Nora. The Brents run a little Café in Soho, assisted by a cockney girl called Pinkie, who lives with them over the shop; Mr. Brent is a liberal-minded old gentleman with a philosophic turn of mind, and Nora dances in the chorus at a non-stop variety theatre. Maria herself is of foreign birth (her nationality is not specified), and her country is now under a totalitarian government which has imprisoned her brother Philip. The narrative begins with the visit to London of a dignitary of this government, General Albern; Maria and old Mr. Brent attend a stormy public meeting at which he speaks, and after it Maria attempts to intercede with the General on behalf of her brother. Brusquely rebuffed, she turns away to find herself face to face with an old friend, Louis Kelman, with whom she had worked as a revolutionary many years before, and from whom she had been separated by the hazards of their occupations. Unknown to Maria, Louis is in London with Steenie Green (described in the script as 'a killer, a little middle-aged Englishman') to assassinate General Albern: he is still working for the same international revolutionary organisation. Meeting Nora, Louis decides to make use of her and Maria; he arranges that she shall perform in the cabaret at a private party given for Albern some days later, and that she shall be accompanied by her mother. He persuades Maria to carry with her a bomb, which she will hand over to another member of the organisation at the party.

The plan misfires: the bomb kills a waitress, who bleeds to death in Maria's arms. Returning, horrified at what she has seen, Maria threatens Louis that she will inform on him to the police if he does not abandon such methods. He lies to her; when she realises that his purpose is unshaken, she goes to Scotland Yard. Louis, Steenie and other members of the gang take refuge in the Café. The police close in and shooting starts. A bomb is thrown. As a result, the members of the organisation are either killed or (in the case of Louis) presumed so. Maria, unconscious, is removed by the police under cover of the confusion. Recovering, she is told that by turning King's Evidence she has earned a pardon for her offence, but that if she is not to be murdered by Louis' confederates, she will have to change her name, submit to plastic surgery, start life afresh elsewhere. She agrees. Maria Brent becomes Lena Martin.

An epilogue comes some years later, after the intervention of the war. We are in the Middle East, where Lena Martin is working as a nurse in a military hospital, tending the victims of civil violence. Nora Brent comes to perform in a touring revue, and her mother goes to see her dance. After the show, she visits her daughter. Nora does not recognise her, but Louis, who suddenly appears, does. Seeing that he is making use of Nora just as he made use of her, Maria pleads with her daughter to leave him. She signals to the Police who have been following her; in fury, Louis turns on her and stabs her in the breast. Maria dies in Nora's arms as Louis is led away by the Police.

This was a full treatment of Dickinson's original idea, but from a script-writer's point of view it represented only a beginning. The next necessity was to 'break it down' into true script form, work out the visual progression of the story with indications of cuts and camera behaviour—the translation of the bare prose narrative into the peculiar language of cinema. But in films the unexpected always happens. Two Cities suddenly acquired the rights of Somerset Maugham's novel 'Then and Now', and Dickinson was assigned to it. So 1947 was spent instead on the production of a full shooting script of this subject. By the end of the year designs were complete, locations chosen and a budget allocated when the Production Chief of Two Cities resigned and the project was written off. Dickinson left the company a little later, taking his own subject, *Secret People*, with him.

The year 1948 saw no further progress on *Secret People*. For Anatole de Grunewald, Dickinson directed *The Queen of Spades*, an assignment which occupied his full attention for nearly a year. After it, when there was time to look around again, two subjects presented themselves. One, of course, was Dickinson's own, the other a property owned by Associated British and being considered by them as a vehicle for one of their stars, and a prestige production for Festival year. Of these, the latter—*The Mayor of Casterbridge*—won priority, and in collaboration with the screen-writer, Wolfgang Wilhelm, Dickinson set to work on an adaptation of Hardy's novel. This had been brought to the same state of readiness as *Then and Now*, when the British cinema plunged into its latest, still persisting crisis. It became evident that an undertaking so ambitious would run considerable risk of loss unless it were either cut into incomprehensibility or produced virtually as an American film. Rather than attempt a butchered version, Dickinson abandoned it; with Wilhelm he turned again to *Secret People*.

Though the way was yet far from clear for the production of the film, we can say that the last lap had begun. After some months of work, Dickinson and Wilhelm produced a new treatment of the story, preserving its feeling and implications, as well as its general outline, but embodying also substantial alterations: Maria and Nora now became sisters, arriving in England as refugees; Philip, the brother, was replaced by Pietro Brentano, the father; Mr. Brent became Anselmo Porri, an émigré café-proprietor and friend of Brentano's. The meeting between Maria and Louis was sited at the Paris Exhibition of 1937, and the last stages of the story were telescoped to some eight months after the fight in the Café, with no interlude of war. Undoubtedly this version presented the subject in a more readily cinematic form, and Dickinson was determined that, with so much thought and work sunk into it, *Secret People* should now be brought to life—if not by an established studio, then by himself, in independent production. Fortunately, this last remedy proved unnecessary; for this is where our wheel, through its long circuit of nine years, comes full circle, and there appears on the scene a producer who shows sympathetic interest in the subject. In Sir Michael Balcon's own words: 'During this period, Dickinson and I used to return home after Film Academy meetings, and since, in a manner of speaking, I had been in at the conception of *Secret People*, he used to tell me of the progress he was making. When, therefore, in June, 1950, he told me that he would not be able to make *Secret People* at Elstree, I was most anxious to help. We discussed the possibility of his setting up to produce it independently or, alternatively, of coming to make it at Ealing. With this in mind I asked him to send me a copy of the script, which fully confirmed the impression I had received from our talks: here was a project which should definitely be given every encouragement, and which would be well worth having at Ealing. The latter alternative, for Dickinson, had the advantage of liberating him from many of the economic and administrative duties that would have fallen on his shoulders as an independent producer, so he accepted . . .'

The Ealing to which Dickinson thus returned in 1950 was in many respects a different studio from the one he had left nine years before. Though its record for continuity of production had always been an enviable one (unique, in fact, in the British cinema), its progress during the war and the years that followed had been remarkable. With an emphasis generally on realism of setting and everyday qualities in stories, relying on craftsmanship rather than extravagant spending to achieve polish and showmanship, Ealing had succeeded in building up a reputation out of all proportion to its size, as the makers of films of quality and enterprise. To take a few examples at random: such pictures as *Went The Day Well?, San Demetrio, London, The Overlanders, Hue and Cry, It Always Rains on Sunday, Kind Hearts and Coronets, Whisky Galore!, The Blue Lamp,* were mostly written, and all directed and made by the small nucleus of writers and technicians under regular contract to the studio; continuity of production and a strong tradition of team work secured for the Ealing film a certain familiarity of tone, a recognisable bias in approach to subjects, characterisation and treatment.

Such an achievement—and in the British cinema at least it has been a very rare one—is not without its dangers. There comes a point where consistency declines into sameness. Besides his interest in the script and his respect for Dickinson's ability as a director, Sir Michael was influenced to make his offer by his awareness of such a risk: '*Secret People* came as a welcome blood-transfusion, a stranger bride in a family tending towards inbreeding, bringing to Ealing a new director and with him new actors.

There is one final aspect of this renewed collaboration about which Sir Michael has written, and which deserves full quotation—not merely for its relevance to *Secret People*, but for the cheerful light it throws upon this relationship between producer and director (a relationship whose importance is too seldom recognised outside the industry). 'There was . . . one more major factor: my admiration for and interest in Thorold Dickinson. Although I had worked with him only rarely, I had watched his work closely, and it seemed to me that he had been given little opportunity to do himself—and the British film industry—justice. All too often he had been given scripts not of his own choosing, scripts not worthy of his great ability. In *Secret People* he at last had a script of his own making, something essentially of the cinema and not adapted from novel or play, something in which both emotionally and intellectually he was very much involved; in fact a subject to which he could bring his full enthusiasm as well as his usual skill. It seemed to me it would be a tragic loss if he were not able to go ahead. Besides, I was concerned at this time with the groundwork for the plan that was to become the Group scheme of the National Film Finance Corporation. I felt that this scheme, by leaving the independent producer the freedom to make films of his own choice, while removing much of the business responsibility that is so irksome to people concerned with artistic problems, would above all profit such a man as Thorold Dickinson; and, in fact, that if the scheme were to function at all as a worthwhile contribution to the fight against the producers' difficulties, it needed such men, bringing to it their ability and experience. With his possible membership of the Group in mind, I wanted to renew my friendship with him, and to come into closer contact with him at work.'

Such then was the long record of endeavour, disappointment and eventual good fortune which lay behind this subject before it ever got near a studio floor. In the late summer of 1950 agreement was reached as to terms and divisions of responsibility: as the first film to be made under the new system of organisation at Ealing, *Secret People* would receive the overall label of 'A Thorold Dickinson Production', and Sidney Cole, an Ealing associate producer, would act as producer. In all other respects, the picture would go through in the routine way, with finance, facilities and technicians provided by the studio. Contracts were signed, and *Secret People* was entered into the Ealing schedule for production in the early spring of 1951.

Preparation

The façade of Ealing Studios, where it fronts on to Ealing Green, is, for a film studio, remarkably unpretentious. Discreet behind a little stone wall, a clump of green and a semi-circular strip of grass, the 'Front Office' resembles a private house rather than a factory; its whitewashed walls are unadorned, its front door is sheltered by a neat, columned portico. Were it not for the words 'Ealing Studios' on the wall above the first-storey windows and the commissionaire at the gate, you would almost certainly pass it by. Nor is this first pleasant impression dispelled as you penetrate further. Walking down the bottleneck which leads from the road to the studio proper, you pass on your left, behind the front office block, a row of domesticated pines, a lawn with flower beds, and a pair of beehives. Within, there is an absence of vast perspectives; the sound stages do not loom, the decor is comfortable rather than spectacular, and easily assimilable.

These things are important in the sense that the atmosphere in which any creative, co-operative work is done is important. Ealing has for long prided itself on being 'the studio with the team spirit'—the slogan, inscribed large on one of the walls, dates back to the days of Basil Dean, but its message remains valid. Its relative smallness, its continuity of policy and employment, have resulted in an atmosphere of friendliness, of at least superficial intimacy, which contrasts markedly with the less personal climates of the larger film-producing plants. By nothing is this better exemplified than in the universal use (in the canteen, on the telephone exchange as well as on the floor) of Christian names. The practice is common, of course, throughout the cinema-- even more so than in the theatre; and it is a good one in so far as it expresses, or helps to create, a genuine camaraderie of endeavour. It can be overdone: the prop man on the floor of *Quartet* who invited the author to 'have a cup of char, Somerset,' was certainly going too far. But at Ealing the habit comes naturally. In the words of a critic, 'its films, one feels, are made by a family for the family'.

Granted this state of affairs, the introduction of an 'outside' subject, with an 'outside' director, into the schedule was an experiment that might easily have been unwelcome; but if *Secret People* caused any resentment in the family circle, it was never even slightly evident. Inevitably there was an admission that this was not, in the usual sense, an Ealing subject; but this seemed to be considered by most people, as by Sir Michael, a refreshment rather than an imposition. So, from the beginning of October, 1950, when Thorold Dickinson moved into an office with his name on the door, gathered around him the tiny nucleus of a unit, and started to prepare for the production of his film, he was welcomed freely into the fold, as a *revenant* rather than a newcomer.

For a film scheduled to go into production in the Spring, October may seem an early date at which to start preparation. The two primary characteristics of film-making, however—its complexity and its expense—make exhaustive pre-planning of the utmost importance. While a film is on the floor—in the process of shooting—it is saddled with the overheads of the entire studio, in addition to the expenses in the wages of the unit, actors, film stock and processing. Obviously, if an extra month of preparation by an advance guard of two or three can save even half a day of shooting, it will represent time and money well spent. Ahead of most subjects at this stage, *Secret People* arrived at Ealing in the form of a full and already much-considered treatment. From this (before contracts were signed) the Production Department had satisfied themselves that the film could be made within a budget and a schedule which conformed to the general practice and resources of the studio. But in spite of this agreement that the subject could and would be produced on a relatively modest scale, its scope was such as to involve a greater amount of preparatory work than usual.

This sprang directly from the nature of the script. For instance: the action takes place chiefly in London, with exteriors to be shot in a number of streets and at a palatial country house. Important episodes also occur in Paris and Dublin. At an early stage it had to be decided exactly where these scenes were to be shot. In or out of the studio? If outside, locations would have to be searched for and picked. Starting from the assumption that at least some of the foreign sequences would be shot on the spot, it would be necessary to make preliminary trips abroad as soon as possible. A further complication of setting was provided by a sequence to be played at the Paris Exhibition of 1937. This could hardly be recreated entire in the studio; material shot at the actual exhibition would have to be found of sufficient quality and variety to submit to re-editing and incorporation in the film as an 'establishing' sequence. The story is set in two periods, neither the present: a prologue in 1930, and the main action in 1937. This would raise certain problems for research. One of the principal characters is a dancer: an actress would have to be found who could dance, or a dancer who could act; a choreographer would have to be engaged to design her dances and the ballet in which she stars; a composer would have to be brought in to work on this well before the film went into production (much earlier than would normally be the case).

Most urgent of all was the question of casting. Few of the supporting characters in the story presented much difficulty, but the two principals would call for a search. From the start, Dickinson was sure that neither Maria nor Louis could be satisfactorily played by British actors. Each (Maria especially) was an arduous part, demanding acting of intelligence and experience; each would need previous knowledge of English. Unfortunately, Britain's economic position, and the scarcity of dollars, seemed to rule out the possibility of signing any of the English-speaking Europeans who had acquired familiarity with the language—together with drawing-power at the box office—in Hollywood. It had been agreed by the studio that the first consideration in casting these parts was quality rather than commercial appeal; it would be pleasant, though, if the two could be combined.

Besides these particular problems, there remained the steps of preparation that are common to every film: designing sets and costumes, budgeting the production, scheduling it for the most efficient and economical progress possible through the period of shooting. Most of these routine (and therefore vital) arrangements would be dependent on the form of the final, elaborated script. Before they could be proceeded with, the 'Full Treatment' would have to be expanded into a 'First Draft Shooting Script', broken down into shots

17

specifying intended positions and movements of the camera; from this estimates of time and finance could be drawn.

Between reading about these routines—basically the same for every film that is made—and witnessing them in operation, there is likely to be a vast difference. On paper they are apt to be neatly subdivided into mutually exclusive categories; as we read, we hear the machine tick over sweetly, harmoniously efficient. In practice, the effect is more confused. As Thorold (the reader must now consent to enter the charmed circle) remarked early on, after a day spent researching into the details of the Paris Exhibition, viewing a documentary on Montmartre, interviewing actors, giving tea to a visiting journalist, discussing casting possibilities for Maria and Louis: 'It's like preparing an enormous meal, in which you're getting the *apfelstrudel* ready at the same time as the meat-and-rice dish.' Any outline of the process which simplifies away this untidiness, this simultaneity, presents a false impression; to be truthful we must go, as far as is possible, chronologically. Unfortunately, the relation of such events with absolute fulness and freedom would result in a volume about the length of 'Ulysses', and almost as sensational. Considerable condensation will be necessary; but it will be possible to supplement the bird's-eye view occasionally with glimpses from closer at hand, as the months dwindle into weeks, into days, until the prepared film goes in front of the camera.

October

When work first starts on Secret People, five months, spacious as eternity, yawn betwen us and the start of shooting (tentatively fixed for early March). On the floor, Basil Dearden is shooting the final scenes of Pool of London, as Charles Crichton starts The Lavender Hill Mob. This will be followed at the end of the year by Sandy Mackendrick's The Man in the White Suit— also to be produced by Sid Cole. This means that Sid will have to divide his time between the two assignments, so it is as well that Thorold is provided with a personal assistant—Freddy Shaughnessy, a post-war recruit at Ealing, officially employed as reader and apprentice script-writer, in practice ready for any function on his way up to the position of Associate Producer. At this stage, this trio is the unit. The others who will comprise it are either as yet unappointed, or—as in the case of William Kellner, who will be Art Director —too busy on the studio's current productions to be available for anything more than an occasional consultation.

Researches into the Paris Exhibition and the hunt for suitable newsreel material; preliminary investigation of London locations; first steps towards the planning of the ballet; tentative casting of the leading supporting parts— these are some of the occupations of the month. But its chief feature is a twelve-day trip abroad by Thorold and Sid, Paris-Rome-Paris, in search of Paris locations, further material on the Exhibition, and, most important, a Maria and a Louis.

OCTOBER 2ND.—Location cruise by Thorold and Freddy locates the script's Morton Street (for Anselmo's Café) in Paddington; a likely-looking café is already in position, and opposite is a greengrocer's which will transform easily into Daly's Chemist's Shop.

OCTOBER 4TH.—Four actors whom Thorold has in mind for important supporting parts are invited to the Studio, and given scripts to read: Megs Jenkins, for Penny; Irene Worth, for Miss Jackson; Charles Goldner, for Anselmo; Reginald Tate, for Inspector Elliot. So far ahead nothing definite can be fixed, and some testing will be necessary; at this stage one can only establish contact and attempt to generate interest. Irene Worth, it seems, will need persuading.

OCTOBER 5TH.—To the Ministry of Works, Exhibition Dept. Interview with the Assistant Commissioner, in charge of the British pavilion during most of the 1937 Paris Exhibition. Illustrated literature is borrowed; the architect of the Pavilion is contacted; he arranges to let us have his original plans.

Hitchcock's Sabotage (1937) is shown, and seen by Anthony Mendleson, costume designer for the Studio. He has not yet read the script, but is intrigued at the idea of dressing his characters in costumes of this period. Difficulties: 'Men's clothes weren't so very different; the women's will be far more difficult —old enough to be dowdy, but too recent to be costume.' He would like a

19

talk with Thorold soon. 'It'll be a change if I can design the clothes *before* the scenes are shot.'

OCTOBER 11TH.—Material on the Paris Exhibition is viewed at Movietone (Newsreels) and at the National Film Library, where Ernest Lindgren has found a print of a film made by Philips' Electric—*Lumière, L'âme de l'Exposition*—celebrating their installations. This turns out to end half-way; perhaps the second reel can be located in Paris.

OCTOBER 12TH.—Before setting out for Paris, Thorold manages to borrow William Kellner off *The Lavender Hill Mob*, for a discussion of general principles. The plan at present is to shoot at any rate the night exteriors on location: this involves a *bistro* where Louis and Steenie meet the Paris members of the organisation, and a *quai* on the Seine for Steenie's murder of the informer. Also originals are wanted for Louis' lodgings in Paris and the *Vieux Chapeau* night club. Further talk explores some of the difficulties presented by economic reconstruction of the Paris Exhibition.

OCTOBER 13TH — OCTOBER 25TH.—Foreign reconnaissance, Paris - Rome - Paris, by Thorold and Sid. Paris first, where work is started at once on the three objects of the expedition. Pathé newsreels are contacted, and promise to look out their coverage on the Exhibition. The original site is inspected. Various theatrical agents are put to work on suggestions for casting. Principally, for Louis, Thorold has François Perier in mind, whose recent appearance in *Orphèe* contrasted so with his generally light performances. But Perier is in a play and may not be free. His agent suggests Serge Reggiani, out of town at the moment, but available for interview when Thorold and Sid return from Rome.

The next four and a half days are full. Films and shows are vetted—*Vulcano, Domenica d'Agosto, The Empire Revue, Manèges, Bobosse* (Perier's play), the *Cirque Medrano*. Perier is met and Thorold recounts the story of the film in tortured French. Evenings in gay *boîtes* (*Vieux Chapeau?*) Trips to the Seine quayside. Dinner with *cinéaste* and old friend Berthold Bartosch ('Louis' lodgings?' Thorold murmurs to Sid, looking round the apartment). Newsreels are inspected at Pathé, and a 'scratch print' ordered of possible useful sequences. (*Scratch Print:* a print disfigured by a continuous scratch down the centre of picture, to prevent pirate infringements of copyright. In London a final choice of usable material can be made with the editor of the film while the print is still held by customs. Thus the footage of film actually imported—on which duty must be paid—can be reduced to a minimum.) Philips think they can locate the second reel of their film in time for viewing next week.

Mid-day on Wednesday the 18th, by air to Rome, where assignments are simpler. Here the search is purely for actors—above all for a Maria. Of the two actresses in the world who come to mind for the part, one is beyond reach, under contract to a Hollywood company. But Lea Padovani, whose performance in *Give Us This Day* made such an impression, is in Rome. Contacted on Thursday, she is introduced to the subject. She is interested, but warns that her plans for next year may make a visit to Britain impossible. By Monday, countless other actors have been seen—an Italian Louis? Nora? and the idea of an Italian Anselmo is not yet ruled out—but none has aroused unmixed approval. Time off at the end for a couple of hours sight-seeing, and back to Paris, with the fair hope that Padovani will be free to play Maria.

In Paris Madame Dorisse, of the Cimura agency, confirms that Perier will not be free from his theatrical commitments, and produces with a flourish Serge Reggiani. This young actor, already known to Thorold for his work in *Les Portes de la Nuit, Manon, Les Amants de Verone,* surprises by appearing in a beard, grown for his most recent film. His English is not elaborate, but his impact is so striking that it is settled on the spot that he shall come over to Ealing next month to test for Louis. The last day of the trip brings to light the missing reel of the Philips film, and more newsreel material, at Gaumont. Scratch prints are ordered. Aerogare. Home.

In the Studio, things have been quiet; but Freddy has been investigating choreographers. Authority Arnold Haskell suggests Andrée Howard.

OCTOBER 26TH.—Scripts to Andrée Howard, and to Ernest Irving, head of Ealing's music department.

OCTOBER 30TH.—Interviews with Geoffrey Hibbert, possible Steenie; and Audrey Hepburn, possible Nora. With Padovani and Reggiani at least tentatively in mind for the leads, the height of potential members of the cast begins to assume importance. Neither of them is tall, so to a certain extent the rest of the cast must be scaled to them. This of course applies particularly to Nora—a slight discouragement to Audrey Hepburn. From now on all actors interviewed are sternly measured against the office wall.

OCTOBER 31ST.—Talk with William Kellner, passing on the results of the Paris trip. As soon as his commitments on *The Lavender Hill Mob* are finished, he will go across to inspect the proposed locations for himself.

November

Locations and actors are still in first priority, but other departments start to open up. As tests start, a cameraman is appointed to the picture; composer and choreographer are engaged; detailed discussions start on design; the breakdown is begun of treatment into shooting-script.

Starting with a number of definite ideas on casting, Thorold has considerably lightened the task of Margaret Harper-Nelson, Studio Casting Director. A test confirms his intuition for Serge Reggiani as Louis; though Maria continues an unsolved problem. On the smaller parts, Margaret's suggestions are of great help, and during these weeks a steady flow of actors whom she considers may be suitable arrive at the Studio for inspection. As well as her recommendations there are independent applications from actors who have heard about the film and write in for interview, and visits from agents who can produce entire casts from their lists of clients. It is humanly natural to regard failure to secure a part as in some way a reflection on an actor's ability, so one cannot mention these applicants by name unless they eventually appear in the picture. In fact, though, incapacity is scarcely ever the reason for such lack of success; questions of height and feature, non-conformance with the director's physical conception of the character are far more often responsible.

NOVEMBER 1ST.—Fresh recruits to the unit: Gordon Dines (now finishing off *Pool of London*) will be cameraman, and Terry Bishop will direct the second unit.

Sir Michael sees *Give Us This Day* (Padovani and Charles Goldner.) Visit from Padovani's agent.

NOVEMBER 2ND.—Andrée Howard comes to lunch, discusses the story, and particularly Nora's part in it. She undertakes the choreography, and suggests a dancer who might be tested for Nora.

NOVEMBER 3RD-5TH.—Reconnaissance to Dublin: Thorold and Sid fly over for the week-end. The Gaiety Theatre is exhaustively surveyed, with special attention to all parts of the theatre mentioned in the script—stage, backstage telephone, auditorium, bar, stage door. Dublin Castle (H.Q. of the Irish Police) interior and exterior; and finally Phœnix Park, which Thorold finds an exciting location for the climax of the story. Just how much will be shot in Dublin is not yet certain: the maximum of authenticity for the minimum of expense.

NOVEMBER 6TH.—(Monday).—Reggiani flies from Paris; in the afternoon he is shown *Give Us This Day*. With his test (script scenes B.50/1) fixed for Friday, he will spend the week working with Thorold and going over his lines.

NOVEMBER 8TH.—Thorold inspects the set which William has had erected for Friday on Stage 1. We still have no Maria to play the scenes with Reggiani; for an occasion so delicate, an actress of exceptional quality is needed. Can

Irene Worth be persuaded to help out? Freddy is dispatched to the New Theatre, where she is appearing in *The Cocktail Party*. Over a chat and a glass she agrees.

NOVEMBER 9TH.—At the Studio, Reggiani spends the morning in the Sound Department, trying his lines back and forth on a tape recorder. His make-up for to-morrow is decided—almost none, a little ageing. In the afternoon to the New Theatre for a run through with Irene. By the evening, everything is wound up, including nerves.

NOVEMBER 10TH.—An important day in any film's life: to-day the camera will turn for the first time on *Secret People*.

Stage 1 at nine o'clock presents the traditional illusion of chaos. In the clattering, the shouting, the sawing and the hammering it is difficult to sort out who exactly is doing what. At the far end of the set (not very far, for this is a tiny stage) Thorold is sitting with Serge and Irene, outlining the emotional background of their scene. This comes immediately after the meeting of Louis and Maria at the Paris Exhibition: a first dialogue is played in the taxi; a second in Louis' flat, as Maria cooks a meal, and they are interrupted by a telephone call from Louis' associates. The continuity girl, beside Thorold, follows in the script as Serge and Irene run through their lines. Gordon Dines, camelhair-overcoated, gloved, and elegantly scarved, disposes his lights round the taxi; inspects Maria's apron (for the second scene) and orders it to be dirtied down; calls for a gauze frame to soften the top-lighting of the taxi. The electricians are singing 'Down in the Glen'.

Serge gets up, stretches his legs in an anxious stroll. Isolated in this foreign babble, the face with which he fronts the ordeal suggests the liveliest of temperaments under the strictest of controls. 'Vous avez dormi bien?' 'Pas du tout.' He gestures graphically about his stomach: 'Butterflies . . .' Then, with sudden self-irritation: 'J'ai fait quatorze films . . .' 'Et c'est toujours comme ça?' 'Jamais.' He turns back to resume rehearsals with Irene.

The camera—which has by now acquired something of the menace of a dentist's drill—is wheeled up on the dolly (i.e trolley) before the taxi shell and positioned by the operator. 'Can I help you, Louis?' comes Irene's voice. Gordon is complaining that the set is not clear for his lights; the assistant director defends himself. With his light meter, Gordon takes readings in the taxi, glances distastefully at the seat. 'Clean this cab up a wee bit.' A prop man moves forward with a duster. In their corner director and actors continue with their subdued run-through. A line is giving trouble; Irene makes a suggestion. 'Try it,' says Thorold. 'Yes, that's much better, you're quite right.'

Gordon is ready; the actors can take their positions in the taxi. Irene is too high ('I have a long waist,' she apologises), so Serge is given a cushion. Thorold comes round to the camera, saying 'Can I have a peek?' and takes one. He asks for a slightly lower angle, and calls for a rehearsal so that he may watch the action through the camera. The scene is to be played to a gradual track-in. 'Shall we put tracks down?' wonders the operator. The dolly-pusher shrugs: 'He didn't ask for them.' 'We must have tracks.'

Waiting for these, and for final lighting adjustments, Irene discusses with

Thorold her feeling about acting for films. 'I don't mind acting to the camera —as it moves, I can identify myself with it—I enjoy television acting. But it's the constant cutting I can't get used to. Why can't you film in long takes; or use several cameras picking up after each other from different angles?' 'It can be done,' Thorold explains, 'but it depends on the style of picture. If you want something exquisitely photographed, it's absolutely impossible to film continuously like that . . .' They are out of the taxi now. Restlessly on the move, tracked by the continuity girl, Serge still repeats his lines. He breaks off. 'My poor heart . . . It boxes . . . comment?' He mimes. 'Shadow-boxes?' 'Oui, c'est ça.'

The lighting is finished. We can return to the taxi for a sound rehearsal. A deep breath. Serge rises to it, and the run-through goes without a hitch. The sound-recordist reports one or two imperfections: feet are tending to rustle on the floor, so a strip of carpet is produced (from where?). There is another, less identifiable sound. 'I think I must be making a noise rubbing against the back,' Irene volunteers. 'Harry,' calls Gordon, 'anything to stop this noise of Miss Worth's back?' The camera operator calls Gordon: 'For some reason we're getting a reflection—not much—about the size of a penny.' While he adjusts, Gordon wonders if we can have a slight shake on the cab, but an attempt by hand produces a barely perceptible tremor. 'God, it is solid, isn't it?'

'Shall we take one?' Thorold announces. A last check on focus and make-up. (By now, an outsider might suppose, the actors are either on the verge of hysteria, or hopelessly dulled, though they continue to look in command of themselves.) 'My hair hasn't been combed; is it all right?' queries Irene. Where is the hairdresser? The assistant goes to the phone, but Irene has borrowed a comb and fixed it for herself. 'Red light. Quiet please for a take.' The clapper board is interposed between the players and the camera: 'Scene One. Take One.' He withdraws. Thorold says—he does this always with a sort of gentle urgency—'Begin'.

They begin. Serge lights his two cigarettes; Irene tucks a flower in his buttonhole. The dialogue comes with such smoothness that I'd like to applaud. The camera tracks in. They embrace. 'Cut.' And Thorold steps forward as his actors relax. He makes one or two points. 'Il faut penser quand elle dit, "Who gives you orders?" . . . And the very end is not coming quite right.' He wants more acceptance in Irene's embrace. She finds this difficult after her previous lines. 'Perhaps if we looked at each other a bit longer?' They try it. 'C'est ça. Now may we have another?'

Two takes on this are satisfactory, and after the second we break for lunch. Serge makes for the sound recordist: 'How was it?' 'Fine, fine.' 'You really understood?' he presses incredulously.

After lunch we return to the set. The taxi has gone, and the stage is set for the second scene—Louis' flat, with Maria cooking at the 'practical' gas stove, and Louis looking on. A table laid in the centre of the floor, the telephone on a shelf in the corner. The morning's smooth passage has encouraged everyone; tension is noticeably less. Lighting is again followed by run-through, discussion and take. The scene is covered in three set-ups, finishing on a close-up of Louis at the telephone. Irene disappears for her play, while Serge is positioned alone before the camera for lighting tests. 'Look left—right—up— down.' He welcomes the end of a gruelling day with a sigh of relief—qualified only by the thought that to-morrow we will have to see it.

PRODUCTION: " SECRET PEOPLE". DIRECTOR: THOROLD'DICKINSON.

ARTISTES TESTS.

DATE: FRIDAY, 10th. November, 1950.
TEST SET: Paris Taxi, Louis' Pan's Lodgings.
TEST SCENES:B50, B51.
STAGE: 1.

Room. Artiste.   Character. Wardrobe. Hair. Make-up. On Set

71 Mr. Serge Reggiani LOUIS   9.15   9.45.a.m.
73 Miss Irene Worth   MARIE   9.30   8.15 8.45   9.45.a.m.

Technical crew from "Pool of London".

Special Requirements:-

                Practical gas stove.
                Table laid for two.
                Salad and salad dressing.
                Bread.
                Knives and forks etc.
                Condiments etc.
                Packet of cigarettes.
                Pocket cigarette lighter.
                Carafe of wine.
                Glasses.
                Two roses for buttonholes.

                Kitchen apron for Miss Worth.

                UNIT CALL: 8.30 a.m.

                ASSISTANT DIRECTOR J. O. Connolly...

*Note typing errors—'Pan's Lodgings' for
Paris Lodgings, MARIE for MARIA.*

25

NOVEMBER 13TH.—Thorold sees rushes in the morning, and expresses his approval. This does not entirely quiet Serge's nerves (he is to see them in the afternoon), and during lunch he finds butterflies in his stomach again. After lunch Thorold goes to see rushes again with Sir Michael, while we wait anxiously in his office: small talk about films flows in a spasmodic way. A telephone call summons us to the theatre, but Sir Michael and Thorold have vanished. We sit, and more conversation is squeezed from suspense, till another phone call tells us not to wait: Thorold and Sir Michael are continuing to confer. But Sir Michael likes it. Margaret Harper-Nelson arrives with her assistant. Freddy presses the button.

At first you cannot look at it objectively at all—see it as an audience ignorant of what had gone on, what was going on out of camera. Two chairs along, Serge is undergoing the familiar agony of the hyper-sensitive: he writhes nervously and bows his head. After a minute or so, though, you attain greater stability. As Thorold has said, the test shows work in progress; and remarkably. The test close-ups at the end, free from language strain, surely clinch the matter.

The lights go up, and Serge groans. 'My English! Terrible . . . *terrible!*' 'Nonsense,' we hasten, sincerely, to disagree. But he is ruthless in his self-criticism. 'I *eat* my words did you not see? And so tense with nerves—like this—" and he knots his left eyebrow hideously. But the ladies, who have not even read the scene, are whole-heartedly enthusiastic. 'And so attractive . . .' Back in the office, Thorold returns, somewhat exhausted, from his economic conference with Sir Michael. The test is discussed. 'What did you think?' asks Serge, with sympathetic directness. Then, quickly, 'No, before you say anything, I will tell you what *I* think. The language is, of course, very bad, and the playing very nervous . . .' As his rather astonishingly objective analysis proceeds, he goes into French. 'Je n'ai pas joué assez ouvert . . . Mais ce que je pense est que je trouve le personnage séduisant—Louis. De la manière générale a n'est pas une catastrophe.' He thinks he can do it, in fact. Thorold agrees.

There remain the *choses economiques*—to be discussed now only in the most general terms. First the difficulty of paying a foreign actor enough to cover the weeks of necessary rehearsals, and a double deduction of tax, without unduly inflating the casting budget. And then the likely opposition of distributors to a picture with stars not familiar at the British box-office. Serge points out that this cuts both ways—French and Italian distribution will be correspondingly easier. And anyway you cannot have your cake (authentic performances in parts such as these) and eat it (with stars beloved by the *Daily Mail* National Film Award).

Tea (of course) and departure. Serge visits Sir Michael for a farewell shake of the hand, and is escorted by Freddy to Northolt. On the way, Freddy volunteers instruction: the pronunciation of—cough, plough, enough, thought, dough.

Serge groans and shows us his English reader—*Alice in Wonderland*, heavily annotated. At the airport we say goodbye. Or *au revoir?*

NOVEMBER 14TH.—Amongst to-day's actors, Lionel Harris *looks* like Frack. He takes a script.

Thorold talks with Ernest Irving about the kind of music he wants for the Ballet, and throughout the film: Mediterranean in flavour, not positively identifiable by nationality. 'The trouble is,' says Ernest, 'You can't ask a composer for a sample.' 'Why not?' Thorold suggests commissioning a sample theme, in piano arrangement, from Roberto Gerhard, the Spanish composer. A letter is dispatched, with a copy of the script.

NOVEMBER 15TH.—Definite news on Serge's test. The Front Office agrees to his casting, and bargaining can start. This afternoon brings a visit also from Padovani's agent for discussion of possible terms. This prolongs itself over tea-time, and is carried up to Sir Michael's office.

A note from Hal Mason, General Manager, brings the unwelcome news that we must postpone further tests till after the first week in December—extra scenes on *Pool of London*, shooting on *The Lavender Hill Mob*, tests on *The Man in the White Suit*, will be occupying all available crews and space till then. A protest goes off by return: we need to test for the parts of Anselmo, Steenie, Frack and Nora as soon as we can.

NOVEMBER 16TH.—Thorold and Sid to Scotland Yard, to hear the police comment on the story.

NOVEMBER 20TH—22ND.—Thorold, out of town, starts work on the development of treatment into shooting script.

NOVEMBER 23RD.—Margaret Harper-Nelson reports the arrival of a letter from Serge's agent refusing the terms which the Studio has offered and sticking out for an equivalent sum to what he earns in France, plus expenses. 'A very reasonable letter,' says Thorold. The Front Office attitude, on the other hand, is that Serge has no pull at the British box office, and so is worth less to us than he is to a French producer. Thorold and Margaret visit Sir Michael and carry a contrary point, with the proviso that Margaret will fly to Paris for reassurance on the authenticity of the figures.

Now that Thorold is beginning to go into the script in detail, it is useful if he can at the same time have detailed talks about chief problems of setting and design with William Kellner. This afternoon is set aside for consideration first of all of the Exhibition. Of this sequence in general Thorold remarks: 'I'm no believer in a sketch artist telling you how to compose your picture. If you can't do that, you might as well chuck your hand in right away. But here I think we'll have to work the whole thing out beforehand—exactly what we'll have in the frame.' The size of the set must be as limited as possible. At present we follow Maria and Louis as they leave together, buy some roses and hail a taxi. Thorold settles to change this to a direct cut: 'We'll carry on the conversation between Anselmo and Rodd (Script scene B.48), then cut to Louis and Maria *in* a taxi, in a different locale altogether. All we've got to do then is to link the Terrace with the Buttery exterior . . .' For the night Café exterior (B.59): 'The effect we want is a blaze of light from inside; utter darkness in the street outside. We'll shoot it on the spot, except for the odd close-up which we'll do in the Studio.'

The return to England. The script shows this in detail: Louis landing from an aircraft on the Downs; Anselmo and the girls arriving at Victoria, on the same train as Steenie; Steenie making contact with a London member of the Organisation. 'I suppose all this is necessary . . .' Thorold sighs. William is worried by the idea of a location at Victoria. 'This is one of the things we'll have to think very carefully about—to get real facilities you want to shoot at night. To avoid all that trouble we shifted an arrival at Victoria to an arrival at Northolt on *The Lavender Hill Mob*—very much simpler; and, as a production point, it'll cost you a tenth the price.' But the social level of the characters, and the period, make it too improbable that they should have flown. Thorold has another idea. 'What about Gordon Dines? Hasn't he got a steady Eyemo arm? Why couldn't we get them off an ordinary train?' William is sceptical. 'I don't think it would work. You'll have to go to a lot of trouble and expense if you shoot it at Victoria—lamps, generators, arcs, crowd. People will be crowding round you . . .'

NOVEMBER 24TH.—We have won the argument about tests. Next Friday (December 1st) we can test Geoffrey Hibbert (Steenie), Charles Goldner (Anselmo) and Lionel Harris (Frack).

NOVEMBER 27TH.—With a pleased surprise, somehow reminiscent of Mr. Brontë's discovery of *Jane Eyre*, Thorold announces that Roberto Gerhard has submitted a piano-sketch of the Ballet, and that it is exactly the sort of thing he wants. Next step: an orchestration, on which the final decision can be made. Andrée Howard introduces her suggestion for Nora.

December

The first week of a new month brings two decisive steps in casting: Serge Reggiani signs to play Louis; Lea Padovani announces finally that she will not be available for Maria. Thoughts turn back to Hollywood, where Valentina Cortesa is under contract to Fox, and negotiations are opened—though, in view of the dollar situation, without high hopes of success. The search in Europe must accordingly be carried on simultaneously, and lists are endlessly compiled of actresses who may possess the necessary qualifications. Halfway through the month, Thorold flies again to Paris where he investigates a couple of likely candidates, and is confirmed by a viewing of Cortesa's latest film in his conviction that she will suit the part ideally.

Two Anselmos are tested, two Steenies and one Frack; tests for Nora are held over to the new year. Work on other aspects of production gathers momentum. Roberto Gerhard orchestrates his 'sample'; it is approved, and he is commissioned to develop it into a score. Detailed discussion of the shape and style of the Ballet start with Andrée Howard. Newsreel material on the Paris Exhibition arrives in London, and useful excerpts are chosen by Thorold in collaboration with Peter Tanner, who will edit the picture. Finally, as the year comes to an end, Thorold gets down in earnest to the shooting script. This must be ready for Sir Michael to read over the first week-end in January.

DECEMBER 1ST.—Further tests. First Geoffrey Hibbert for Steenie (B.69); a simple assignment—from the camera point of view—shot in close-up, with Freddy reading in for Louis at one side, and the actress who will stand in for Maria in the day's later scenes playing 'the woman'. Since Geoffrey is appearing without make-up, he is on his way out of the Studio by nine-fifteen, while the second test is lined up: Charles Goldner for Anselmo, Lionel Harris for Frack (A.40, 41, 44). Lastly Charles plays B.7 in close-shot as a final test for Anselmo.

DECEMBER 4TH.—All but free now from *Pool of London*, Peter Tanner is named as editor of the picture. His first contribution is made this morning: he accompanies Thorold to the Bonded Film Store (where film is held by the Customs until duty has been paid) to view the Exhibition material which has arrived from Paris. First Thorold explains what he wants from the sequence: 'We've got to get up to such a lick that it's just simply a rain of images.' It is easy to see the sort of stuff that will be useful—low-angle shots of pavilions, snatches of fountains and fireworks, the Russian forward-marching group of statuary, endlessly recurrent. No one could ever be bothered, apparently, to devote film to the British Pavilion. At Peter's side his assistant notes the shots which director and editor agree should be printed up. With duty payable at 5d. a foot, it is important that wastage be kept to a minimum.

A letter from Padovani apologetically announces that she cannot after all come to England. This takes us back two months, to fresh memory-searching for actresses capable of such a part. Were we right to imagine Valentina Cortesa out of reach? Thorold and Sid confer with Sir Michael, and he agrees to contact Fox's London office; meanwhile a short list of European possibilities is drawn up. A phone call to Paris discloses that Maria Casarès signed yesterday to go into a play, so will not be available.

DECEMBER 5TH.—Recording session on the sample Ballet music by Roberto Gerhard. Ernest Irving presides over the composer at the piano, a violinist and a flautist. Firmly he asserts his control over every aspect of the proceedings: 'I'm going to prevent you becoming too subtle,' he warns the composer, with a little joke about his predilection for 'bitonal' music. 'We must stop him getting too *Wozzeck*.' 'I shall look on you as a real mentor,' says Roberto tactfully. Not that there seems anything very *Wozzeck* about this combination of the two elements asked for—the lyrical-nostalgic (a rich, elegiac melody) and the harvest dance (with harmonies less familiar, rhythms more broken). 'It is of personal significance to me,' says Roberto, once a refugee (from Spain) himself. Everyone is happy about it—'We'll get something out of him we wouldn't get out of a hack,' explains Ernest.

Lionel Harris comes to look at his test, and judges his performance as geared rather to the theatre than the screen. His only previous film performance—in *The Tales of Hoffmann*—was 'no real use from that point of view—I was even encouraged to overplay. But this shows how much less you must do in front of the camera to achieve much more.' 'Don't act it,' Thorold urges. '*Behave* it.' He will have another go on Friday, with a different Anselmo.

DECEMBER 6TH.—The rushes from yesterday's recording are heard and approved by Sir Michael. Roberto can now be commissioned for the full Ballet score.

A telegram from Serge in Paris tells us his joy at the signing of the contract, and to expect him early in January. Meanwhile Fox have been contacted about Cortesa and are in communication with Hollywood. But Thorold is worried that, if she proves unobtainable, there may be pressure for a 'name', popular in Britain, to play opposite Serge. This seems a question intimately connected with the whole selling-angle on the film: he visits the publicity department to discuss possibilities for a campaign based on title and story. He is even ready to change the title, to *The Secret People*—'Particularise it: Who are The Secret People? and so forth . . .' Other ideas are thrown up: shooting behind locked doors? A clause in the contract of each artiste that he is forbidden to reveal details of the story? The Story Scotland Yard Denied? If a report is prepared stressing the opportunities for a novel campaign along these lines, it may help to prevent insistence on an unsuitable star name for Maria.

DECEMBER 8TH.—A different Anselmo and a different Steenie are tested in last week's scenes; Lionel Harris again does Frack.

DECEMBER 11TH (Monday).—Rushes of last Friday's test are inspected, and personalities discussed. Someone suggests trying an Italian Anselmo—if necessary not a professional actor. 'We're not making a Documentary,' says William. Thorold's comment is more explicit. 'That sort of thing depends entirely on the weight of the part and the style of the picture. If you use actors who aren't skilled technicians, you have to sacrifice so much of what you can do through the camera—all the balletic qualities of movement—because they simply can't perform with the necessary precision Not many of the parts in these Italian neo-realist films have demanded much acting *technique*—which our script emphatically does.'

DECEMBER 12TH.—Work is resumed on the shooting script.

DECEMBER 14TH.—Morning: Wolfgang Wilhelm comes to discuss progress on the script breakdown. Afternoon: Andrée Howard, for first thoughts on the Ballet. First the music is heard, then Thorold outlines his ideas. He wants the Ballet to reflect the background, and even to some extent the story of the principal characters of the film. 'We want cheerfulness and positiveness—nothing negative, nothing black on the whole . . . We could even work it within the conventions of musical comedy: use a gay mountain dance to begin with, and have the last section showing the lovers parted by the girl's father—a change in the character of the music and a quiet curtain. Then the music opening the second act picks up on this—which gives added emotion to what Maria hears coming over the telephone' (in scene F.48).

The motivation of the story? Not really important. What matters chiefly is the mood. Thorold wants 'a kind of whirling gaiety.' It needn't necessarily have the usual Mediterranean atmosphere of heat: 'I always had the feeling they came from the mountains—perhaps we can get that feeling into it—more of the Dolomites or the Pyrenees . . . I'm sure the Ballet has to be absolutely direct, so that the audience can get it at once.' In which case, Andrée emphasises, Roberto will have to keep his music simple; she finds its rhythms at the moment somewhat too sophisticated. With this approach settled, Roberto and she must get together for mutual discussion, so that he can proceed with the score.

DECEMBER 15TH-19TH.—Thorold to Paris again. Serge has had an offer to appear in an Italian film before *Secret People* starts: can he accept? After some wrangling between agents, the Italians agree to a 'stop date' in late January, which will still leave him adequate time in London before we start shooting. He proceeds to Rome. Thorold inspects more actresses, and is particularly impressed by one, the rough-cut of whose latest picture he is able to view at the Studio. She is younger than Maria should be, but speaks good English. A possibility.

Also seen: Cortesa's *Donne Senza Nomme — Women Without Names* (Wardour Street title: *Unwanted Women*.) This precipitates a phone call to Sid at Ealing: redouble efforts to get Cortesa.

DECEMBER 20TH and following.—Concentrated work on the script.

January, 1951

The New Year takes the Studio's programme forward decisively: The Lavender Hill Mob *comes off the floor, and* The Man in the White Suit *goes on. As a result, preparation of* Secret People, *now the next for production, perceptibly accelerates. Already, looking back over the past three months, a good deal of ground has been covered: with two important exceptions, all the leading parts are now cast, most of the locations have been chosen, specific discussions have been held on design. The Ballet is under way. The principal members of the unit have been appointed (cameraman, art director, editor), and have started preliminary work.*

As the weeks draw on, attention concentrates more and more closely on the practical details of production—how exactly, when exactly, and where, and at what cost the story can be translated into film. For all such calculations a fully detailed script is, of course, the indispensable basis; from this the unit's production manager (who comes on to the picture in the middle of the month) prepares his estimate of the number of days that will be necessary for shooting. This will then be brought up for round-table discussion between representatives of the unit (director, producer, writer) and the Studio Production Department (General Manager, his assistant, the head of the Costing Department). The first step towards this is taken at the beginning of the month, with the completion of the breakdown of Treatment into Shooting Script; but this is only a first draft. It will have to submit to detailed examination not only for length and cost, but also (by Sir Michael and the head of the Studio Script Department) for points of characterisation, dialogue, movitation and clarity of development. First draft must be revised into second, second into third, before the final shooting script is reached, with which the film will go on the floor.

It is about now that you begin to appreciate the complexity of the business— interesting in itself, but more important for the pressure with which it bears down upon the artist. However sympathetic his associates, it must sometimes seem to the writer-director as if he is fighting alone for his subject against a host of critics, business men, organisers, whose sole aim is to pervert or to maim it. Yet without them, he is powerless; indeed, by the qualities of imagination and efficiency possessed by any of a very large number of these associates, the nature of his film can be affected, and its success enhanced or diminished.

Happily, one vexed problem at least is settled during the month, greatly to everyone's satisfaction: Cortesa is signed for Maria.

JANUARY 2ND.—First draft shooting script readied for typing and duplication. Sir Michael will have it next week-end.

JANUARY 3RD.—Gordon and Thorold discuss the lighting of the picture. From his reading of the script, Gordon has formed his idea of how he wants to photograph it—in dramatic, low-key images (which means in sharply contrasted tones, ranging from dense black to white), a violent lighting which will reflect the violence of the subject. With this conception Thorold wholeheartedly agrees. Gordon's only doubt is over the scenes actually in the Café. Should these be pitched higher, or in the same key as the rest of the picture? They decide, for continuity of style, to treat them in the same way.

Specifically, Thorold is worried about the Phœnix Park sequence at the end of the film. 'If we talk about Phœnix Park, it's got to look like Phœnix Park—and that means no lamps. If the scene is played at night, the only illumination is by flashlamp. If it was an artificial story, it wouldn't matter: either you have to play it for moonlight, or for filtered daylight, which would look terribly phoney in this story. Or if you have the old trick of so many candlepower on every face, willy-nilly, people will ask where the light's coming from . . .' 'Could we do anything with cars?' 'To anyone who knows Dublin, there just aren't enough cars around there to justify it.' 'How about using infra-red stock in daylight?' 'What does that do?' 'We could get outlines of trees, the rest dark . . . The trouble is, it costs a small fortune: you have to buy a whole batch of 40,000 feet, and it has such a short life. We tried to use it before—one of those shots where they have a black cat being chased by a nigger through a tunnel at midnight, and they wanted to see it . . .' 'Well,' Thorold sighs finally, 'you may say we've got to change the location; but it's so suitable . . . Better wait till you see it.'

JANUARY 5TH-11TH.—Paris again, for Thorold, Sid, Gordon and William. The purpose of the visit is twofold: first to inspect the locations picked by Sid and Thorold previously. William makes sketches and commits details to memory of the Seine Quai, and the Bartosch's flat (which will definitely serve as the original of Louis' lodgings.) Various night clubs are investigated which will compositely serve for the *Vieux Chapeau.*

The other objective is a possible Maria. Though enquiries, cables to Hollywood, are flying, the lack of a definite answer from Fox makes it essential that the search for a Maria be continued in Europe—in case . . . Thorold meets again the young actress whose film he viewed in rough-cut on his last visit. He discusses modifications in the script by which Maria might be played as twenty-one instead of twenty-six, decides to try a make-up test at Ealing.

JANUARY 12TH.—Make-up tests on this younger possibility for Maria.

JANUARY 15TH.—Conference on the first draft shooting script. Relaxing in an assortment of chairs round the edge of the room, Thorold, Sid and Wolfgang Wilhelm assemble with Sir Michael in the Script Department office. The object to-day is to get the fresh view of someone who knows the subject, but has not been intimately concerned with its development over the past few months.

Sir Michael starts, speaking from the notes he made while reading the script last week-end. He has two primary criticisms: first on the opening sequence. 'I think this rather gives the idea that you're *planting* your characters. That possibility arises from the fact that two of the most important people—Brentano and Galbern—are talked about but not seen. Which of course is inevitable if you're not to have any preliminary scenes.' Thorold takes this up: 'We did originally have an opening scene—a sort of prologue, which we rejected because it broke the geographical unity. A little Southern European town, with a hilly street, overshadowed by mountains. Dawn. The police making their way up the street; window curtains being tweaked aside as people watch. Then inside the house: Pietro Brentano, Louis, the girls, perhaps Marco. Pietro sends the girls off, and Louis too, then waits to be arrested . . . It's an effective

33

opening, but we decided against it, both to preserve unity, and because it presented language difficulties.' Sid: 'And it brings up other related problems. If you show this country, and the police in their uniforms, it makes it difficult to keep it generalised. Unless you invent your own.

My feeling about this sequence is that Maria's story about their flight comes at a difficult time.' (This version of the script gives us the girls' story in Anselmo's voice, told over images of Maria unpacking her things, just after she has learned of her father's death.) 'I do think all this would be better from Maria herself, with concentration on her playing. After all, her emotion about it is more important than the fact itself.' Thorold: 'Yes. We were rather influenced by this post-war realism craze. I think—feeling that if Maria speaks herself, it should be in her own language. But I think probably we must make that concession.'

The other main point stressed by Sir Michael is the danger of the film leaving a sense of futility. 'I think this arises because the ramifications of the movement are so enormous. When Maria dies, you may feel it's not worth it: the activities of the movement will continue just as before. Does Louis give himself up because there's no point in resisting, or because he's realised the movement's not worth it? I'm not sure that at Maria's death Louis doesn't have a change of heart.'

This comment sets off a long and animated discussion. Thorold maintains that the positive principle—of the sacredness of human life, and the evil of violence —is clearly upheld in the behaviour of Maria. 'Years ago, when this thing first began in our minds, the idea was that once you *see* a thing, your attitude towards it is liable to change completely. That is what gets Maria at the core . . . She goes away, finds that her sister is threatened, goes back. Only by dying can she convince her sister of what she herself has learned.'

But Sir Michael feels that the defeat of evil should be more externalised, made concrete. 'Within the limits of the story—which is the only thing that counts—they have made no impression on the movement.' Wolfgang points out that if Nora has undergone a change of heart, she will be able to give the police valuable information. This could be stressed. Sid: 'There's no harm in hammering home Nora's change of heart.' But Sir Michael is not sure whether the point can be fully made in Nora: 'You see, no single person has a change of heart who is a member of the organisation.' Thorold: 'Except Nora.' 'She's not really a member; she's a victim ' Should there be indications of a change of heart in Louis? Wolfgang: 'If he was covering someone with a gun in the last scene . . . We could have him purposely not using it.' Sir Michael: 'This is conventional I know, but suppose Louis dies at the same time as Maria, and at the point of death there's some contact between them?' Finally Thorold suggests that this last sequence is one which cannot be adequately described on paper: the essential feeling and implication of it can only come in the shooting. But it looks as though Steenie is going to be provided with a sticky end; and that Louis refuses to run for it for other reasons than the purely politic.

Minor points: Sir Michael is not altogether happy about some of the dialogue, Anselmo's in particular. 'We can make the experiment of writing it "straight" in the next draft.' And some of the 'plot points' obtrude rather. He would like to try the experiment of a reading. And as regards Friday's tests for Maria: he is not reconciled to the idea of the character played so young, because the

34

altered age seems to destroy the existing Maria-Nora relationship. 'I'm looking forward to a rewrite,' he finishes. 'And it will be all to the good if we can get the length down a bit.' (At the moment, the rough estimate is for twelve weeks' shooting.) So, with these numerous considerations in mind, Thorold and Wolfgang press on to a second draft.

JANUARY 16TH.—In the light of last week's expedition, it is decided to eliminate any Paris location shooting. Chiefly this is a matter of finance. French unions demand that any foreign unit working in France must employ an equivalent number of French technicians—if necessary to do nothing but be paid. This additional expense would make it an unjustifiable luxury to shoot in Paris. Louis' lodgings would anyway be a studio set; now the Seine Quai and the Café exterior will also be built in the studio, from sketches taken on the spot. On the Paris Exhibition Thorold has to agree also to a disappointing restriction. He has been particularly anxious that this should be an exterior set; but William now declares this an impossibility. Apart from weather risks, there is no room on the 'Lot.' (There is, in fact, no real Lot—or open space for the building of exterior sets—at Ealing.) 'I don't see why we can't split it up inside.' 'But I don't want to do it inside. We *must* have daylight.' 'Then we'll have to go to another studio—Pinewood or Denham. And that'll cost you a pretty penny.' Money has talked

JANUARY 17TH.—Bright news. Fox are ready to loan us Cortesa; she has read the script and is interested in the part; the Studio can obtain the necessary dollars to bring her over from America. We may expect her early February, for a week in London on her way to Italy for a holiday before the picture starts. At the same time a post-card from Serge in Rome tells us that the weather is bad, and that he is working hard at *Alice in Wonderland*.

JANUARY 22ND.—The picture acquires a Production Manager. Returning from a holiday after winding up *Pool of London*, Ralph Hogg opens up the production office from which he will plan and guide the immediate day-to-day organisation of *Secret People*. His first responsibility is to devise (in collaboration with the studio production department) a shooting schedule which will suit everybody from every point of view. To this end, he starts breaking down the shooting script on to a series of cards—one card for each setting in the film. Each of these details the number of scenes played in each set, the characters involved, day- or night-time, and Ralph's estimate of the time (in quarter-day units) needed for shooting. These can be used as the basis of a preliminary schedule.

JANUARY 25TH.—Thorold and Wolfgang complete their labours on the second draft script. The beginning and end have been slightly rewritten, and the girls' journey across Europe now comes in a short impressionist sequence (A.25-33) introduced by Maria herself. Of the scenes which have been eliminated, the most useful cut takes us straight from the *Vieux Chapeau* to the beginning of Sequence C.—losing the inconvenient scenes of arrival in England, saving time and money, and giving a good quick start to this new section of the story.

JANUARY 29TH.—Conference on the second draft script, same attendance as before, with the addition of Bill Lipscomb, head of the script department. It is he who starts, with a vehement attack on a story point which has aroused his disapproval—Maria's action in carrying the bomb to the garden party. 'Louis has persuaded her in cold blood to do something that is absolutely against all her principles. I began to hate her: she's so cold-blooded . . . Would you take a bomb to a party where your sister's just got her first chance to dance? . . . If the audience is not in the fullest sympathy with her, I think you wreck your story.'

Then Sir Michael comes in to the attack. 'Do you mind if I'm awkward? Would you mind telling me exactly what happens to the characters after the moment of the bomb explosion in Anselmo's Café?' He is, in fact, worried that, as the script stands, the audience will not be convinced at the progression of events—at Anselmo's and Nora's acceptance of the report of Maria's death, and of Louis' and Steenie's escape. 'We had it all scripted,' Thorold explains. 'Fire engines, the police roping off the Café, the cellar after the explosion with Louis and Steenie escaping through the back, and Inspector Eliot dragging Maria out of the wreckage and getting a C.I.D. man to rush her to hospital. Sir Michael says: 'Well, I think those scenes have got to be played out in front of the camera.'

Bill Lipscomb says: 'You just cut them out for length, did you?' Thorold says: 'No—just for the balance of the thing. You could do it as a police drama, but every time we developed it in that direction, ·we found we were losing the thread. Then, if we have a high climax here, we have to cap it later, or we risk ending the film on an anti-climax.'

For this reason—and to avoid further expense—it is agreed not to make any additions to the explosion scene. Sir Michael finds the revised beginning and end. 'a great improvement' but feels it should be made clearer that an attempt has been planned on Galbern's life in Paris, and has failed. At the moment the Paris activities of the Organisation are too reticently scripted. And he is not quite happy that Nora and Anselmo should accept apparently so easily the news of Maria's death. 'I would like some scene in Scotland Yard where the news is broken to Anselmo. We could even have him told the truth, and warned that, for Maria's sake as well as his and Nora's, he must accept the report of her death.'

WEDNESDAY, JANUARY 31ST.—To everyone's chagrin, Ralph's preliminary schedule works out at 57½ days. Suppose this can be got down to 55, it still means 11 weeks' shooting (on the five-day week) instead of the desired 10; to which we may expect resistance from the production department. The morning is spent examining Ralph's estimate of necessary time on the Café set. Present are Thorold, Sid, Ralph, William, Gordon and Wolfgang, peering at each other through cigarette smoke, over a desk littered with William's plans. Shot by shot, the schedule is combed out; where possible, camera behaviour is simplified; where necessary, alterations are suggested on the designs.

The layout of the kitchen in particular causes discussion. A.39. Thorold explains how he sees it: 'This is a standard kitchen shot, with this wall' (pointing on the plan) 'floated' (removed). Sid: 'We want her at the stove—that affects the position of the stove.' 'Also,' Gordon is quick to worry, 'which is her best profile?' But William has equipped the kitchen with a range as well as a gas fire, and this threatens to cramp the action. 'Do we ever use the range?' Sid asks. 'It would be there,' declares William firmly. 'We don't want it if it isn't used.' 'We could put it in the corner; it would never be there, but I don't suppose anyone will notice.' So the range is moved. Thorold begins to worry about the gas cooker. 'Wouldn't she have something more elaborate? The place is a sort of hot snackery isn't it? And talking of snacks . . .' It is time for lunch.

During lunch, a suggestion from William eliminates another short scene; and after it other suggestions are considered. With the happy result that another half page is lost. And so, at 2.30 to:

First Production Conference On Schedule

This assembles around the large circular table in the directors' (company-, not film-) dining room, beneath huge framed stills from the Studio's latest production. Our party moves across entire, to be joined by the General Manager, Hal Mason, his assistant, Simon Kershaw, and Orlando King from Costing. The document before the meeting is headed 'Breakdown Summary,' and dated 31.1.51. On it are tabulated all the sets and locations stipulated by the script, and against each the shooting time which Ralph and Simon have estimated they will need. The procedure is to go through this, set by set, and check the estimates—bearing in mind those extra days which must, if it is humanly possible, and perhaps even if it is not, be lopped off the schedule.

First on the list is the Café set; it is agreed that a last word on this must wait till Thorold has finished his detailed examination of it with Gordon and Ralph (they have saved a quarter of a day already). We proceed to the lesser sets, to Daly's shop, the manager's office at the British Pavilion (play in one set-up and reduce from ¾ to ½ a day), the Quai on the Seine where Steenie murders the drunken informer (¾ day if we can prelight it) . . .

In general, Ralph's estimates are agreed on, but here and there they can be reduced. Sometimes he had allowed for the insertion of close-ups into dialogue scenes where they have not been specified by the script; these can be eliminated. 'I think we can take it,' says Sid, 'that the script is now largely as Thorold intends to shoot it.' 'Yes,' Thorold agrees, 'unless someone breaks down on a shot, or we have to cut for any other reason. But we just can't afford too many close-ups.' We plough on. The *Vieux Chapeau* is listed for 2½ days. Gordon comments: 'From my point of view this is a difficult set to light, with the ceiling and all. We might reduce, provided we can pre-light it.' Schedule it for a Monday, so that Gordon can come in and light it on the Sunday? Hal remarks drily that it may not be possible to schedule *every* set for a Monday; and anyway the union rules forbid lighting on two Sundays running. 'We must leave time for the dancing shots, too,' adds Thorold. No change then. Paris Café exterior (¾ day). 'That's a bit excessive isn't it?' wonders Thorold. Ralph: 'Well, you've three set-ups.' 'Yes, but all in the same direction.' 'What about these lorries?' (The script specifies lorry wheels passing in the street.) 'Oh, we'll just suggest those, by light- and sound-effects.' Down to ½ a day, then. The Dublin Theatre set, on the other hand, seems rather tight at two days. 'Mind you it doesn't cover everything.' 'No, but it covers the ballet— and that's designed to run three minutes on its own.' 'Another ½ day?' Agreed.

The atmosphere thickens as the talk goes on; eyes begin to water; tea is brought in, and sandwiches filled with an anonymous brown paste. We are on to the locations. Morton Street: Café exteriors. We have four days for this— if the weather is favourable we may manage in less, but that cannot be relied on. 'Don't forget,' says Thorold, 'the police say we've got to be finished a fortnight before the Festival of Britain begins.' This brings us to April, which means we will have to work on alternative calls over that period— interior sets must be ready in case the weather prohibits exterior shooting. Chancery Lane and the street outside the rehearsal rooms call for Sunday shooting; which takes another day off the schedule. And the Garden Party— which will be shot on a night location—wants to be done as late in the Spring as possible, unless half the cast is to go down with pneumonia. This precipitates a complicated and indecisive argument about the length of the nights at this time of the year: does the clock go forward or back? Does it make the night longer or shorter?

Finally, Hal sums up. Total shooting time subtracted from the estimate: four days, leaving us with, at the moment, a 53½ day schedule. 'So we're still 3½ days out.' He adds optimistically: 'Of course, we've still the big set to go through . . . Anyway, we're not going to be arbitrary; a day or two over doesn't matter. But if we go to an 11 week schedule, we've got nothing to spare for retakes.' The next step is for Thorold to finish his examination of the Café schedule, to see if anything can be chopped off that. 'When you're determined you've got it down as low as you can, we'll start a cross-plot and cost. If the cost comes out all right, we'll let it go at that. Otherwise, we'll have to have another go at it.'

Hal says: 'The point is, having gone through it—do you think you can do it?' Thorold says: 'We'll do our best.'

February

By the advance schedule which still obtains (these things have a habit of changing), Secret People is due to go on the floor on Monday, March 5th. Twenty-two more working days.

Activity centres on the script, which—minor excisions and dialogue changes apart—may now be regarded as complete, unless either of the stars presses hard for more considerable changes. On it the spearhead of the unit is bringing to bear their various specialised skills. William Kellner has been for some time at work on his designs: starting on the Paris scenes, with his visit still fresh in his mind, he has completed plans and sketches for the Paris bistro, Louis' lodgings, the Seine Quai, and the terrace at the Exhibition where Maria and Louis meet again. At the moment, the Vieux Chapeau is on his drawing board, and a cardboard model of Anselmo's Café is being built by his senior draughtsman—for examination by director and cameraman before the plans are finalised. Costume design has started: Cortesa's measurements have been cabled from Hollywood, and Anthony Mendleson has been able to sketch first designs for her eight changes of costume. Otherwise he can only draw up his list (to be checked through with the director) of small part costumes called for by the script, and await a casting decision on Nora. Thorold, with Gordon and Ralph, proceeds with his shot-by-shot examination of the Café scenes; on the result of this hangs any further scheduling, as well as costing, arrangement of a building schedule, and a 'cross-plot,' detailing just when and for how long each member of the cast will be required. During the month also, the Ballet must assume musical and choreographic shape, must be cast and go into rehearsal. Final decision must be taken on where it is to be shot. The exact extent of the Dublin location must be determined.

What of the actors? As far as the stars are concerned, we are at the mercy of the Ministry of Labour. Applications have gone in for their labour permits; it is hoped that both will be through within a week. The rest of the casting must wait until Thorold is free to test for Nora, and to resume interviews for the smaller parts.

FEBRUARY 1ST.—*East* (why *East?*) *of the Rising Sun* is viewed. Unanimous verdict: M-G-M unfair to Cortesa.

A letter from Cortesa in Hollywood puts forward some points on the script from her point of view. Chiefly, these concern Maria, whom she would like to give some evidence of the intellectual interests one might expect from a girl of her background. It is agreed to make certain dialogue changes to meet this view.

FEBRUARY 2ND.—First discussion on the Ballet between Andrée Howard and Roberto Gerhard. Refereed by Thorold, Sid, Wolfgang and Dock Mathieson (from the Studio Music Department).

To begin with, Andrée has some queries to raise about Roberto's rhythms, which he endeavours to elucidate. 'But anyway, we don't want the dancing to follow the music pattern too slavishly.' It has already been agreed that the

39

skeleton of the ballet is to be the parting of two lovers by an angry father, against the background of a wine harvest celebration. Out of suggestions from all round, a workable synopsis grows: the harvest dance; diversion by three drunks; the girl's father forbids her to dance with her lover and is whirled off by the revellers; the girl dances alone, and is joined by the boy for a final *pas de deux*.

This sketch has general approval. 'Yes, it's beginning to shape,' says Andrée. And Roberto: 'This conversation has been very illuminating to me. I must say, I begin to see how it should all look.' And Thorold feels it is developing into something 'which I can see it would be very exciting to photograph.' He goes on: 'What I think would be fun, if you agree, is that when Andrée has laid out her pattern, we can then break it up into shots—and Roberto can then know what the camera will be doing when he writes his music. And in turn, camera movement and choreography can be adjusted to the music, so that the whole thing will be a threesome. I do think the difference between stage and film ballet is that the camera should be an element—not just the dance, but the dance seen through a lens . . .'

MONDAY, FEBRUARY 5TH.—A tentative shooting schedule, drawn up by Ralph in collaboration with Simon Kershaw (assistant to General Manager), is produced for inspection by Thorold, Sid and William.

The problem of scheduling is briefly this. There is not enough floor space in the studio to allow one to build all the sets for a film simultaneously, and shoot the story from beginning to end, moving from one set to another as the script demands. So a shooting-order must be devised, by which filming can proceed continuously on one stage after another, while the Construction Department is given sufficient time between sessions on any one stage to dismantle used sets and put up new ones. But the practical necessities of construction are not the only considerations which apply. Dramatically, it is an enormous advantage (for the director, and even more for the actors) if the schedule keeps as close to the script-order of scenes as possible; and on *Secret People* it has been agreed to give this consideration particular weight. Financially, it is desirable not to spread the actors' engagements over too wide a period (it is more expensive to engage an artiste for five days' work over seven weeks, than for five days over a fortnight). Locations must be kept as late as practicable (on the off-chance of a little summer sunshine), and be provided with alternative scenes in the studio in case of bad weather.

Working out the schedule is like playing a rather intellectual nursery-game Ralph does it on a tall 'ladder' of his own devising—a wooden board divided vertically into six columns: one each for the studio's five stages, and a sixth (on the left) for a cardboard strip of dates, in this case running from March 5th to June 1st. Into the empty columns have been fitted strips of varying lengths, standing for the various sets. Thus: opposite the first four days, in the Stage 2 column, runs a strip labelled 'Café 1'; then (Stage 3a) 'Daly's Shop' and 'British Pavilion: Manager's Office'; then back to Stage 2 for 'Café 2', and so on. Everything seems to work beautifully, until we reach mid-April, and the shooting of the Ballet, on Stage 2. Sid reminds us that Andrée has asked that her concentrated work be got over by the beginning of April, to leave her free to rehearse the ballet she is arranging for the opening of the

40

Festival of Britain. Can we shove the Ballet back earlier? But that would mean breaking the continuity of the Café scenes—tidily arranged in three chronological blocks on Stage 2. And anyway, we cannot dismantle the Café set to make room for the Theatre, then rebuild it again. Can we build the Theatre set anywhere else? The Model Stage? William is very dubious, and certain that Gordon would object—it is so poorly equipped for lighting. How about 3a and 3b? Too small. But if we open the connecting door, build on 3a and shoot on to it from 3b? Let's go and have a look.

As we move off, we become conscious that Sid is crouched over the telephone in the corner, talking French in a sort of low shout. 'Oui . . . c'est presque certain . . . mercredi . . .' At the other end, apparently, is Serge, anxious to begin work. Valentina's permit is through, and his should come in time for him to fly over the day after to-morrow—in which case both our stars will be arriving on Wednesday.

FEBRUARY 6TH.—It is agreed that the Ballet *can* be shot on Stages 3a and 3b, and that it will be most useful all round if it can be cleared out of the way as soon as possible. So it is moved up to the beginning of the schedule, which has the advantage of keeping the three blocks of Café scenes intact and virtually in script-continuity. The schedule is O.K.'d, and can now be finally drawn up and duplicated.

FEBRUARY 7TH.—Valentina flies in from Hollywood, Serge from Paris. Press reception at the Dorchester; pictures in the evening papers.

At the Studio: budget meeting on casting.

FEBRUARY 8TH.—Meetings on Sets budget; Costume budget; Small-part and Crowd budget.

An announcement from the production office pushes our starting date forward a week, to March 12th.

FEBRUARY 9TH.—At the Studio, Valentina meets Ernie Taylor, make-up artist on the picture, and Barbara Barnard, who will dress her hair. Together with Thorold, they plunge into the problems presented by Maria's three variations in appearance—on arrival in London, as a girl of nineteen; seven years later; and as transformed into 'Lena Collins.' Thorold and Ernie are both anxious that this shall be done with a minimum of 'surgery': Ernie is sure that a most convincing change can be effected using make-up alone. Barbara advises a blonde wig for Lena, and long plaits for the arrival. Valentina, seated in front of Ernie's mirror, tries the effect of a blonde switch; likes it; pours out a torrent of very practical suggestions; pulls her face recklessly this way and that. 'For Maria,' she muses, 'I might wear a chignon. And for Lena, perhaps, glasses?' Thorold does not agree: 'I want Lena to be just as attractive—in a different way—as Maria.' ' "Men seldom make passes",' quotes Valentina, ' "At girls who wear glasses." Do you know that rhyme? It is very cruel. And anyway it is not true.' She will make tests for wigs and make-up on her return from Italy.

Later, and over the week-end, Valentina discusses the script with Thorold, and makes some suggestions.

41

FEBRUARY 12TH.—Further modifications to the script embody points made by Valentina. One, about which she is vehement, reduces Maria's evident preoccupation with food. It is now Louis who is cooking the prawns at the beginning of the scene in his Paris lodgings.

In the main projection theatre, Roberto plays over his Ballet score for Andrée, while director, producer, writer, deputy musical director huddle round the grand piano. 'I can't *quite* get your rhythm,' Andrée interposes rather frequently. Roberto finds this difficult to understand; he repeats the passage with increased emphasis. 'Can't you give us something absolutely simple, though?' Without thought, he ripples out a long, melodic phrase. Andrée is delighted. 'That's the sort of thing exactly. I'm afraid the audience may get lost in that more complicated music.' Roberto promises to simplify his score, still apparently astonished at the necessity.

Valentina confers with Anthony, and falls upon his designs with enthusiasm. She hands over to the Publicity Department a bundle of letters which have arrived at the Dorchester since her arrival. This is the sort of thing a film star is liable to be confronted with over the breakfast table:

'Dear Valentina Cortesa,—Hoping you will forgive an Englishman not as old or as young as your lovely self according to the *Mirror* photograph. It would be the greatest pleasure of my life to just have a good Cup of Tea with you. My assets are the finest Sight in the World and three small pensions. If I told I have eyes of all birds and animals, Millions of Human Beings see under water like fish, whales, sharks, crocodiles and all Electric Rays from Earth to Beyond the Sun and Moon. This letter is actually written by Radio. I have sent a Ray through the wireless around the Earth, as I am the only one who causes faults at night. I should like you to answer this letter from a lonely Englishman Who has eyes like you, hands and feet as the Master you see in all your Churches . . *Post-script*: I see more than anyone else when I go to the pictures. I can throw your pictures off the screen.'

Valentina's comment: 'Yes, it's horrible—but that's nothing, darling.'

FEBRUARY 13TH.—Sets and costumes for the Ballet discussed between Andrée and William and Anthony. 'Don't forget we're going to use a priest-character.' Anthony is delighted: 'I've got just the thing—a wonderful chasuble Alec Guinness wore in *Kind Hearts*. It was so elaborate that it provoked a furious complaint from a retired Protestant missionary in Finland. With any luck it'll do the trick again.'

FEBRUARY 14TH.—Valentina to Italy. Serge, now equipped with labour permit, identity card, ration book and income tax demands, moves from the Dorchester (with a sigh of relief) into a flat of his own, where he will be joined at the beginning of March by his wife, his little boy, and another baby who will put in an appearance during shooting. Meanwhile he gets to grips with the script, checking pronunciation on a tape-recorder, working with a tutor four or five afternoons a week.

FEBRUARY 15TH.—First test for Nora (using scene C.21, without Penny's entrance). This brings another, and distinctive character into the picture: Spike Priggen, who as first assistant director will be responsible for discipline on the floor and—with Ralph and Thorold—for the day-by-day administration and adjustment of the schedule. A humorous tyrant, Spike early bares his teeth at Andrée — who is cueing and encouraging her protégée with the kindliest of intentions, and the completest ignorance of union etiquette. 'If she doesn't watch out, I'll have her branched,' threatens Spike. 'She'll be moving the lamps next.'

After the test, Serge complains perplexedly of his nerves. 'And I don't sleep well.' Sister Ross provides him with some sedative pills and fixes him an appointment with the doctor. 'It's the artistic temperament,' she pronounces knowledgeably.

This evening Thorold and Sid travel down to Brighton to inspect a musical clown (needed for the Galbern garden party scene). No success.

Third draft shooting script appears.

FEBRUARY 16TH-18TH.—Flying visit to Dublin: director, art director, production manager, 2nd unit director, and a stills cameraman. Costing meetings on the picture have shown that the budget must somehow be reduced, and overseas locations are a particularly expensive item. So over this week-end, the Dublin schedule is shredded down to a total of three or four establishing shots, without artistes—all sited by Thorold in consultation with Terry Bishop, who will shoot them. Ralph meanwhile makes contact with the various authorities whose co-operation will be necessary—the Irish Army, the Police, the Electricity Supply Board.

At the same time, it is decided that a great saving will be effected if we abandon the attempt to reconstruct the interior of the Dublin Gaiety, and find a London theatre where we can shoot instead.

FEBRUARY 19TH.—Final discussion with Sir Michael on the shooting script. The chief points made concern dialogue. It is agreed that some additional writing could with advantage go into Maria's part, and accordingly a new writer—preferably a woman—will be brought in to do this. About the end: Sir Michael still feels it is 'a bit negative. I wish I could feel more strongly that Maria's death had not been all for nothing.' Alternative, or rather additional, endings are debated, but the general response is not enthusiastic. Thorold says: 'It's tricky, I know. I think whatever scene we devised, the audience would go home while it was playing. I think they'd just go home.'

Last week's Nora is reluctantly turned down. Her eyes, strangely enough, are *too* expressive: experience shows in them. Further tests will be needed, soon.

FEBRUARY 20TH.—Eighty theatres are telephoned in an attempt to find one suitable to represent the Gaiety.

FEBRUARY 21ST.—Andrée conducts an audition for the Corps de Ballet in a studio off the Marylebone Road. 'It's vivacity we want.' Thorold and Gordon attend, on the look-out for possible Noras: two are chosen for testing. Her partner, it has already been arranged, will be danced by John Field, from Covent Garden.

FEBRUARY 22ND.—In the projection theatre, Roberto runs through his final ballet score for Andrée, adjusted to meet her points of ten days ago. Agreement is reached. 'And you must remember,' he cautions, 'this is only the bare bones —I have concentrated on giving you the rhythm and the tunes. The feelings come after, in the orchestration.' Andrée replies: 'Well . . . yes, but you know, to a dancer it's the same whether it's played on a piano or a symphony orchestra.'

They proceed to dissect the music, establishing the dramatic significance of each section—rather like (as Sid remarks in an aside) two people speaking in different languages, but contriving nevertheless to hold a fruitful conversation. Andrée will seize on a bar: 'Now what exactly is happening here?' 'That is where the young man enters—that sustained note . . . You see?' She listens, makes a grimace. 'No, it isn't quite right. Couldn't we have it a little longer?' So here the music is extended, here emphasised, and here contracted, so that the finished piece may be dramatically as well as musically correct. Particularly admired is the melody for the *pas de deux*. Thorold demands that this be extended and repeated: 'And the second time we want it to *flower out*.' Roberto jumps at the phrase: 'Flower out—I shall remember that word . . . I like to be given words—adjectives—they seem to give me images.'

In the afternoon, Roberto, in consultation with Andrée, records the music in sections, for the Ballet to be rehearsed to. While over on Stage I another possible Nora is being tested.

FEBRUARY 23RD.—Two more tests for Nora: in the morning a dancer; in the afternoon, our first choice, Audrey Hepburn.

Lunch time is spent on a reconnaissance to a likely theatre—the Bedford, Camden Town, sad, damp and cold after the failure of its most recent actor-managers. Stills are taken of the boxes (each flanked by near-nude goddesses, gloriously moulded), while William notes and sketches, the Studio electrician acquaints himself with the installation, and tape measures are run out in all directions. Thorold, with a viewfinder, tries out a few angles. Though guarded in conversation with the owner, he and Sid admit themselves pleased as we return to the Studio. The location is all but fixed.

Audrey Hepburn's test. After the first run-through people start eyeing each other meaningfully; she has the quality all right. After another rehearsal it seems almost a waste of time to shoot the test.

FEBRUARY 26TH.—Now, and over the next few days, Thorold and William apply themselves closely to a duty which—if films could be made as the theories specify—should have been done simultaneously with the breakdown of treatment into shooting script. (At which time, however, William was still caught up with *The Lavender Hill Mob*.) Set by set, shot by shot, they work through the script, sketching each angle on the appropriate plan, making sure that the layouts will be adequate for Thorold to shoot the scenes as he visualises them. To each sequence the approach varies. On the Paris Exhibition set one principal angle is chosen (shooting towards the door of the British Pavilion) and all comprehensive shots in this direction are labelled MAIN; detail shots on the same bias are 'main'. Long shots in the opposite direction (towards the Terrace

44

Café where Louis is waiting) are REVERSE, with corresponding detail shots 'reverse'. Everything is quite straightforward until Anselmo, Maria and Nora break away from the crowd and make for the Terrace (B.37). William had imagined that this would be a static set-up, but Thorold asks for the camera to track and pan with them. William's face falls. 'That means I shall have to put something in there . . .' and his pencil jabs at an empty space at the back of the set. He ruminates. 'Or perhaps we can float this wall from here . . . Anyway . . .' Then Maria and Louis meet ('reverse') and talk ('If we have time, we'll have two close-ups there'). But how exactly has Maria been separated from Anselmo and Nora? 'I tell you what,' says Thorold, his finger tracing their route. 'If you could have a narrow way down there . . .' William interrupts: 'A statue—they can be separated by the statue.' So the scene is built.

The *Vieux Chapeau* sequence, when analysed in a similar way, reveals a more awkward snag. Starting with William's design before him, Thorold extends a swift clockwise arrow on the dance floor. 'That's the direction of the dance. Now we want to start on a close-up of Maria and Louis dancing— track back so as to reveal Steenie, in close-shot, watching from a corner. Then, if we cut back to a shot from over the bar, we have Louis and Maria dancing towards us.' Then suddenly it is realised: the dancers are moving in the wrong direction—the flow round a dance-floor is anti-clockwise. This affects the set: the same movement in a reverse direction brings Steenie to an inconvenient corner of the floor. Can the set be readjusted to satisfy all considerations without wholesale re-design? Reverse it? The drawing is turned back to front and held against the window. The arrow is now going in the right direction, but we lose the forward movement of the dancers when shot from the bar. To gain this, we will have to re-position the band. William frowns; this will mean extending the set, and additional expense. Pros and cons are debated; finally it is decided to sacrifice the effect of the dancers moving towards the bar, and settle for the original opening shot, with the original design in reverse.

At tea Thorold is contacted on the subject of crowd auditions by Muriel Cole, director of casting for small parts and crowd. (Muriel has a way of her own. She starts: 'May I bleat away rather pathetically for a moment and see what happens?'). Thorold is wondering about French types for the *Vieux Chapeau*: 'Can we go outside the union?' 'Frankly, no.' Before any extra can be engaged who is not in the union, every union member must have been auditioned and declared unsuitable. And in London—since to get them down to the Studio costs 10/- a head. Thorold agrees to attend an audition the day after to-morrow, for the patrons of Anselmo's Café.

Audrey Hepburn is Nora.

FEBRUARY 27TH.—Valentina returns from Italy, and starts fittings. Bad news is that she is not too well: she must return to Milan for a week's treatment before shooting begins. So our starting date goes on to Friday, March 16th.

FEBRUARY 28TH.—Crowd audition. Thorold and Muriel Cole meet in the West End for a lunch-hour tour through an assortment of cafés, followed by the audition of Anselmo's patrons. Serge accompanies them, dutifully absorbing *ambiance*. Successive cups of strange coffee are drunk, and, in a Soho café whose crammed horseshoe bar is the original of Anselmo's, brawn sandwiches are consumed and the clientele inspected.

The audition room is a brown, Victorian Gothic hall, ornamented with wooden carving and stained glass windows patterned with the heads of deceased composers. Anselmo's patrons (pre-selected by Muriel) ring the room. In the rounded tones of one who declares a bazaar open, Muriel introduces Thorold, who inspects the company, pairs them off, checks heights, and finally passes the lot.

March

Nearly there. The indisposition of one of the stars puts the starting date on from the 12th to the 16th—and the amount of additional preparation done in the unexpected lease (of three working days: in the end, shooting begins on the 15th) makes one wonder how the film could ever have started on the original date.

Over the beginning of the month, director and art director finish the shot-by-shot examination of the script which is designed to ensure the impossibility of arriving on the set to discover odd projections, levels or gaps which might make it impossible for Thorold to shoot a scene as he has imagined it. In the case of major sets, most of which have been already drawn out to scale, this has resulted only in detail alterations and expansions; the smaller sets, not yet designed, can be conceived from the first in terms of character- and camera-movement.

The other specialists are making ready simultaneously. Andrée puts the ballet into rehearsal, to Roberto's piano records, while the composer works on his orchestration. Anthony Mendleson designs costumes, and carries off members of the cast and corps de ballet for a succession of fittings. Ralph, reinforced by first and second assistant directors, is occupied with the formidable quantity of paper-work on which the organisation of production must be based. Casting of supporting parts, selection of crowd proceeds; and a full unit list is circulated, detailing names and addresses of all the principal members of the unit. Make-up tests are carried out on the leading artistes. For the dialogue revisions in Maria's part, a writer is contacted, introduced to the script, and gets down to work on it in consultation with the director and producer.

And on the second day of the month, Anselmo's Café begins to rise from the floor of Stage 2: an event as significant, and even more decisive, than the first turn of the camera four months ago.

MARCH 1ST.—Christianna Brand, writer, comes to the Studio to discuss possible dialogue alterations. She has read the script, and agrees that more colour can be put into Maria's lines. This she settles down to, working sometimes at home, sometimes at the Studio, submitting the revised scenes for Thorold's approval before they are passed on for duplication and incorporation into the script.

MARCH 2ND.—On Stage 2 the first set, Anselmo's Café, starts to grow. It is designed in two units: at one end of the stage the Café itself, with steps leading down into the cellar (a tank recessed into the floor, usually boarded over, but useful for constructions such as this, or to hold water for river or sea scenes) and a staircase up to the first floor landing. To facilitate lighting and shooting, the rest of the first floor will be built on ground level, at the other end of the stage.

By midday, floors are down, and a few flats are positioned around them. Against a far wall a couple of scenic artists (call them scene painters at your peril) are painting an exterior view, as it will be seen through the Café windows, of the houses opposite; they take the design from a drawing, and the details from stills taken on the actual location in Paddington. Note that the floors on this set have been specified for an absolutely smooth surface—obtained by basing them on sections of three-ply wood covered with linoleum. (The routine basis is felt under hessian under paper). This will enable Thorold to manœuvre his camera with complete freedom—for the tracks used in British studios are uniformly straight, with no provision for the diverse movements which are made possible by the curved tracks commonplace on the Continent and in America. The only disadvantage to our method is the resulting clatter of footsteps on the wooden base: the artistes' shoes will have to be felt-soled. Across the way, in the workshops, the rest of the Café—staircase, counter and kitchen—is under construction.

Michael Allen and John Chandos are interviewed in the Casting Office and cast—Rodd and John (of the London Committee).

MARCH 5TH.—In the Production Office Ralph is joined, for the duration, by Spike Priggen and John Meadows, first and second assistant directors. Together they go ahead with preliminary work on organisation, preparing Dope Sheets and Dress Charts—breakdowns of the script in terms of practical requirements necessary for its realisation. Thus Dope Sheets are essentially directives to all servicing departments, detailing all bodies, and everything those bodies wear, or use, in every scene in the picture: the script is divided into sets, the sets into sequences, the sequences into scene numbers; against each scene is listed an outline of the action, artistes involved, requirements from Prop Department, Construction, Special Effects, Wardrobe. Thirty-odd copies of these are circulated, to everyone who can use them. Similarly the Dress Charts list, under characters, full details of their several changes of costume; then, under scenes, the particular costume needed for each. Besides all this, the schedule is searched through endlessly, for any possible hitches, and to ensure that all casting is complete for the first scenes to be tackled

Valentina flies to Milan.

MARCH 6TH.—Andrée's second ballet rehearsal, in an all-purpose Church Hall. is attended by Thorold and Sid, Gordon and Wolfgang. At this stage the presentation is naturally rough. Under a garish mixture of neon and electric light the dancers perform in a wild variety of costume—the boys in tights or jeans or corduroy trousers, shirts or pullovers; the girls in sweaters, and tights, trousers or skirts. On the wall the clock sticks depressingly at twenty past nine. 'Pom-pom,' Andrée calls out, 'One-two-three-four. *Rum*titi-*rum*titi. Shuffle-shuffle . . .' Watching the run-through, Thorold begins to develop ideas on the behaviour of his camera; he makes suggestions to Andrée, who adjusts her choreography obligingly. 'I think,' he murmurs to Gordon, 'We'll have a nice long crane back during that first ensemble, when we get the whole company lined up on the stage together.' Lighting. 'We'll keep to one single source as much as possible,' says Gordon, 'I don't like double shadows thrown by dancers. And we should be able to get an effective change when Audrey is left alone on the stage; from evening to night, and bring up the lanterns. Then during the *pas de deux* we'll have no light at all on the scenery—just a misty darkness behind them.'

Timed on a final run-through, the whole ballet is found to run just short of four and a half minutes. 'Don't you think it's still a bit "plotty"?' someone asks Wolfgang. He shrugs: 'Look—I wanted *Spectre de la Rose* . . . .'

48

LOCATION   PRODUCTION 741 "SECRET PEOPLE"

SET: EXT. PHOENIX PARK
        - DUBLIN

SCHEDULE: 3 nights.   SCRIPT PAGES: 4¼

LOCATION: Gunnersbury Park. W.3.   SCRIPT SCENES: 25
          (to be confirmed)

Sc. No. D. or N.	Artistes.	Action.	Props,Effects & Remarks.

NIGHT-1938
 	
F.55.56.57.
58.59.60.
61.62.63.
64.65.66.
67.68.69.
70.71.72.
73.74.75.
76.77.78.
79.
	MARIA(LENA)
	NORA
	STEENIE
	LOUIS
	MISS JACKSON
	IRISH INSPECTOR
	IRISH SERGEANT
	TWO PASSERS-BY
	
	Taxi-driver
	Steenie's
	Driver.
	Irish Police
	Passers-by
		Maria breaks
		in on Nora's
		meeting with
		Louis,
		convinces her
		that she is
		wrong to get
		mixed up
		with the
		organisation.
		Steenie
		kills Maria.
			MAKE-UP: MARIA as
			LENA
			
			MARIA'S Irish Taxi,
			Irish Station-Wagon,
			STEENIE'S Car
			(these three
			   vehicles continuity
			   from NIGHT LOCATION
			EXT.STAGE DOOR &
			STREET - DORIC
			THEATRE)
			Other traffic
			(Irish, 1938)
			
			LIGHTING: Spec.
			headlamps for
			Station-Wagon (see
			Script F.67.68)
			
			Torch (specially
			powerful)for MARIA
			
			Another torch for
			STEENIE.
			
			Cigarettes &
			lighter for LOUIS.
			MARIA'S handbag,
			with contents, to
			include her
			father's fountain-
			pen.
			Knife for STEENIE
			(prop one with
			handle absorbing
			blade)

*Dope Sheet prepared by the production
office to cover the Phœnix Park scenes.*

MARCH 7TH.—Make-up, lighting, costume tests on Serge, Audrey, Charles Goldner.

MARCH 8TH.—Thorold, Charles and Spike make an expedition into Soho, in search of further atmosphere. Over cups of coffee they sit in the original of Anselmo's Café and observe and talk to the customers. Charles inspects the kitchen, assimilates the techniques, and spends a long time watching the boss tie his apron on. Thence to another ballet rehearsal.

At the Studio the Café nears completion. Time now for the set to be 'dressed' —i.e. clothed with furniture and props. First the upstairs unit, which is comprised of Anselmo's bedroom and the sitting room. The flats are papered with dowdy Victorian floral designs in brown and green; a heavy marbled fireplace carries an elaborate wooden-framed mirror. The furnishings are consistently late Victorian, of a solid ugliness which makes Andrew Low, the set-dresser, shake his head and think nostalgically back to the elegances of *Saraband For Dead Lovers* and *Kind Hearts and Coronets*. (Under William's general instructions, the set dressings are his particular responsibility, their acquisition the task of himself, in co-operation with the studio buyer.) Local colour is provided by a clutter of dusty medicine bottles on Anselmo's mantelshelf, an array of pictures and photographs (Relatives, Venice, the Pope), and a rosary which hangs at the head of his brass, beknobbed bedstead. A prop man makes up the bed, with the blue sheets and pillowcases which the eye of the camera will see as white. Above the set, level with the top of each wall, is lined a battery of spotlights, mounted on a continuous catwalk which is suspended from the roof on chains, and held firm by tubular scaffolding, also sprouting from the roof. The electricians who already stand by the lights, looking down with their peculiar air of distant attention, seem almost to have been moved in with the props.

After viewing yesterday's tests, Thorold announces that he intends to play all the cast in as little make-up as possible. 'It isn't really necessary, particularly for a story like this, where the whole emphasis must be on realism. Generally the only result of all that make-up is to take personality away from the faces and living texture out of skins.' In addition, this will have the advantage of easing the transformation of Maria into Lena Collins: since Valentina will have worn almost no make-up for the first two-thirds of the picture, it will be all the simpler to make the disguise convincing without over-elaboration.

MARCH 9TH.—Thorold flies to Glasgow to inspect a possible Clown act—the Rastellis, who shoot at each other comically with pistols. This might work effectively into the explosion scene; but commitments for the team in Germany over the next month or two may rule them out.

MARCH 12TH (Monday).—A day earlier than expected, Valentina returns from Milan. The starting date can accordingly be brought forward a day, to this Thursday (the 15th).

MARCH 13TH.—Getting off to an early start, a preliminary conference is held on Publicity—attended by Thorold, Sid and Ralph; Jack Dooley from the Stills Department; Pat O'Connor and John Newnham from Publicity; and John Woods, who supervises design and production of posters for Ealing films. Hal Mason presides.

First, how long is it likely to be before the picture is publicly shown? Hal: 'It usually takes us between 14 and 17 weeks from the end of shooting.' So, if nothing holds up any of the various stages, say early October in the West End. What about the poster campaign? John Woods says: 'I think it would be useful at this stage to have tentative ideas, particularly in relation to stills.' Thorold says: 'I don't want to lay down the law, but I think there's a tendency for publicity to get too geometrical—lacking in heart. We don't want the old melodramatic "story" poster, but it's equally wrong to have just an abstract design . . . I feel so intensely about show business—that it's an affair of emotion. The good taste end is subsidiary.'

Then there is the question of publicising the stars. Hal emphasises: 'We've got to do something about putting these personalities over. We've started with a week at the Dorchester . . . We do want to follow that up. Presumably the poster campaign will focus strongly on Cortesa and Reggiani . . .' Thorold: 'One important thing: on the Continent we'll be able to work through these stars, where they both have considerable reputations already. And at home, Cortesa is already a star, through her American pictures. But I agree that we do need to concentrate on getting these two known and talked about before the film comes out—most particularly in the case of Reggiani, since this is his first English-speaking film.' Pat O'Connor: 'Reggiani has already broadcast in the B.B.C. European service . . . .'

On stills. 'The difficulty,' says Jack Dooley, 'is in really getting the atmosphere of the picture if you start on portraits and groups right away.' Ralph points out: 'Cortesa has scarcely a free day in the schedule to squeeze stills sessions into.' Hal: 'All the more reason for starting straight away. We can grab anything that's missing later.' John Woods: 'Could we try and get all persons connected with the film in publicity stills? I'm always in difficulties, particularly with Major Baker.'

MARCH 14TH.—The lines converge. The set, ground- and first-floor, is complete, and Gordon spends part of the day prelighting it for to-morrow's shots. Further make-up tests are shot—on Audrey in her ballet costume and make-up; and on Valentina as Lena Collins. (This appears—to the naked eye—to succeed astonishingly. Blonde, exquisitely painted, Lena has that rather forbidding, surfaced beauty one associates with photographs in *Vogue*. The distinction from the fresh, life-like charm of Maria could not be more complete.)

The director's day is spent in almost continual conference. With Christianna Brand, reporting her task accomplished, debating a few final suggestions. With Ralph and Spike, conferring on the scenes scheduled for to-morrow and the best order of shooting. With William, inspecting the set and props for use during the coming week—Maria's photograph album ('Entirely wrong: it couldn't take the size of picture we need—not less than postcard size'); Pietro Brentano's pen ('It should have his name on it'); designs for the front cover of the Ballet programme . . . With Margaret Harper-Nelson and Muriel Cole, discussing casting and viewing possibilities (Dublin theatre barmaid; Woman on Paris Committee; Commissionaire of the British Pavilion at the Exhibition). Andrée reports the Ballet all but ready for shooting; the costumes have all been fitted and will be delivered to the wardrobe department to-morrow; Roberto's full orchestral score is being copied in the music department in readiness for a recording session on Friday.

Late afternoon, Valentina and Serge report at Thorold's home to be given the last batch of new script pages, and to essay a trial read through their principal scenes together. Since many of the lines are new to them, this does not go without stumbling. 'We are *lousy*,' calls Valentina. Serge grins, and blesses the schedule which gives him ten further days of preparation. 'My lousy stars,' says Thorold, with a benignant smile.

Studio Unit List

ISSUED FROM THE STUDIO MANAGER'S OFFICE
1st March, 1951.

This is the unit assigned to the making of *Secret People*, who will be engaged on it five days a week (excluding week-end work) for the next eleven weeks; from eight-thirty in the morning to five-fifty (Wednesdays and Fridays) or six-twenty (Mondays, Tuesdays and Thursdays)—excluding overtime. The list is not exactly as published. I have divided it into departments and appended nicknames where people are mentioned by such in the Diary.

PRODUCTION
Producer: Sidney Cole (Sid).
Director: Thorold Dickinson.
General Manager and Production Supervisor: Hal Mason.
Studio Manager and Technical Supervisor: Baynham Honri (Bay).
Production Costing: Orlando King.
Production Buyer: F. Lacy.

Unit Production Manager: Ralph Hogg.
1st Assistant Director: Norman Priggen (Spike).
2nd Assistant Director: John Meadows.
3rd Assistant Director: J. O'Connolly (Jimmy).
Continuity: Phyllis Crocker (Phyll).

CASTING
Casting Director: Margaret Harper-Nelson.
Assistant Casting: Thelma Graves.
Casting (Crowd and Small Parts): Muriel Cole.

CAMERA
Lighting Cameraman: Gordon Dines.
Camera Operator: Chic Waterson. (For the first fortnight this was deputised by Ron Taylor).
Camera Assistant: Herbert Smith. (Deputy: Ken Westbury).
Loading and Clappers: Ken Westbury. (Deputy: Michael Shepherd).
Camera Grips: Ted Lockhart.

ART DEPARTMENT
Art Director: William Kellner.
Assistant Art Director: Bert Davey.
Scenic Artist: G. Dickinson (Dicky).
Set Dresser: Andrew Low.
Special Effects: S. Pearson.

STILLS DEPARTMENT
Stills Supervisor: Jack Dooley.
Floor Stills: R. Penn (Bobby) (Deputy: Roy Gough).

SOUND DEPARTMENT
Sound Supervisor: Stephen Dalby.
Sound Mixer: A. Bradburn (Brad).
Sound Camera Operator: E. Stockl.
Boom Operator: Cyril Swern.
Assistant Boom Operator: R. Healy.
(Deputy: Martin Maclean).

EDITING DEPARTMENT
Editor: Peter Tanner.
1st Assistant: Alastair McIntyre.
2nd Assistant: Roy Baker.

Make-Up Supervisor: Ernest Taylor (Ernie).
Make-Up Assistants: Harry Frampton, H. Wilton.
Hairdressing Supervisor: Barbara Barnard.
Hairdressing Assistant: Daphne Martin.

COSTUME DEPARTMENT
Wardrobe Supervisor and Costume Designer: Anthony Mendleson.
Wardrobe Master: Ernest Farrer.
Wardrobe Assistant: Ben Foster.
Wardrobe Mistress: Lily Payne.
Ladies' Wardrobe Assistant: Edith Crutchley.

ELECTRICAL DEPARTMENT
Chief Electrician: Jack Ford.
Floor Electrician: Tom Chapman.

PROPERTIES DEPARTMENT
Property Master: Bob Tull.
Floor Props. I/C: Harry Phipps.
Floor Props.: W. Hill.

CONSTRUCTION DEPARTMENT
Construction Manager: George Speller.
Stand-by Carpenter: J Forret.
Stand-by Stagehand: W. Gunner.
Stand-by Rigger: A. Leonard.
Stand-by Painter: A. Radford.

MUSIC DEPARTMENT
Director: Ernest Irving, HON. R.A.M.
Assistant Director: Dock Mathieson, A.R.C.M.
Librarian: James Crawford.
Secretary: Una Bart.

54

Schedules

'Read in conjunction with the Cross Plot on page 57, the
Schedule on page 56 shows the progress of the picture in
terms of sets worked and artistes employed. Crosses, letters,
or figures in the squares indicate the proposed course of
shooting; diagonal shading represents work actually carried
out. Thus by reading vertically down any column it is
possible to see the set scheduled for any particular day,
with the artistes involved; and (by the shading) the sets and
artistes actually used.'

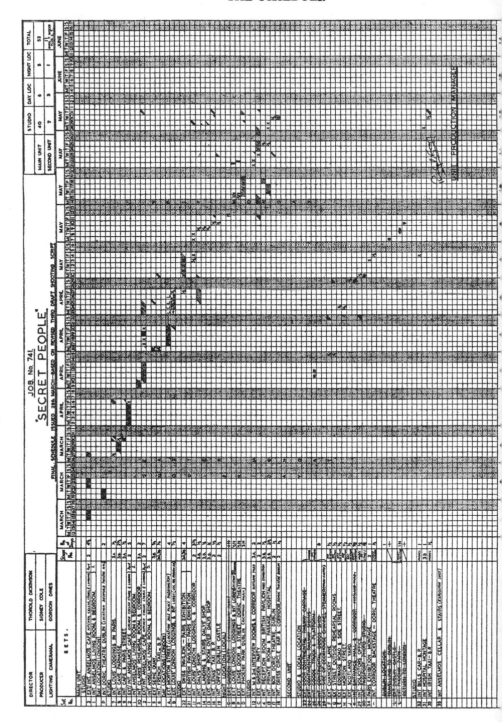

THE CROSS PLOT

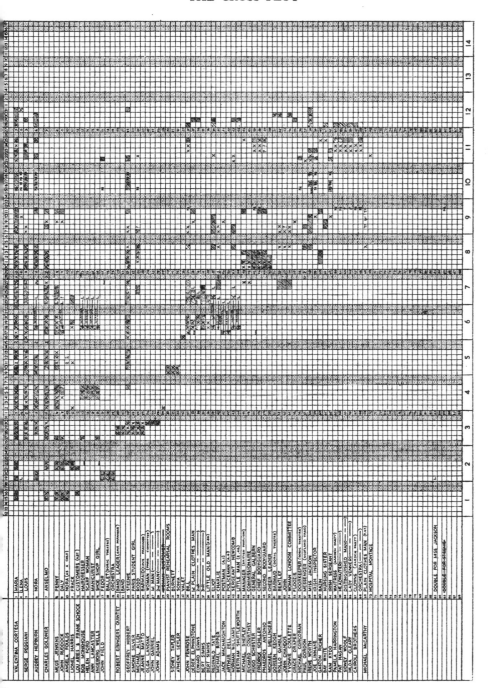

Diary

First Week

After the various alterations of starting date, 'Secret People' finally goes on the floor on Thursday, March 15th, 1951. For the first week the schedule concentrates primarily on the first slab of scenes in Anselmo's Café — the prologue to the story proper. This will take us up to the end of Part I of the script: the arrival of the girls, and the news of Brentano's death. Sandwiched into the middle of this concentrated shooting on Stage 2 are three days (including Sunday) on location at the Bedford Theatre, Camden Town; here we will be shooting the Ballet which Maria (now Lena Collins) watches Nora dance at the end of the picture. Preparations for this start on Friday, when equipment will go out from the Studio while the unit continues work on the floor; at the same time the Ballet music will be recorded at Denham to be available for the dancers' final rehearsal on Sunday.

Of the cast, the first day introduces Charles Goldner as Anselmo, Megs Jenkins as Penny, and John Ruddock as Daly. Valentina Cortesa will make her entrance as Maria on Friday, and Audrey Hepburn will appear for the first time at the Bedford. Serge Reggiani, whose first call is not till the seventh day of shooting, can meanwhile continue to work on his part.

THURSDAY, MARCH 15TH

Would you expect the kick-off to be accompanied with flags, bands and a sense of the momentous? If so, you would be wrong. On the production notice board at the gate is pinned call sheet number one, a sober enough document, with calls for Mr. Charles Goldner, Miss Megs Jenkins and Mr. John Ruddock. Stage 2, at 8.15, shows little activity: a few advance members of the unit have begun to collect round the top-floor set of Anselmo's Café, otherwise the floor is quiet and unlit. In Thorold's office the cleaner is surprised at my arrival: 'You're not usually in as early as this.' (Indeed no.) Thorold himself arrives on my heels, hoarse but apparently recovered from his incipient 'flu; there is a nostalgic glitter in his eye. 'Isn't it extraordinary how the types vary in the underground according to the time of day you travel? It's years since I've come to Ealing by a train as early as that, but I'm positive I recognised lots of the old faces.'

Making for the stage, we find it now fully alive. Besides electricians, carpenters, propmen and all the other anonymous craftsmen, the featured specialists find themselves gathered together for the first time: Barbara and Ernie, Arthur Bradburn with his two assistants on sound, Gordon, Ron Taylor and the camera crew, Phyllis with stopwatch and notepad, William, closely flanked by Andrew and Bert. And, of course, Ralph and Spike, the brisk co-ordinators. Before anything gets under way, Ralph calls the unit together for a brief address—the name of the picture, mostly studio work, about a week of night locations, any questions? Someone suggests a fortnight on nights would be more amusing. 'Most of you know the story, I expect,' Ralph proceeds imperturbably. 'If you don't there are scripts available for you to borrow.' Would Thorold like to say anything? No: Thorold prefers to conserve his voice. 'Oh, and finally let's remember that we have two stars not used to work- ing in this country. Let's make them feel we're right behind them.' 'Very moving,' comments Gordon as the group disperses

We are starting on A.10: Anselmo's bedroom, Anselmo on his bed, replete with ham, listening to his gramophone; Penny disturbs his siesta with the news of Maria's and Nora's arrival, and the letter from Pietro. (This is the shot which the script specifies as one set-up, but which has since been split into two.) One wall of the bedroom—that facing the bed—is floated away; the camera wheels in on the velocilator; and Charles, fully padded and moustached, is deposited on the bed, to be sited by Thorold through the viewfinder. In con- sultation with Ron and Gordon, viewpoint (mid-shot, lowish angle) and lens (35mm.) are chosen; the camera is wheeled up to the chalk mark, and Gordon proceeds to light the shot.

It all goes with a somehow unexpected ease. Before we know where we are (or I know where I am) Spike has called for one bell and the action is being finally rehearsed. This involves the timing not merely of Charles's movements and speech, but also of Penny's knock on the door (provided by one of the carpenters with his hammer). In the process a few details are added: Charles is given a Toscana to smoke; a little sweat is sprayed to his brow. Then we are ready to go. The tape is run out. Spike calls for the shooting bell. 'Camera.' Ron starts her up; his assistant comes forward with the clapper board— Secret People: camera No. 7; slate No. 1; take 1. 'Ready,' says Thorold, and then, softly, 'Begin.'

On the first take the knock is mistimed and Charles is left dangling. 'Cut it.' The timing is explained and we go again, this time without a hitch. 'That'll do,' says Thorold. 'Print it?' someone queries in surprise. 'Yes, why not?' The stills-cameraman nips in to take his set still (each set must be covered in case any have to be reassembled again for retakes); and Brad interjects a query on sound. 'I'm getting a slight noise off that gramophone' (it has been turning silently but for the hiss of the needle on the surface of the record). 'Could we have a wild take, without the gramophone playing?' 'But you'll be dubbing music on anyway,' Thorold comments; but Brad is not convinced. 'Well, let's not argue.' And, for sound only, the scene is repeated.

'O.K. two bells.' This is the signal for activity to break out all over: the camera pulls out; the microphone slides away; led by Thorold with the view- finder, Gordon, Ron, Spike and the rest of the unit make for the point of view of the next shot. In this case the wall behind Anselmo must be quickly floated, as the wall through which we have been shooting is replaced: this is for the reverse set-up, in which we will cover Penny's entrance, the delivery of Pietro's letter, and Anselmo's reading of it. By this time Megs has arrived, to walk through the scene while Thorold decides on his camera angle and movement— tracking into Anselmo, an abrupt stop as the contents of the letter hits him, then a resumed movement into medium close shot as he continues to read.

Once actors' and camera's movements are decided, the stand-ins take over as the business of lighting begins again. But Charles is not allowed to rest: on the living-room set he is meanwhile rehearsed by Thorold in the action of the next shot—Anselmo's hurried progress from his bedroom, through the living-room, to the head of the stairs, to inspect the new arrivals. 'A little more *delicatesse*,' beseeches Thorold, as Charles bounces ebulliently across the set . .

This flying start sets the key for the day; by twelve we have covered the delivery of the letter, a close-shot of Charles reading it, an insert of the letter, and Charles's dash through the living-room. This brings us to the Café: Anselmo, Daly, Penny and the Red Cross parcel. John Ruddock appears from makeup and the unit streams up to the other end of the stage, where a sudden flood of light has conjured into life the Café interior, the street outside (complete with furniture van), and the reduced-scale façade of the houses opposite. The action, more complicated here, takes a little time to get right; Gordon starts lighting; we break for lunch.

This unanticipated speed calls for a change of plan; we will be through to-day's schedule with perhaps a couple of hours to spare. Surveying the possible alternatives with Thorold, Ralph and Spike pick four shots out of to-morrow's schedule, and call Maria and Nora when young, for three o'clock. After lunch, and rushes (yesterday's make-up tests on Maria show her transformation is as effective through the camera as to the naked eye), back on the floor again; the interrupted shot is rehearsed and captured on the first take. Round to the kitchen, where we shoot Penny depositing the Red Cross parcel on a shelf, then pan down to 'the magnificent fatty ham'. An insert of a denuded ham bone follows; then back to the Café. From the top of the stairs Anselmo views the new arrival with alarm (one set-up); and the day finishes with the appearance in the set of Valentina and little Angela Fouldes, to greet Anselmo for the first time.

Breaking off with eleven set-ups to our credit, we feel we have made a good start. Phyllis tots up her estimate of the total screen time on the used takes: two minutes, fifty-seven seconds. Scenes disposed of: A.10, 11, 12, 13, 7, 8, 9, 15, 16, 18, 20, 10a.

FRIDAY, MARCH 16TH

The four extra shots taken yesterday set Ralph busy with alternative schedules—in case we catch up still further. Typical point: to-day we could do with Frack, who will have to be present in one of the Café shots. But Lionel Harris has been cleared for a BBC programme; so we will have to make do with a double, and keep him well in the background. Next week's shooting at the Bedford represents another chore for the Production Department—not least the victualling of the unit. Lunches for 120: a figure which pleases Ralph by corresponding exactly to his rough guess. ('My private system: estimate the number of hands you'll need, double it, and add 10 per cent.')

In the studio, work proceeds on the 'A' Sequence Café scenes. Meanwhile a party from the Sound and Music Departments sets out for Denham, where the ballet is to be recorded for playback at the Bedford on Monday and Tuesday. The operation is conducted by Ernest Irving, with the Philharmonia Orchestra; in close attendance are Roberto and Andree, with Audrey, John, and a skeleton troupe of dancers. (Not to mention Steve Dalby, to supervise the recording; Mac, to hold a brief for the Editing Department; and Sid, to keep all the wheels oiled.)

In a recording theatre the size of an Ealing stage—or a small concert hall—we first of all run through the ballet for Roberto to approve three cuts which Andrée has made in his score. This, and the ensuing discussion, takes till lunch; after which we reassemble, with the addition of the orchestra, to start the recording proper.

Seated on his rostrum, white coat, white hair, white beard gleaming in the shaft of a brilliant spotlight, Ernest is in unmistakable charge of proceedings. Behind him, anxious in defence of their own, stand Roberto and Andree, the one jealously attentive to his orchestration, the other stressing always the claims of movement. After a trial run-through, we try it with the ballet: it is as though the dancers have slid into slow motion. Roberto and Andree are eager with their comments. Ernest listens, then announces to the orchestra, 'It's got to be played faster than you'd think it should be.' For convenience, the score is split into six sections: taking the last first, we get down to detailed work on the *pas de deux*. At last a tempo is achieved that seems to satisfy everyone: the buzzer sounds for the first take. By 3.45 the version is approved.

By this time we are beginning to look anxiously at the clock: we have got to be out of the theatre by 5.30, and the process of reaching tripartite agreement is not a speedy one. Switching to the opening of the ballet, we achieve Part I by 4.50, and Part II by a quarter past five. The session ends with a rush. Part III is recorded by 5.26; then, in an atmosphere tense with the desire to depart ('I'm missing my massage,' one of the ballet boys complains) Ernest sweeps the orchestra through another section. On the dot of 5.30 instrumentalists and dancers are streaming to the door, and somehow—we are mystified to hear—the recording has been successfully completed.

Scenes shot in the studio: A.14, 17, 19, 21, 22, 24, 36, 22a. Screen time: 1 minute 47 seconds. Thorold and Sid make straight for the Palladium, to inspect yet another Clown for Galbern's party.

SUNDAY, MARCH 18TH

Temporarily, the centre of interest shifts from the Studio to the Bedford Theatre, and from the beginning to nearly the end of the picture. On Thursday and Friday, advance squads have been at work, checking, installing and constructing; arriving early on Sunday morning we find the ballet décor in position, the built-up tracks erected for the culminating track-in on the *pas de deux*, and on them the 2,000 lb. camera crane which somehow someone got in here on Friday morning. The stage lighting has all been inspected, the footlights rewired and replaced; dressing rooms have been (partially) cleaned; fire appliances checked. The morning is occupied largely with the unloading and installation of electrical equipment from the Studio, under Gordon's supervision: a snag is struck when it is discovered that no one knows how to get into the gallery—the street entrance is bolted on the inside. Half an hour's search discloses a camouflaged door in the least likely part of the theatre, and up go the arcs.

Dancers, called sharply for ten, spend most of the day sitting despondently in the stalls, wondering why it is always like this. How are they to know that we are held up by the discovery that the camera-head on this crane will not take our camera (standardisation in such matters being evidently a thing of the future), and a replacement has to be fetched from Walton-on-Thames? Even after the lunch break there is much to be done before we can get down to

61

actually looking at dancers through the camera: a cloud glass (to project cloud-shadows, magic lantern style, on the backing) is installed in the circle; saws are produced and William's decor is simplified by the excision of a vine or two; the playback is positioned and tested; the public address system is put in working order. The music is several times played through and minutely timed by Phyllis.

To guide her through the shooting of the ballet, she prepares a 'breakdown' of it to stopwatch—one column for its timing in seconds, the next detailing the principal points of action on the stage, and a third for the camera directions which are given her by Thorold. This last is as yet only skeletal.

It is halfway through the afternoon before we can start lining up the first (which is the ballet's last) shot; Gordon lights as Thorold watches Audrey and John through the viewfinder, sighting also on to the box where Maria will be sitting. Once this last angle is chosen and lit, we can rehearse the whole movement to music—the slow track-in, halting halfway; the resumed track, the pan round on the revolving figures of Nora and Fedor, the descent of the curtain.

This brings us to five o'clock when the day's work is due to end; but the Unit has volunteered (through their shop steward) to go on an extra half hour, so there is just time for a complete run-through of the ballet. Not surprisingly the dancers show the effect of a day's wait in a chilly theatre; but 'It'll all be all right on the night,' murmurs Thorold undisturbed as we break for home.

MONDAY, MARCH 19TH

Eight-thirty at the Bedford, and we are ready to embark on the arduous task of shooting the ballet entire in two days. Yesterday's long preparation gets us off to a good start, with first set-up and movement already established, but has infected Thorold also with a dense cold—not the best incentive to creative improvisation. To-day the theatre presents a livelier (or at least more populated) appearance: 47 crowd artistes, half of them in evening dress, are here—for although we will have none of the regulation shots of audiences watching, dreamy-eyed, we have to cheat the impression of a crowded theatre. Chilly, the ladies shiver and draw their wraps around them: the exit doors are lodged open by the cables which carry power to the lamps from the Paxman generator in the alley outside.

(The Paxman, by the way, deserves a page all to itself. It is unique in the world—the largest single-source generator ever to be put on a lorry—and the pride and joy of Ealing in general, and Jack Ford (Chief Electrician) in particular. Mounted on an eight-wheel lorry, weighing twenty-one tons, it can generate up to 2,300 amps. 'ABPC have got two which go to 2,000; and Pinewood have one at 1,700,' Jack admits indulgently, 'but we're still unique.')

Positioned in the stalls by nine o'clock, our audience sits waiting patiently for further instructions, for their tea break, for lunch, for another break, and finally for their pay. The Corps de Ballet show themselves less familiar with film routine. They imagine, apparently, that yesterday's rehearsal should make to-day's first shot a simple matter: by 9.30 they are dressed and in the stalls, waiting their turn to perform. By 12.30, with Roberto's lyric theme flooding from the playback for the fiftieth time (it seems), and the camera moving in for the seventh take, their ready interest has congealed into bored acceptance. Only Audrey and John, on the stage, seem to have an endless fund of vitality to expend.

62

SOUND SCENE REPORT
CAMERAS: MITCHELL A. 7

Prod....741.............. A......35..mm.   Day.....................   Int.   ....DORIC..THEATRE

Date ....19th..March.51.. B..................   Night...NIGHT... Ext. ....

Script Scene....F..40............ C.................   Fig...........................

Takes ....4.7.8...... D...................

Slates ....20.........GUIDE..TRACK...   Time ....

PLAYBACK "BALLET"

CRANE SHOT TRACKING ON TO STAGE.	MARIA & MISS JACKSON (DOUBLE) WATCH NORA DANCING HER SOLO & THEN PAS DE DEUX WITH FEDOR. THE TABS DROP & NORA & FEDOR CLASP EACH OTHER HAPPILY.

Camera shoots from HALF WAY DOWN RIGHT SIDE GANGWAY OF STALLS, across AUDIENCE seated in LEFT FRONT STALLS, looking r. and holds STAGE r. and TWO CIRCLE BOXES 1. MARIA sits in BOX NEARER STAGE, leaning forward, r.h. shielding her eyes, looking r. with MISS JACKSON (DOUBLE) sitting to r. and behind her. MISS WARRENDER & MR. C. BROWN sit in BOX FURTHER FROM STAGE. ORCHESTRA PIT with CONDUCTOR standing, conducting.

MARIA watches NORA dancing her SOLO and then the PAS DE DEUX with FEDOR. CAMERA TRACKS FORWARD ON TO   STAGE, CRANES UP & SWINGS ANTI-CLOCKWISE and finishes shooting from BACK OF STAGE past NORA & FEDOR dancing in foreground, over ORCHESTRA PIT & AUDIENCE in STALLS and holds CIRCLE BOXES in background. TABS DROP SLOWLY until MARIA is hidden from view. NORA & FEDOR pivot in foreground and when MUSIC FINISHES, clasp each other happily, standing in profile, NORA r. and FEDOR l. of screen.

MUSIC COVERED.

Mins.	Secs.	
2.	15.	PLAYBACK commences.
2.	28.	NORA pirouettes down to footlights.
2.	33.	SOLO commences. (1st TANGO).
2.	45.	NORA kneels in 'obeisance' as if to MARIA.
2.	58.	FEDOR reappears from wings l.
3.	10.	PAS DE DEUX commences.
3.	20.	FEDOR lifts NORA (1st TIME).
3.	25.	CAMERA TRACKS FORWARD ON TO STAGE AS FEDOR LOWERS NORA.
3.	30.	(2nd TANGO)
4.	05.	FEDOR lifts NORA (2nd TIME)
4.	25.	CAMERA IN FINAL POSITION ON STAGE shooting past NORA & FEDOR with CIRCLE BOXES beyond. TABS START TO DROP SLOWLY. NORA & FEDOR pivot.
4.	47.	MUSIC FINISHES. NORA & FEDOR clasp each other.

Take 1. 240 ft. N:G: crane.

2. 170 ft. N:G: CUT. FEDOR'S wig and bandeau flew off.

3. 240 ft. N:G:A: NORA & FEDOR wide on crane's final position.

4. 245 ft. PRINT.

5. 240 ft. N:S:G: for Crane. (Slowed down too much).

6. 255 ft. RESERVE. (NORA & FEDOR pivotting off marks at end).

7. 235 ft. PRINT.

8. 245 ft. PRINT.

Continuity sheet for the first set-up in the two days' shooting on the ballet. (See illustrations on plate 3.)

It proves a shot as difficult as it is important. Time and again the record starts, and the dancers go into their *pas de deux*. Thorold stands, attentive to the music, until he recognises the cue, nods sharply, and gives the word to start. Smoothly the crane moves forward down the tracks; the camera stretching out on its streamlined arm; the crew (operator with eye glued to the viewfinder; assistant with fingers gently adjusting focus) clinging on with devout intentness. While behind, placid and unfaltering, marches the acolyte whose touch propels the whole, on whose sense of rhythm and timing, as much as anything, depends the success of the shot—Ted Lockhart, Camera Grips. As we move in, holding on the left of frame Maria and Miss Jackson in their box, and on the right the dancers on the stage, Ron has to watch his angle with care—if he comes as far to the right as ideal composition would demand, the tracks come into picture; as it is, they are covered, for safety's sake, with a strip of black curtain, whisked away by the prop man as the camera rolls in. Then there are the dancers themselves, to present inevitable variations of positioning, and the problem of the final angle, to which our lens—from the necessary finishing position of the track—will only just subtend: the box now top right in frame, the dancers revolving slowly in mid-shot on the stage, the curtain descending like doom between. On the first take the crane movement is mistimed; during the second, John's wig flies off in the middle of a pirouette: the third spreads the dancers too wide on the stage; the fourth we can print. But on a shot of this importance we must have cover, and we proceed: fifth take —camera too slow; sixth—possible, reserve; seventh and eighth—both print. We break for late lunch (ten past one) with the assurance that at least one of our takes must be good; on return the orders can be given to strike the track and shift the camera for the next set-up.

The achievement of what we know to be the trickiest shot of the sequence breaks the back of the day. Now it is a question of covering the rest from the series of (except one) static set-ups which Thorold planned on our first reconnaissances and yesterday. While the crane is manhandled off the stage, we cover a shot on the conductor; then up to the back of the circle for the opening shot of the sequence—a programme held in close-shot during the first few bars of the Overture, then whipped away to disclose the stage and the entry of the dancers. With three cameras now on the job, we cover the action simultaneously from further angles. The Corps de Ballet have no call now to complain of inaction.

William, visiting his set during the day, hears the ballet music for the first time, and finds it less Spanish than he has been led to expect. 'If I would have known it was like this, I would have made my décor much more Central European,' he explains, pained.

Scenes shot: F.29, 30, 31, 40, 46. Screen time: 2 minutes, 27 seconds.

TUESDAY, MARCH 20TH

Attempting to defeat his throat infection, Thorold retired last night with penicillin and a sleeping draught. This has kept him under only too well, and he does not appear in the theatre this morning until half-past nine, to find the first set-up prepared, and the unit waiting, a certain smugness tincturing their patience. This check, together with the discovery from rushes (viewed during the morning at a cinema round the corner) that the opening shot must be retaken, presents a challenge. We set to under pressure, the ballet sections, liberally overlapping, repeated over and over, the three cameras shifting between positions in the circle, rostra and ground-level in the stalls, and Maria's box. (We are restricted to audience viewpoints, for otherwise the surprise and particular quality of the last movement would be diluted.) Time is lost sight of, or rather signalled only by the break for lunch, and the arrivals, mid-morning and afternoon, of the mobile canteen from the Studio. *Note:* Tea and solids provided free when on location. Teacups litter the stalls and the music goes around and around. Under the stress nerves do not snap, but they tend to fray. Andrée, ceaselessly vigilant of her dancers, is inclined to call out instructions when Spike thinks she should not. He gives her one of his looks. 'I'd sooner work with animals from the zoo,' he grunts, not out of earshot.

Of the members of the unit who remain unaffected by vagaries of temperament, Phyllis, Continuity, is surely the most unshakably under control. Script open in her hands, pencil perpetually at the ready, she shadows Thorold round the theatre, plotting the course we have run, mindful of what yet remains to do. If she has a somewhat intimidating appearance, an earnestness about her not encouraging to the idle questioner, it is really only because she has so much to do, and is so busy doing it well, that there is no time for her to gossip or relax. (Though of course there is, too, her strict and kindly personality, which would not in any event, one suspects, extract much pleasure from chatter.) 'Don't ask me what Continuity is—you either talk about it for five hours, or you just say nothing at all . . .' But over a cup of tea, she will be more indulgent, and explain enough of her job to make it clear that the term 'Continuity Girl', with its implication that her function is chiefly to see that a man wearing a spotted tie in long-shot does not mysteriously appear with a striped one in close-up, is quite misleading. She is here, in fact, to record on paper, as fully as possible, all that is said, done, worn, moved in front of the camera; the behaviour of the camera itself; she must safeguard the director from possible mistakes (a fragment of scene left uncovered, a glance that will not cut in with a shot already taken), check the artistes on their dialogue, keep record of the way the day is spent. Her instruments are stopwatch, script, propelling pencil, typewriter, and a plentiful supply of carbons. During rehearsals and takes, you find her by the camera, at Thorold's side, noting, checking, till the blank backs of her script pages are covered with shorthand scribbles—clothes worn, positions of artistes, action, dialogue changes and variation from take to take. And in the intervals she will retire to her desk (placed usually at a vantage point removed from interference, but near enough to the set for observation) to type her 'sheets'—informing editor (two copies), producer, and studio general manager of the details of every shot we cover: camera position and movement, action and dialogue, length of shot, number of takes, lens, focus and lens-aperture. Besides these, Phyll is responsible each day for a diary of activity —a bare hour-by-hour report of how time has been spent on the floor (to-day's for instance has the ominous note against 9.15 that we were 'waiting for director'); and also a daily Progress Report, summarising the day's continuity sheets.

About this work on the ballet, Phyll is quite sanguine. 'This isn't as difficult as some things, because of course the dancers know what they have to do— and they do pretty well the same thing every time. Unlike some artistes. . . . The only tricky thing is to be sure we cover every bar of music not just on film, but from the right set-up. I'd prefer to be doing this from a score, but apparently there just isn't one available. . .' And she is away to where Thorold is siting a new set-up from a rostrum in the stalls.

Last shot to-day finds us tracking away from a crowded stage up the centre aisle—fortunately just wide enough to take the wooden tracks which carry the crane and give it smooth passage. Anxiety proves unjustified, and we get there with half an hour in hand: so up on the stage again, and we take a final close-shot on Audrey and John, embracing excitedly after the curtain has descended.

Scenes shot: *F*.32, 33, 34, 36, 37, 38, 39, 32*a*, *b*, 34*a*, *b*, 40*a*, *b*. Retake *F*.29. *Screen time*: 2 *minutes* 17 *seconds*.

WEDNESDAY, MARCH 21ST

A few days on the floor are enough to make plain the formidable nature of the task: to translate just a little of this atmosphere into words, this atmosphere compounded of so many elements, so variously coloured, so many skills, so variously applied.

There is the outsider's view: the cavernous stage, like a vast, soundproof aircraft hanger, with a few rather weakly burning lamps dotted across the roof. And in the centre of the floor, or perhaps in a corner, an area where light and activity intensify. Inside a structure of unpainted wooden flats, ringed by lights, connected to the roof by scaffolding, trestles, chains, is your Soho café, your Paris nightclub, your Paddington boarding house. To the uninitiated the excitement of this discovery soon pales; for most of the time little appears to be happening, people are standing about, sitting about, or, if occupied, performing mysterious, unrelated functions. A camera is to be seen, and a microphone, stretched into the set on the long, slender arm of its boom; in the background a girl is typing busily; all around, in amongst a flotsam of lamps, cables, canvas chairs, are people (some of whom one seems to recognise) sitting in various attitudes of boredom or exhaustion, hammering, carrying objects this way and that, or standing about in little, loquacious groups. Comparatively rarely there will be silence on the stage and action on the set; and even this is apt to resolve itself into intimate conversations between director and actors, or cameramen, or sound men, so quiet as to be without significance to the eavesdropper, and probably incomprehensible when overheard. And even when the actors are allowed to perform without interruption, their scenes are so short that they are almost over before the spectator has realised what is going on.

Such is one view of the floor—an incomplete one it is true, but then no view can be wholly objective, and the outsider is perhaps more alive to the elements (which certainly exist) of mystery and magic in film making than the initiated. For inevitably with knowledge there disappears some of the romance. Familiarity having bred contempt of the exotic qualities of the setting, the initiate sees the sound stage in a very different light. The atmosphere approximates to that of a battlefield: we are fighting for the film, and the enemy is time. Members of the unit are like soldiers in an army. exposed as much to the inevitable tedium of inactivity as to excitement of action. All, that is, but the few who know what is going on and why, and have no leisure to be bored: Thorold, the commander-in-chief and architect of the campaign; Spike, his indefatigable adjutant; Gordon, who can rest neither while a shot is being taken, nor while it is being lined-up; Phyllis, recording angel of the conflict.

This metaphor of war can be extended. For, just as no army is ever committed entire to the field, so the set is manned only by the spearhead of the unit whose mission is the realisation of the film. From time to time it receives visits, inspections by back-room boys who are equally part of the effort, but whose functions are performed elsewhere: Anthony appears fleetingly to inspect a costume or consult with Thorold on a design; Barbara drops in to appraise a hairstyle, or Ernie to reassure himself on a make-up. (Each of these is represented permanently on the set by a subordinate.) Well after the picture has started there will still—it is apparently inevitable—be parts for Margaret to cast; there will certainly be crowds and small part possibilities for Muriel to organise and present. Planning proceeds steadily in the art department; sets are under construction for us to move on to weeks or days ahead; in the cutting rooms the fruits of yesterday's victories are being amassed and refined; future stages of the campaign, from this afternoon to a month from now, are being plotted by Sid and Ralph from the Production Office; and every now and then a visit from Hal Mason reminds us that we are part also of a larger struggle —that *Secret People* is not merely a picture on its own, but one of five in the year's production schedule for the Studio.

Does any art offer a stiffer challenge to its practitioners, or provide a texture (of personalities, of crafts) more fascinating?

Back in the Studio, we press on with the Café scenes; rushes show that the filming of the ballet has been successfully completed.

Scenes shot: A.37, 38, 39, 40, 41, 42. *Screen time*: 2 *minutes* 57 *seconds*.

THURSDAY, MARCH 22ND

The end of the first week's work (five days, that is) brings us to the end of Section A's scenes in the Café. In the morning Valentina reads the note informing her of Pietro's death (Kitchen set), then, in the Café, Frack makes his insinuations while Maria disappears forlornly up the stairs in the background.

The afternoon is devoted to the remaining set-ups in the living-room. The last of these, which is also the last shot in the sequence, gives us an interesting glimpse of co-operation between director and artiste. As scripted, the shot presents Maria returning to the living-room, where Nora lies asleep, after hearing of her father's death: the significant elements in the scene (which is silent) are Maria and Nora themselves, the parcel, the girl's belongings, the photograph of Louis, and Nora's ballet shoes, 'neatly placed on her little pile of belongings'. Though movement of the camera is not specified in the script, a fairly extensive one seems to be implied, starting on Maria, proceeding subjectively to cover her field of vision (the photograph, the parcel, Nora's bed) and finally including Maria again, as she looks down at her sleeping sister.

We complete the preceding shot by 3.45. Viewfinder in hand, Thorold crosses the set and surveys it from the wall opposite the door; the left-hand wall, through which we have just been shooting, is missing; the door is at the back and to the left; the table in the centre of the room is piled with the girls' battered packages. 'We'll need to lose that fireplace' (in the wall now behind the camera), 'bring in the couch' (against the absent wall on the left), 'she comes in there' (through the door). As the electricians pour on to the set to move the lamps, prop men get busy on the fireplace and Thorold starts moving tentatively around with his viewfinder. At the door Valentina suddenly chafes: 'Please may I go to my dressing-room?' 'Just give us a few minutes, dear, then you can have a nice long rest.' Thorold straightens up, arranges Louis' photogaph so that it is plainly visible in the basket on the table, and turns to Gordon with a grin: 'Deep focus again! From the picture to the door—how close can we get?' Gordon has a look: 'I think we might be able to do that for you'.

Thorold has another look, then: 'Valentina—would you come through the door?' Valentina goes out. A slight pause, then the door re-opens and she slowly enters, tears welling from her eyes. For a moment or two she stands, then turns tentatively to sob against the door. She looks up: 'It's very uncomfortable, all this . . . it doesn't want to move too much . . . tell me, suggest me . . .' Thorold crosses nearer to her; gestures to the baggage on the table: 'Does this mean anything to you?' He suggests a move. Valentina ponders 'At this moment I am thinking of my sister—we are alone now—I have got to work hard for her . . ' She would prefer not to include any action with the belongings.

A break is made as the couch is moved in on the left, and Angela appears, to be embedded in it. 'And get that wall out,' demands Thorold, finding that the carpenters have taken only the fireplace and left the rest. He turns again as Valentina calls out: 'I come in here—you will cover the things with the camera?' 'No: the camera doesn't want to move . . ' Undistracted by the violent hammering which has started up behind him, the director stands in thought: 'What about the ballet shoes?' He looks at Nora. 'Where are her clothes?' Valentina tries again: 'Thorold, what would you like me to do? I don't want her to see me crying . . . how about if I just turn into the corner?' 'She's asleep isn't she?' 'Yes, but maybe she can hear me; I can't tell . . .'

Thorold has now retired to the foot of the couch; squatting, he views the scene from a low angle. He looks up. 'Where are her clothes?' Enter Lily, with Nora's clothes in a neat little bundle. 'Sorry to interrupt your tea, dear,' murmurs the politic Spike, as she positions them on the chair by the bed, ballet shoes prominent on top. Indeterminate minutes follow as Thorold moves restlessly about with his viewfinder, balancing one angle against another in the effort to find the perfect visual presentation of the scene. He speaks: 'The trouble for me is, I can't . . . The whole thing is . ' Then he gets it into words: 'The foreground is so inanimate. I'd like to start with the baggage in the foreground, then move so that Nora takes it over . . . but it's so difficult if Maria is just a motionless figure. Couldn't you cross from the door to the table, and finish up looking at Angela?'

Valentina tries this move, and doesn't like it: 'I don't find an excuse. I see the things with my eyes when I come in. I don't want to move.' 'Can't you feel you can't support yourself any longer? Remember the strain of the journey, and now this news.' 'That's why I turn away.' 'Couldn't you cross over to this chair for support?' Doubtfully Valentina agrees to try. She goes out through the door, closing it behind her. A few seconds' pause. The door opens cautiously. Weeping bitterly, the letter clutched in her hand, she enters, stands for a moment by the door, then closes it softly. She attempts to move; but undeniably it does not fit, it comes out too sharp, too staccato, breaking the

68

mood of the scene. Valentina goes back to the door and plays it as before, to herself, standing for a moment quite still, then suddenly caving in against the door. She looks up, her face streaked with tears, and remarks: 'I'm afraid to come in, you see . . .'

But Thorold has capitulated: 'No, you needn't . . ' From the foot of the couch he contemplates Valentina, now blowing her nose at the door. Then the shot starts to crystallise. 'Look, let's lose the clothes off the chair, and we'll have them at the foot of the bed. Now put the basket on the chair, with the photograph in it. I think we can do it like this.' He sketches out a short track back, starting with Angela in medium close shot and moving back to disclose the chair by the bedside. 'Now, Cortesa, come in and let's have a peep.' Valentina repeats her action as Thorold demonstrates the movement to Gordon and Ron. 'Yes,' Gordon agrees, 'the pull-back can be going on as Valentina closes the door. 'Yes,' says Thorold, 'let's do that'; and, calling for chalk, Ron proceeds to mark out his camera position, and Gordon begins to work out his lighting.

'Just five minutes,' comments Valentina, mock-indignant, '—and you keep me half an hour!' She makes off for her dressing room as her stand-in takes over her position by the door. But she does not get long: in twenty minutes she is back again, and by 4.50, after two takes, the shot is in the can.

Scenes shot: A.34, 35, 43, 44, 45, A.35a. Retakes A.8, 9. Screen time: 2 minutes 30 seconds. Total screen time to date: 14 minutes 55 seconds. The unit breaks gratefully for Easter.

Second Week

A good start: we go into the second week dead on schedule. With only four working days to fill, we plan for another half day on the Café, which will take us to Anselmo's announcement of the trip to Paris. The Exhibition itself has to be skipped; with this exception we preserve continuity by taking the scene between Louis and Maria in Louis' Paris lodgings on Tuesday afternoon. Wednesday, Thursday and half Friday will be spent on the 'Vieux Chapeau' sequence, and on Friday afternoon the Paris café and street. This week will bring Serge Reggiani into the picture for the first time; also Geoffrey Hibbert as Steenie and Michael Allen as Rodd.

TUESDAY, MARCH 27TH

After a holiday, they say, work always seems stickier. Back on the Café set after the Easter recess this is proved true, though with excuse, for to-day's scenes are exceptionally complicated. First, in the Café itself, packed tight with extras (hardly summer clad, by the way), Maria receives congratulations on her naturalisation. In the seven years since their last appearance, both Maria and Penny have changed hairstyles: Megs now has a period close-bob, while Valentina sports an unexpected chignon—her own idea. 'I think it's a great success,' murmurs Barbara, who knocked it up this morning. 'Of course it *looks* very nice,' replies Anthony, hurrying past with his usual air of worried efficiency, 'but now *none* of her hats will fit.'

It is one of those days. The tea urn turns out to be insufficiently practical; the lemonade supplied to Valentina tastes as dubious as it looks; Thorold, in one of his rare, effective excursions into obscenity, administers reproof to the property department. Progressing at length into the kitchen for the long dialogue between Maria and Anselmo, we run into even trickier problems, with the obstinate misbehaviour of spaghetti and salad and thick soup to complicate further the ordering of lines, business, action and camera. Serge turns up at midday, for after lunch we are scheduled to move to the scene between Maria and Louis in his Paris lodgings. But when we resume again at 2.0 we are still in the kitchen, and Valentina is still struggling to register pathos and serve spaghetti (with meat sauce) simultaneously. Tension is further stretched by a visit to the set by Richard Basehart, who played with Valentina in her last Hollywood picture. The last shot of the sequence is split into two: the latter half, leading up to Anselmo's production of the Paris Exhibition leaflet (designed, incidentally, by Thorold at 11 o'clock this morning), calls for endless retakes. Charles fluffs, Valentina fluffs, the track-in is mistimed, a hair is caught in the gate of the camera . . . Meanwhile Serge wanders from one corner to another, going over his lines and gulping continually at his bottle of nerve tonic.

It is almost five by the time we have a take that Thorold is happy to print. Pause for the recording of a wild track, then : 'O.K. boys, break to 3a. Louis' Paris Lodgings,' yells Spike. One by one the arcs dim out, the portcullis-like entrance to the stage yawns up, and tepid daylight breaks in as lamps camera and unit begin to move for the new set. But Serge is not fated to break silence to-day : for a number of reasons (the lateness of the hour; to-morrow morning we must move on to the *Vieux Chapeau*; Valentina pleads for rest) the plan is changed. We abandon the scene for to-day, and give the rest of the afternoon to pre-lighting the *Vieux Chapeau*.

Off the floor, through the lunch hour, Thorold, with Sid, Peter, Gordon, and the camera crew, have viewed the ballet, now assembled in rough editing order. The climactic track-in presents difficulties, with two balletic blemishes in the take which is best from the camera point of view. Andree has already expressed herself forcibly on this, but it looks as though she is fatally outnumbered.

During the afternoon Roberto, Andrée and the orchestra for the *Vieux Chapeau* arrive and record dances for to-morrow: a foxtrot (improvised by the band leader), the ballet *pas de deux* arranged as a tango, and a waltz which Roberto has composed for Nora's solo.

Scenes shot: B6, B7, 7a. Screen time: 2 minutes 33 seconds.

WEDNESDAY, MARCH 28TH

'Why they don't do all this months before, I don't knew . . . If you ran a business firm like a film studio . . .' It is a sound recordist talking, disgusted at the rush in which the foxtrot and tango for the *Vieux Chapeau*—which were recorded on to film only yesterday—have to be re-recorded on to disc for use on the set. Even more hurried than he, though, is Mac, who has already this morning cut the sound rushes, abstracted the good takes, and delivered them to the Sound Department. As a result, the discs are on the set before the first set-up is lit, and by 9.40 a remarkably authentic-looking crowd is dancing, sipping aperitifs, and doing a gallant best to give the appearance of past midnight in a Paris nightclub. (The French words which have been cooked up for Roberto's tango delight Serge. 'It's exactly the sort of *connerie* they do sing in these places.')

Complicated though the first shot is—camera tracking back as Louis and Maria dance past the band, stop, ask for a tango (all to be timed so as to match the changeover from foxtrot to tango on the playback), dance on, pass Steenie, who exchanges significant glances with Louis—a certain zest is given to proceedings by the gaiety of music and decor. A check is caused when the smoke, which is sprayed through the set before every shot, is found to fly straight up to the roof; we have to wait while the offending ventilator is boarded up. Otherwise the day goes well: the dancers prove malleable, and two complicated tracking shots are covered as well as other, less difficult set-ups. As it is impossible to record sound direct through all this shuffling of feet, creaking of bodies, playing of music, we record only guide tracks during the takes. After the camera is satisfied, however, the microphone comes into its own: the players line up in front of the mike, for all the world like a team of close-harmonists, to speak their lines without action. If they can preserve the timing of the scene they have just played, the editor will be able to cut these 'wild tracks' on to the scene without any apparent discrepancies between lip movements and sound. Otherwise the dialogue will have to be 'post-synchronised'—recorded by the actors in front of a microphone with the scene projected before them as they speak. (A technique colloquially referred to as 'post-sinking': written 'post-synching' by purists.)

This is the first day for three of our characters: Louis, Steenie and Rodd. Serge takes to the intricacies of the tracking shots with enjoyment: 'This is what I like in the cinema—this precision . . . It's the real problem of acting in films.' The recording of the wild tracks, on the other hand, must be something of an ordeal; but he carries it off . . .

Not the most enviable job in the unit is that of Stills Cameraman. Bobby Penn is on the floor continuously, except for brief excursions across to the stills department, to inspect his negatives or prints of the day before; it is his responsibility to provide Publicity with their full complement of 'Production' (scenes from the film) and 'Publicity' (informal shots of unit and artistes off the set or in rehearsal) stills—as well as to compile a pictorial record of every set in the film, in case any need to be reconstructed in whole or in part for retakes.

It is not so much pressure of work that makes Bobby's a tricky job, as the conditions under which he has to carry it out—subject to the same pressure of time as all other activity on the floor, with the additional handicap that what he does is more often regarded as an inevitable evil than as an integral part of the business of film-making. For production stills, for instance, the procedure is that during a shot which Bobby feels would suit his purpose, he asks Spike for a still; provided there is no overriding necessity for speed, permission is given, and when the shot is taken, Spike will call out: 'Hold it for a still.' The camera is wheeled back, and Bobby must nip in, set up in the same position, direct the artistes to the moment, gesture, expression he wants, then beg them to 'hold it' for the second or two exposure which his plate camera demands. 'And just one more . . .' The general sensation of impatience has taught Bobby that his soundest principle of work is to get the best he can in the shortest possible time. 'The trouble is, you know you're holding things

71

up; and if the picture is at all behind schedule, you daren't ask extra time for stills. Some directors seem to resent them anyway, and of course their attitude gets picked up by the assistant. On some pictures it becomes quite a fight to get stills at all, let alone good quality.'

Mention of 'quality' leads to the enquiry: why this use of a plate camera, whose 5in. by 4in. negative demands a long exposure and a consequent sacrifice of spontaneity and expression in the artistes? They freeze very expertly of course, but you need only compare a blow-up from the frame of the cine-film with the equivalent still to see how much 'edge' (just that extra sharpness of emotion and drama) is lost in the process. Couldn't results far more exciting be got with a miniature camera? The answer is to be found in a definition of the function which these stills have to perform. They are taken for use; each must be passed by the publicity department as useful material for their campaign. And for this it is not the arty 'effect' shot that is most valuable, but the straightforward group or two-shot or close-up, with the greatest possible clarity and the most flattering lighting, suitable for reproduction on the coarsest newsprint, for the inspection of that vast majority of filmgoers who are suspicious rather than appreciative of variations from the norm of expression, lighting and composition.

The same general principles apply to publicity stills. No wonder Bobby gets sometimes depressed, and looks with an envious eye at the photographer from *Picture Post*, flashing off his high speed candid shots on a Leica. For their equivalent he must use a flashlight, and say farewell to interesting photographic quality as well as to any hope of remaining unobserved. It is a question of markets.

Scenes shot: B.53, 54, 55, 56, 57, 58, 60. Screen time: 2 minutes 23 seconds.

THURSDAY, MARCH 29TH

On the floor this morning Serge asks me: 'Don't you get bored?' And perhaps it is surprising that I should continue to be so absorbed by a process in which I am serving no function. The truth is that by now a rhythm has been established that is quite hypnotic in its regularity: the shots are run through the action, the set-ups are chosen, the camera is lined up and the shot is lit, the actors are rehearsed, and the shot is taken. It is something like watching the sea, except that every wave has its individual shape and fascination. And there is no recoil: the tide is always advancing.

Nevertheless, it would not do to forget, or neglect, the work that is going on behind the camera, out of the range of the arcs. Every day, for instance, at 10.30, there is a Production Meeting, at which the practical problems of work scheduled for the next 24 hours, or for the near future, are discussed by the heads of departments. Consider to-day's: round the large, circular table in the directors' dining room gather Ralph and William; sound supervisor Steve Dalby; Jack Ford; construction manager George Speller; and Orlando King (production costing), to consider what problems are presented by to-morrow's schedule. Bay Honri is in the chair.

Ralph starts: 'It's extremely probable we'll get off the *Vieux Chapeau* set this evening—which'll put us back on schedule. Now for to-morrow we've got the scene in Louis' Paris lodgings, and also the Paris Café scenes. We wanted to shoot them the other way round, but it's impossible as we've got to strike part of the lodgings set to make room for the lorries which drive past the Café.' (The two sets stand cheek by jowl on 3a.) The question is: Can we get the Café set spotted (i.e. the key lamps in position on the spot rails over the set) by to-night? 'You won't get it,' states Jack decisively and immediately. And then: 'Is it ready?' 'It will be,' from William. George: 'We've got three scenic artists working on it now; they should eat their way through it. What we really need is some idea from Gordon as to what he'll want.' It is agreed that immediately after this meeting Ralph and George will make straight for the *Vieux Chapeau* and try to draw out of Gordon the necessary information.

What about props? The Café set is now being redressed for 1937, with a few more modern appliances in the kitchen, and evidence in the bedroom (now Maria's and Nora's) of Nora's passion for ballet—photographs on the wall, and copies of *The Dancing Times*. Props are worried, however, about the prawns for the scene in Louis' lodgings: 'Thorold doesn't want just ordinary prawns; he wants those big ones—*scampi*—and they're not on the market just now. Still, we'll keep trying.' 'What about the lorries?' William: 'Don't forget that French number plates will want to be ready.'

Looking further ahead, Bay runs through the list of sets shortly to be needed. The Drawings for Clark's Rehearsal Rooms? Completed. The French taxi and the Seine Quai? In hand. The Swiss Pavilion at the Paris Exhibition? On the drawing board. 'What we've got to bear in mind on the Paris Exhibition is that we've not got many clear days for building.' William: 'I think all the drawings will be through by Monday. And I have placed it in such a way that, if Thorold will shoot out of continuity, there are some detail shots he can do first—in case the whole set isn't ready in time.' 'I'm sure,' says Ralph, 'he'll play on that.'

This deals with *Secret People* for the day: the meeting passes to a consideration of progress on its predecessors: retakes on *The Lavender Hill Mob;* also title backings and a car crash. And finally the filming of a foreground model for *The Man in the White Suit*, and something informally referred to as 'the split matte job'. Coming away, Ralph remarks that the next stage will certainly consist of the impossibility of getting Gordon away from the *Vieux Chapeau* set, to say what he will want for to-morrow. We are dumbfounded to hear from George (preceding us by a couple of minutes) that, on the contrary, he has already been tackled, has specified his wants, and that all is now in hand.

Meanwhile, on the floor, we continue to carve through the *Vieux Chapeau*. Thorold announces a change of plan on Nora's solo dance: 'I've thought of something to satisfy Andrée's objections.' (She had not much liked the idea of Nora breaking spontaneously away from Rodd into a dance on her own.) 'We'll set the dance deliberately in a carnival atmosphere—everyone wearing fancy dress hats—the band playing faster and faster becomes part of an organised novelty dance . . . I thought of it in my bath this morning.' To the point that we have deserted the script breakdown: 'That's just a basis— in case I turn up with a headache and a temperature of 100: it'll carry you through. But I believe passionately in improvisation—so long as your roots are there. Just as last night, for Louis' exit, we shot into the mirror behind the bar, instead of taking the bar out and shooting straight down onto the dance floor as we'd planned. It's difficult to analyse exactly *why* a shot like that is more effective in this context—it certainly isn't necessarily the sort of thing you can foresee in the script . . .'

73

Ralph's estimation is correct. We are through all the *Vieux Chapeau* shots by the end of the day, which brings us again abreast of the schedule.

Scenes shot: B.61, 70, 71, 71*a*, 71*b*, 72. *Screen time*: 1 *minute* 46 *seconds*.

FRIDAY, MARCH 30TH

Louis' lodgings—a charming garret looking out on a vista of Paris roofs—provokes an immediate protest from Brad. Instead of the usual ceiling of white net (solid to the camera eye, but easily penetrable by sound), it is roofed with a section of scenic canvas, papered. The set is too low to admit a microphone between the actors and the ceiling, and above it nothing will be heard. To make matters worse, Thorold plans to shoot the scene in a single take, tracking from the kitchen in the background, via Louis' conversation on the telephone, to the table by the window. 'Can't be done,' Brad declares flatly, 'why have we got to have a solid ceiling anyway?' 'Because William wants the stripes on the wallpaper to be continued across the ceiling,' says Gordon, 'and they couldn't get the effect on net.' 'You won't see them anyway.' 'Yes, you will.' Feeling the need for support, Brad calls for Steve; Sid appears, peacemaking. By way of compromise, the roof is eventually shifted back, and a portion cut away from the front to allow the mike as near the artistes as possible.

All morning, while the scene is rehearsed and shot—its length and variety of business and feeling makes it a difficult one—work proceeds on the adjoining part of the floor, on the Paris Café exterior: rigging the awning, putting the finishing touches of paint to the perspective of houses opposite. Over the lunch hour the trucks appear, together with Steenie, three conspirators, a waiter, and a handful of loiterers. Meanwhile, before we break, Thorold announces his intention to shoot an extra scene in Louis' lodgings: 'It was in the script before, but everyone insisted it wasn't necessary. After yesterday's shooting I know it is.' The scene is to establish Louis' decision to make use of Maria and Nora. 'It's the hinge,' Thorold explains, 'without it he's just a monster . . .' Michael is called down to the studio at lunch time, and is on the set by four; hemmed in by the trucks (part of the set, fortunately not needed, has been lost to make way for them) he and Serge are rehearsed by Thorold in the few necessary lines.The scene is shot without interference with the schedule.

This morning's *contretemps* results in a conference at the end of the day's work: Thorold, Sid, William and Ralph sit in between Steve and Brad on the one hand, and Gordon on the other. As Sid explains afterward: 'It's always difficult to get the flavour of a meeting you haven't attended yourself.' The essential point is simply that in any picture the claims of sight and sound are bound to conflict, if only because it is the recordist's responsibility to get his microphone in the most favourable position—and it is an intrusive object, which casts inconvenient shadows, and threatens constantly to invade the camera field. 'And in this picture, where we're constantly using low angles, ceilings, and hard floors, the opportunities for friction are obviously even more than usual.' Discussion appears to clear the air, however, and Steve re-establishes his right to inspect all models before William's plans are passed for building.

Scenes shot: B.51, 59, 62, 69, 73*a*. *Screen time*: 4 *minutes* 31 *seconds*. *Total screen time to date*: 26 *minutes* 8 *seconds*.

Third Week

Still on time, though last week nearly threw us off schedule: our delays on Tuesday meant the postponement of B51, and the consequent loss of half a day. However, the two hours spent prelighting the 'Vieux Chapeau' set in the evening paid their way, and we covered the sequence in two days—half a day under schedule—which put us right again. On Friday we again made good time, which allowed us to shoot an extra scene without falling behind.

The third week returns us to Stage 2 for five days solid in the Café. These include some very crucial scenes.

It is always rather strange when we come to one of those scenes used for artistes' tests to see the transformation wrought in them when they are shot for the film. This morning, with C5 and C21, we come to the test scene for Nora. ('I couldn't wait . . .' The line has already acquired overtones.) The action, which we used entire, is now split into two: over Louis and Maria embracing we hear the telephone ring. Cut to Nora answering, and hearing the news of her audition. For the body of the scene we are back in the kitchen, reversed on to the door: Nora enters, and we track back between Maria and Louis to make the three-shot. The whole scene is played from this set-up, with much movement in and out of the door at the back (Penny's entrance, Maria's exit, Nora's exit and re-entrance, Penny's exit, Nora's exit) and excited dovetailing of conversation.

On this occasion, though, Brad remains unruffled; in fact he has an air of positive enjoyment. 'From a sound point of view, a delightful piece of direction,' is his verdict. 'A lot of directors don't seem to realise the importance of composition with reference to sound—particularly when using a wide-angle lens. It's been calculated that on a screen 20 feet across an audience can only focus sharply on an area of four foot square at a time: now since the sound system in a cinema employs a *point* source of sound behind the screen, it isn't possible to *place* the sound. If you have a group of characters spread over the screen in conversation, it can be very difficult to locate with immediate precision exactly which is speaking. Particularly as, by the time they've been through all the processes we subject them to, voices have a tendency to lose their most individual characteristics. Thorold seems to track his sound by movements and eyelines—he manages to keep the point of dialogue at the centre of visual interest, as I'm sure you've noticed.' But of course when these refinements of technique are exercised with skill, the result seems merely inevitable. It is when things go wrong that one perceives the complexity of the task.

To-day brings a change of crew on the camera. 'Bronzed and fit, as from the seaside,' Chic Waterson (Camera Operator) and Herbert Smith (Assistant) return from working on *Where No Vultures Fly* in Africa. Chic takes over from Ron Taylor; Herbert displaces Ken on focus; and Ken steps down to second assistant. What eagle-eyed critic will spot the change, distinguishing between the operation of scenes already shot, and those still to come?

Scenes shot: C.4, 5, 20, 21, 22, 23, 23a. Screen time: 3 minutes 9 seconds.

TUESDAY, APRIL 3RD

You soon realise that from the shooting on the floor it is difficult—and for those who cannot view the action through the camera, impossible—to appreciate the real style of the film, its expressiveness in terms of lighting, camera set-up and movement. We get a certain way towards this at rushes, but even here the glimpses are so fragmentary and discontinuous that it is a considerable exercise to imagine the effect of them cut together, smoothly or impetuously flowing.

It is under the hand of the editor that the images start to coalesce. Peter's office, or workshop rather, seems none too spacious for the job: lengths of film hang into linen-sided bins; a side-bench carries horizontal and vertical winders on which the clumsy stuff can be manipulated; one wall is piled high with tin boxes for the storing of unused takes and fragments. ('We never throw anything away. If a director tells you to junk something, you can be sure he'll be crying out for it six weeks later'.) Most important is the Movieola —the portable viewer through which sound and picture tracks can be run simultaneously for the necessary repeated inspections; this is the editor's basic instrument. Here Peter, and his two assistants, are fed each morning with the fruit of the previous day's work, to be cut together for showing at rushes (in the morning to Sir Michael and the producer, at the end of the lunch hour to the director and the unit). After rushes and consultation with the director, the editor can start work on the material in earnest, taking what is relevant from each shot, striving to build from these lengths of celluloid the ideal pattern towards which the director is striving.

'The great thing is to keep level—to cut the stuff as it comes in, so that you've got your sequences pretty well assembled a couple of days or so after they're shot. Of course, there are bound to be adjustments, so it's better not to cut too tight at first . . .' How often does the editor view the material before starting to cut it? 'Well, I see it twice at rushes—the first time I look at it dramatically, the second time I try and think how I'm going to cut it together. Any particularly tricky sequence (like the ballet, for instance) I may run three or four times, with all the takes strung together in rough cutting order, before I touch it. Then there are always a few cuts in a picture which give real trouble—the danger is that you can go stale on them if you try them too often and too continuously. The only thing is to carry them about in your head, think about them on week-ends, or just forget about them for a bit, and come back to them fresh.'

To-day I squeeze into the cutting room to see Peter at work on yesterday's continuity of four shots: Nora tells Maria and Louis the news of her audition; the girls leave the Café; Louis and Anselmo converse (from two set-ups). Watching the little picture in the Movieola, one becomes excitedly aware of that other property of cinema, more often written about than appreciated: the satisfaction of images which flow like music, their changes of rhythm and tone complementing and enriching the contributions of script and actors. Handling the coils of film with a dexterity fantastic to someone as hamfisted as I, Peter runs through each take time after time, estimating the precise moment of cutting; when he has the rhythm in mind, he starts dabbing at the film with his chinagraph pencil, until he finds that three times out of four he has lighted on the same frame. Here he makes his cut. 'I always try to cut pictorially—silent sequences are the thing the cutter dreams of. They're mostly

76

confined to chases, unfortunately—we get plenty of those.' Of these five cuts, one is on action (Nora's exit from the kitchen picked up by her entry into the Café); two involve a change of subject (after the girls leave, we cut to Anselmo; he glances sideways, and we cut to Louis); and two within the conversation between Louis and Anselmo. The timing of each is a matter of instinct and personal preference: Peter cuts briskly, leaving little to spare. Over the conversation he hesitates a little. There is business with a cigarette which would prove ideal opportunity to cut from one angle (favouring Anselmo) to the other (favouring Louis), but Thorold has asked for the cut back on a specific line ('Her father did'), which makes it impossible to cut on the action. The cut is made instead by dialogue, on the end of the line before.

A quarter of an hour later we are watching the sequence in the theatre; it flows well, but perhaps a trifle too sharply. 'Yes . . .' Peter muses, 'I think I'll put a little more on the end of the first one, and hold the exit from the Café a little longer.' I find particularly interesting the cut from Anselmo to Louis: so smoothly is it covered by Anselmo's glance to the side that the screening is over and the lights are up before I realise that, though watching expressly for the cuts, I have entirely failed to notice it.

On the floor: C.1, 1a, 2, 3, 18, 19, 41, 49. Screen time: 3 minutes 12 seconds.

WEDNESDAY, APRIL 4TH

A rather notorious aspect of contemporary film making, for which any observer is likely to be well prepared, is the extreme insistence by trade unions on departmental rights. Though here as anywhere the authority of the union is sacrosanct, there seems little desire to interpret the law with restrictive literalness. Thorold, Gordon, Spike, Phyllis have laid their hands on props from time to time, straightened a table or advanced the hands of a clock, without the set caving in, or the shop steward calling the studio out on strike. All the same, the pressure is there; and this morning I feel it. I ask Spike if he has any objections against a friend visiting the set with a Leica, on which I should like to attempt to get a few stills for this book. Spike frowns: 'You'll have to ask Ralph about that.' Ralph's response is even shorter: 'No.' My inevitable 'Why not?' proves rash, and I am furnished with some home truths. (Suddenly to be introduced to yourself as others have seen you can be an unnerving experience, and calls forth full reserves of statesmanship). Ralph and I are soon shaking hands, and he agrees to consult the shop steward. It is established that there is no union objection, provided nothing I take is allowed to compete commercially with anything put out by the publicity department. (Though it is a pity I am not a member of the N.U.J.). But my nerve has gone, and when John Fletcher arrives with his Leica it is some time before I can gather the courage to produce it on the floor. When I do, my confidence is not increased by Gordon's stern regard, and his remarking, in tones not calculated to reassure, 'Have you got a ticket for that?'

'But you mustn't forget the other side of the picture,' Thorold emphasises. 'I well remember working here in the old days, and in the cutting rooms we'd still be at it at two and three in the morning. In fact we made such a row that the management got complaints from the neighbours, with the result that we were asked to try to finish work by eleven o'clock—*eleven o'clock!*'

Lunch time is devoted once again to beer and sandwiches in the main theatre,

77

where William produces more models for inspection (including the Paris Exhibition set). These are followed by a play-through of the music composed by Roberto, to Andrée's specification, for Nora's dance at the Garden Party. Thorold is dissatisfied: 'If Galbern liked Bach, he wouldn't be the bastard he is . . . We want something luscious and pretty and sentimental. Can't we use something from Tchaikowsky?' This must be discussed with Andrée this evening.

On the floor, still working through the Café, we arrive at the crucial scene where Louis persuades Maria to carry the bomb to the party. 'Now this scene brings us to the heart of our story,' Thorold announces, 'so while we're on it, to-day and to-morrow, we'll have real quiet on the set, and *no visitors.*' But no gravity can subdue Valentina's satirical effervescence; she finishes the last, tense run-through of the dialogue—with Thorold prowling watchfully around her and Serge with his viewfinder—with an explosive: 'And now let's go home.' And so we do, having covered the opening shots—Louis unwrapping the parcel, Maria's entry, their embrace; the crux of the scene remains to be tackled tomorrow.

Scenes shot: C.48, D.4, 4a, 4b, 5, 6, 6a. Screen time: 2 minutes 24 seconds.

After hours: an evening conference over the music for Nora's dance listens exhaustively to Tchaikowsky; but everything Thorold likes seems to come already in one or other of the ballets—which Andrée is not prepared to rearrange. 'Why not Chopin?' suggests Dock Mathieson; and by chance the accompanist has a book of Chopin waltzes with her. It is produced and almost at random she starts to play. 'That's exactly the sort of thing we want,' Thorold calls out. So it is chosen—*Valse Brillante in A flat.*

THURSDAY, APRIL 5TH

The seriousness of our assignment to-day is pointed by the notices we find posted on the doors of the stage when we arrive in the morning: 'Staff And Visitors NOT Allowed On The Set To-day Unless On Business.' 'You have no idea how terrible it is to play so early,' groans Serge, on the set at 8.30. 'I have no voice, you know . . . I would like to play this scene very quietly, and for that you need a good deep voice.' At home in Paris he is used to working more civilised hours—12 to 8, though this has the disadvantage of involving work on Saturdays. Clearing his throat fiercely, he continues his prowl around the stage, and his muttered attack on recalcitrant consonants and vowel-sounds.

This scene (D7) is certainly something of an ordeal, for besides the emotional pitch of the scene, and its tense development, there is its length to be reckoned with: the first take, triumphantly surmounted, runs for three and a half minutes. At the other end of the stage, hushed in deference to that precious, scarcely audible thread of sound, a little group poise like statues round the teawagon: teacups in hand, immobile amongst scaffolding, Ralph and Muriel might be chorus-leaders in a modern verse play, about to break into colloquial utterances about Fate.

The first take proves an exception: it is followed by several fluffs ('Merde!' explodes Serge. 'Porco Cane!' echoes Valentina. They compare notes rapidly in Italian). We cover the scene eventually in two halves—the first half on Take 8, the second on 10. But this far from exhausts it; we are not sticking to the script's single basic set-up The first half (up to Nora's off-screen call) is taken again from another angle—an intriguing triangle is formed by Maria's face on the left, Louis' back and side on the right, and, between them, his full-face reflection in the mirror. In order to get the right effect in the mirror, Serge has to play the scene looking just right of Valentina's left eye; conversely Valentina has to cheat her eyeline on to Serge's left ear—a comfortable procedure for neither. Close-shots, covering the same dialogue, follow on each. By lunch-time, when it is all over, we have been over the course thirteen times, with an additional nine takes halted half or three-quarters of the way through, and about the same number of rehearsals. 'And you realise,' says Serge, 'we have no idea what it is like. Even when we see it in rushes, we have to think how it will be cut, and what goes before it, and what comes after.'

In the afternoon, we press on in continuity. When we come to D9, Thorold has one of his rare changes of mind. We are setting up for a track through the Café, when he suddenly decides the shot is a bore. 'Oh, let's skip it!' he says, and instead we take the whole scene from the street outside, shooting in through the Café door.

Scenes shot: D.7, 7a, 7c, 7d, 8, 9, 11 (D.10 cut). Screen time: 4 minutes 39 seconds.

FRIDAY, APRIL 6TH

Postscript to Wednesday's encounter with the union: I may *take* stills in the Studio, but I may not have them developed or printed by the Stills Department. A fine example of inter-union solidarity, designed (presumably) to prevent loss of livelihood amongst employees of photographic dealers outside the film industry.

Consideration of last Friday's rushes (B51) has resulted in the decision to do more work on the Paris Lodgings scene. The actors were not too happy with their performances, and Thorold feels that the single camera movement is not successful; the end needs the additional punch of cutting into close-shots on Louis and Maria. The beginning, too, is re-covered; now we start closer in, on an insert of the prawns frying in a fish basket, panning up to hold Louis and Maria—a more decisive opening to the scene. This is followed by an extra close-up of Steenie to insert into B59, which at the moment leaves his identity doubtful. Fortunately we have made such progress during the week that we can take time out for these retakes without setting back the schedule.

Discussing to-day's rushes—the bomb scene in particular—Spike says: 'I think the scene's too long. I can hear lots of rustling and coughing through that lot, especially in the Edgware Road.' And all through the afternoon, as we shoot this intimate, finely-tuned dialogue between Serge and Valentina, you can hear those millions of fingers unwrapping their sweets, see those vacant faces, those desolate Northern queues, who must somehow be persuaded to enjoy what we are doing here.

Scenes shot: C.42, 46, D.3, B.50x, 51a, 51b, 51c, 59a. Screen time: 1 minute 23 seconds. Total screen time to date: 40 minutes 55 seconds

SATURDAY, APRIL 7TH

Reconnaisance party (Thorold, Sid, Gordon, Ralph and Spike) investigate possible locations. The exterior of the Commissioner for Oaths, in Chancery Lane, is viewed for the first time by Gordon, approved, and the set-up chosen.

79

(As so often this includes an anachronistic 'No Parking' sign which will have to be transformed into a lamp post).

For the exterior of the Dublin theatre various possibilities are inspected: Drury Lane, the Cambridge, the Comedy, the New, Wyndhams, the Winter Garden. The best seems to be the Scala, provided the scaffolding which at the moment disfigures the façade is removed by the time we want to shoot.

The rehearsal rooms are sited in West Street, with a pub conveniently next door, and a shop selling ballet shoes for Louis and Maria to walk past. Exterior set-ups are chosen at the entrance to Scotland Yard, the last of which follows Anselmo and Maria away across Whitehall to catch a bus on the opposite side of the street. ('And that *will* be a nightmare'.) Finally Richmond Park is chosen for the Phœnix Park location of the last sequence, with a quadrangle of roads which exactly reproduces the requirements of the script

'And do you get paid for that?' 'Well officially,' says Ralph, 'we all get a day off for it—except Spike, who gets an extra day's pay And' (gratuitously) 'he well earned it.'

Fourth Week

Apart from its effect on morale, the chief advantage of getting ahead of schedule lies not so much in the hope of thereby finishing the picture early, but in the opportunity it affords of taking in one's stride extra scenes and retakes (of which there are always bound to be a few). Last week's assignment, for instance, was completed by 11.30 on Friday; this did not put us ahead, but enabled us comfortably to retake and elaborate B.51, grab an extra close-up on B.59, and move over to next Monday's set into the bargain—still keeping pace with the schedule.

Next week takes us to a new set (Clark's Rehearsal Rooms) for the first two days; then back to the Café for the other three. Prelighting on Sunday for the Seine Quai sequence.

MONDAY, APRIL 9TH

Visitors on the set. These may be divided into two categories: professional and private. The latter—relatives or friends; civilians who have given assistance to the Studio and are being rewarded by a conducted tour of fairyland—are generally little trouble, even if maddeningly predictable in their responses. ('Isn't she *small*!' 'There's nothing much happening, is there?' 'What a lot of people—no wonder films cost so much.' 'When you go to see a film, you never think of all the work that's had to go into it.' When you go to see a film, you never think, madam.) For these blithe innocents ten minutes is generally enough before they are toddled off, making little noises of appreciation and wonder, to the model shop. Professionals—apart from the odd student (rarely English-speaking) who may stand in a corner, observing and unobserved, for anything from two days to eight weeks—means the Press. Native and foreign, singly and in hordes, these appear with regularity. To-day twenty-two Finns (they arrived in a charabanc) are escorted on to the set of Clark's Rehearsal Rooms to interview stars and director.

The general attitude towards this sort of thing is one of resignation. No one on this picture is particularly publicity-hungry, but the necessity is accepted as part of the business. Both Valentina and Serge, however, are vehement that publicity must be kept within the limits of professionalism. 'No,' says Serge, when an interviewer refers to acting as his 'life,' 'it's my job' About his work he is always ready to talk, or rather to answer questions; about his personal life, his family, he is firmly, politely uncommunicative. Valentina, with her experience of Hollywood, has even more reason to be emphatic on this point. 'Of course, I realise that if an actress is popular, it is more than just her acting . . . It's her personality too, and people want to know about her, to feel they are in touch with her. And sometimes that can be very touching. But we must be allowed to have our own lives. In Hollywood it is terrible; they expect you to be their slave; you have to be ready to do anything for them, at any time, not just when you're making a picture.' She shudders, and turns to Audrey Hepburn: 'Think hard before you sign a long-term contract. Liberty is the most wonderful thing of all.' Though still young in her career, Audrey, too, has her worries: she has had a great deal of publicity before anything she has done has been seen by the public. ' . . . And they'll get sick of it. I'd much rather wait until I have something to show—instead of risking a tremendous anti-climax when people finally do start seeing the first little bits I've done in films.' But this would be to contradict the natural order; next week, on one of her days off, Audrey is already booked for the South Downs, where she will feed ducks, paddle in village ponds, and breast skylines to the click of a Leica. Objective: a cover and feature-story in *Illustrated*.

To return to visitors: there is a time and a place for them To the Publicity Department, either an actor is on the floor that day (and therefore accessible) or he is not. To the actor, on the other hand, there is a vast difference between a scene which makes comparatively light demands, and one which calls for intense concentration between set-ups. These are the occasions when mass interviews, arm-in-arm stills with visiting Beauty Queens, cost more than they are worth. Fortunately to-day's shooting does not weigh too heavily on the artistes; they are able to talk to our Finnish guests, answer their questions, be photographed with them, with every appearance of unaffected charm and enjoyment. (*Le terrible don de la familiarité*, in Turgenev's sharp phrase).

Scenes shot: C.24, 25, 26, 27, 28, 30, 31, 32, 33, 34, 35. *Screen time*: 2 *minutes* 56 *seconds*.

TUESDAY, APRIL 10TH

A Day in the Life of an Art Director. William arrives this morning at about 8.45; his first chore is to check the plans for the Hospital set and approve the list of alterations drawn up by Andrew for the Café exterior as glimpsed by Maria on her way to Dublin—an awning, fresh window dressing, new sign boards and lettering. So to the morning rounds.

First to the Rehearsal Room set, where shooting is busily in progress. There is a possible cause of dissension here. Gordon has asked for his overhead lamps to be spotted level with the top of the flats—which means that their supporting structure must be even lower. As a result the spot rail has to be lifted every time one of the flats is moved. 'Fortunately these walls are all bare, so it's possible to tilt them, but of course we couldn't do that if they're carrying pictures or a mantelpiece . . . With a couple of changeovers this sort of delay might cost two hundred pounds in a single day . . ." Also the lino is proving a worry: 'It's the first time we've used it to allow the camera to move without tracks—a very good idea, but we need a better quality lino. This one is only a mixture of asphalt and paper; it warps, and we have constantly to be nailing it down.' All the same, the unit continues to make excellent time.

81

Next to be inspected is the set for the Seine Quai, now well under way on 3a. This makes ingenious use of false perspective, and with its asphalt-lined tank and its midget bridges stretching into the distance, looks really something *like* a film set. Surveying his plasterers, painters, scenic artists at work, William remarks: 'You see human beings are very peculiar. They will never really work intensely until two days before shooting; and no matter how long before you start on a set, it will never be ready before it's needed.'

Continuing the tour of inspection, we visit in succession Carpenter's Shop, Prop Department, Plasterers and Painters. In the first, William surveys the sectioned embryos of future sets with the expertness of the practised *accoucheur;* a couple of featureless flats signalize the beginning of Louis' London Lodgings; this curved structure in hessian is part of the Buttery, and in that corner is the entrance to the British Pavilion. In the office the cost sheet is produced, with the comfortable disclosure that, on aggregate, we are at the moment running slightly under the budget. In the Prop Department the chief current worry is the purchase of leaves for the trees which will grace the Paris Exhibition set; in the first place they have not been budgeted for, and in the second they seem phenomenally expensive (sprays of six small-size leaves, 72/- a dozen; medium-size, 144/-; and large 216/-). 'Anyway, we can eke them out with the plane leaves we're using on the Seine Quai.' In the Plasterer's Shop we inspect a squatting Juno, who will figure in the Exhibition garden, and decide that her buttocks are weak and will probably be improved by a skirting of drapery. The painters are also taken up with gewgaws for the Exhibition, including replicas of the Royal Arms which give rise to the usual disputes over the positioning of lion and unicorn.

What is going on meanwhile in the Drawing Office? On one desk a lay-out for the bus-poster advertising the serialisation of Galbern's life-story in a Sunday newspaper; on another drawings for Maria's room in the hospital; on a third reproductions of Phoenix Park notice boards, for erection at Richmond; and on a fourth the ground plan of the Exhibition garden. Discussion of details carries us to 11 o'clock, and the daily production meeting.

This being Tuesday, the meeting is the full, once-weekly one, presided over by Hal Mason. The directors' dining room fills rapidly, each new arrival ticked discreetly off on her roll-call by Hal's secretary: by the time the meeting starts, there are twenty-seven present—heads of all conceivable departments, and of some scarcely conceivable: Costume Design; Art Department; Camera Maintenance; Music Department; Casting; Prop Department; Men's Wardrobe; Construction; Canteen Manager; Special Effects . . . to name only a few (and in no order of priority). The meeting goes briskly and without dispute. The future schedule of *Secret People* is established, progress on set design and building checked, arrangements for location shooting confirmed. Discussion moves on to final shooting on *The Lavender Hill Mob* and *The Man in the White Suit,* and the meeting breaks. ('You want twelve children?' Muriel calls across to the sound department, 'I'll lay them on!') William remains behind to confer with Hal about those leaves; after hesitation they are conceded, 'but the cost will have to come off the budget somewhere'.

So the pattern of the day establishes itself. The set in use on the floor has to be continually checked for snags; future sets must be supervised on the drawing boards, in the shops, or under construction on the stages. And there are designs still to be prepared. Before lunch William sits in on the floor while Thorold approves Terry Bishop's plan for the montage of the girls' journey to Britain. After lunch the procedure is repeated between William and Terry alone, in a preliminary effort to reconcile the requirements with the three hundred and fifty pound budget. 'I promise you to execute everything,' William assures the anxious director, 'but I must warn you that the final word will be whether the carriage moves or not . . . It may be just too expensive.'

Back to Anselmo's Café; back to the Seine Quai. And only just in time. 'Surely that curb should be four inches higher?' The plans are checked and the error verified. 'It'll be a big job to lift it all up again.' 'Build on top of it then.' And the perspective of the Quaiside has strayed out of alignment, and must be repainted. (Relations between William and Dicky Dickinson, the scenic artist, are jocosely hostile: 'Don't forget,' William cautions, 'a night sky is lighter than the buildings in front of it.' 'It'll happen onc day,' Dicky returns, 'I'll hit you with a bit of iron').

'A typical day?' William ponders, as he puts his feet up and draws on a cigarette, 'Except that I didn't make any sketches to-day—and there's still the Garden Party to be done. Of course a really heavy day is when we're starting to-morrow to shoot on a new set; then I spend the whole day on it. It's only by being there constantly during the last stages that you can be sure of getting what you want—everything depends on the *finish*, the way the paint is mixed, the way it's applied. And then it's more than likely the whole thing will be killed by the director . . . Which does not apply to Thorold. Did you notice the way he brought out the character of the Rehearsal Rooms?' And at the memory of to-day's rushes, the sight of his work well used, William's face breaks into a smile—the artist's true reward.

On the floor progress has been more than good. Nora's audition is finished by midday, and we return to the Café half a day ahead of schedule.

Scenes shot: C.25a, 25aa, 27a, 27b, 29, 32a, 34a, 34b, D.16, 17, 18, 19 (*part*). *Screen time*: 1 minute 58 seconds.

WEDNESDAY, APRIL 11TH

In contrast to yesterday, a slow day. Arriving in the afternoon one seems to sense the stickiness of the morning; there is a certain laxity in the atmosphere; the machine functions, but at a lower pressure. This morning's scenes, too, proved tricky, with complexities of timing and movement which take time to perfect. So the fact that Valentina has been unwell today, and has had to be replaced in a couple of shots by a double, has not held us up: her dialogue scenes are held over for to-morrow anyway.

As the scheduled time draws near for the shooting of Maria's and Nora's montage-journey across Europe (A.25-33), Terry Bishop, who will direct the sequence, has been busy on its preparation. Requirements must be specified, in relation to the modest budget allocated for the construction of sets; and this means a tight plan of shooting. Taking the script directions as his basis, Terry has visualised the sequence in a number of rough sketches, which have been elaborated into a finished series by the Studio sketch artist. To-day he takes these to William for final decision on sets. The assignment is simple enough, but has to be drawn and built in a week, which is not long.

Terry spends the rest of the morning with Anthony, concocting fictitious fascist uniforms from the costumiers' stock of jackboots, peaked caps and totalitarian tunics. In the afternoon he chooses his refugees from a parade of possibles pre-selected by Muriel. In the drawing office, his sets begin to take shape on the drawing board.

Scenes shot: *D.15, 19a, 19b, 19c, 19d, 19e, 19f, 20, 21. Screen time*: 2 *minutes 45 seconds*.

THURSDAY, APRIL 12TH

You find yourself asking extraordinarily stupid questions. For instance: 'Thorold, do you ever find it difficult to direct a film?' This is occasioned by the ease with which this morning's scene (D22) is split into set-ups, made to flow into the camera. The question gets a kinder answer than it perhaps deserves: 'Yes, very . . . It's terribly difficult to direct a film you don't want to make. Almost impossible. That's why I've made so few . . . This comes from here—from the guts.' Then continuing to discuss this relation of what appears on the screen as is specified in the script, of pre-planning to improvisation: 'Well, for example—the script specifies that this shot should be made from the door. I came in this morning determined to shoot it the other way; but it just didn't work . . . Compositions? Half-and-half. For that shot last night (D15) I had the rough balance in my mind, but it wouldn't have come off if the actors hadn't worked in with it. So much depends on your cast; and we've got a remarkable one in this picture. I think if you've got the right idea, and the right artistes and unit, they work together towards it . . . '

(Apropos this scene: Serge, who has also evidently tried to work out a decoupage for it, and found it difficult, remarks: 'You see how much easier it is to criticise something than to do it.' He means, not how much easier to write criticism, but to see room for improvement, suggest refinements in a conception already conjured up out of nothing by the creative imagination of another. An ordinary enough observation, I suppose, but one of those which, made in the right context, strikes home to the conscience, and stays there.)

To-day's group of scenes constitutes our first sizeable leap out of continuity, forced on us by the impossibility of interrupting the Café scenes in order to shoot the Garden Party. The girls' return thus plunges Audrey rather suddenly into drama—as a serious scene tiny enough, but none the less intimidating, for it is the first in her career. 'There was an explosion,' she has to say, in answer to Penny's question; and 'it was horrible,' then run from the room. In the long shot with which we start, the words sound like words, the emotion is being pressed. We move in to a close two-shot, and Audrey consults Thorold. 'I just can't seem to say this line right . . . How should I say it?' 'Don't bother about how you're going to say it. Just think of the experience that lies behind the words. During the war, perhaps you saw something like that—not the same, of course, but its equivalent. Get the feeling right, and the words will look after themselves.' So while the stand-ins are being lit, Audrey sits by herself in a corner, thinking back. By the time we come to the take, the words have become spontaneous (heartfelt); and tears come naturally to her eyes.

The afternoon brings us to D.53, 54 and 55, a scene which Valentina attacks with savagery, and with such sharpness of movement (speaking the lines anywhere, into the wall or down on to the floor) that Brad must remonstrate, 'I just can't get at them with my mike.' 'Well then we'll have to post-synch them, darling,' replies Valentina, and tears once more into the scene.

84

Rushes disclose that yesterday evening's D15 is marred by a blemish on the negative. This will have to be retaken to-morrow—much to Serge's delight, for the scene was brought in unexpectedly from further ahead in the schedule (due to Valentina's absence), and he regards his showing in it without joy.

Scenes shot: D.22, 22a, 22b, 52, 53, 54, 55 (retake D.5). Screen time: 1 minute 33 seconds.

FRIDAY, APRIL 13TH

Another leap in continuity brings us to Maria's return to the Café from Scotland Yard. The scene is shot with a good deal of discussion, for Valentina's playing here must dictate the key also of the Scotland Yard sequence. This, of course, immediately precedes it in the film, but has to be shot three weeks from now.

D15 is retaken, and shows the advantage of preparation. It now runs nine seconds shorter.

Having cleared the day's schedule with half an hour to spare, we move on to the Seine Quai set at the end of the afternoon. Here Thorold establishes his first set-up, and sketches out his plan of action for Gordon's guidance. As promised long ago, at the pre-production conference on the schedule, this scene must be pre-lit if it is to be cleared in a morning: hence its assignment to Monday morning. Gordon, then, will come in on Sunday, with Tom Chapman and a camera assistant: in support will be Dicky Dickinson (scenic artist), in case extra touches or alterations are needed to backings or perspectives; electricians; and "standbys"—carpenter, stage-hand, rigger, plasterer.

Scenes shot: E.2, 3, 4, 52, 54, 55, 57, 63 (retake D.15). Screen time: 2 minutes 52 seconds. Total screen time to date: 52 minutes 59 seconds.

SUNDAY, APRIL 15TH

Birthday of a new British baby: Miss Carine Corinne Jane Reggiani. By God's grace this happy event occurs on a Sunday; for how could you expect an actor to perform with full concentration and effect while he is becoming a father for the second time? All are doing well.

In the Studio: the Seine Quai. Although lighting proper starts to-day, this is by no means a first go on the set. All the week Gordon and Tom have been dodging in off the floor while Thorold chooses a fresh set-up, to inspect construction and decide on general lighting principles.

Its foreground framed by the arch of one of the Seine bridges, William's design presents a vista of the Quai with river (the Studio tank) stretching from the bottom right-hand corner of frame into the distance. As the river and the Quai stretch away, they narrow in false perspective; in the 'distance' bridges, street lamps, houses shrink to dolls'-house proportions. 'Days ago' Gordon has determined his main source of light; on Wednesday he gave his instructions for the disposition of the spot rails, which will carry the main complement of lamps.

For the illusion of distance to be preserved, the set has naturally been designed to be viewed from a pin-pointed camera position. This gives Gordon his start—for he never begins to light a set until he has the initial set-up established. 'The first set-up on a scene is usually a key one, and probably dictates the whole way a set is to be lit. There's no sense in starting before you know what exactly the director wants.'

85

Arriving first, Tom has the lamps switched on, and establishes the key light —the principal direction of light and the primary illumination of the scene. The function of the Gaffer, you discover, is not simply to relay and superintend the orders of the cameraman; like a good sergeant, he can exercise his own initiative and make his own contribution to the speed of working. Tom explains: 'I could just sit back and wait for the cameraman and say, "Well, what do you want?" but why waste time? I've worked with Gordon long enough to know the way he goes about things. . . . When you've been with 30 different cameramen or so, you begin to know the tricks.'

By the time Gordon starts, the main 'spotting up' has been done: the canvas has been prepared. It is now for him to paint the picture in—a process, like any creative work, which can be described only in useless generalisations, or in terms of equally uncommunicative externals. For instance: once the distribution and emphasis of light has been decided (the tones of the picture), it is chiefly a question of achieving balance. Here the keylight floods under the arch, towards camera: the light on the roof of the arch must be balanced against the light in the background. And as this keylight is not going to illuminate the artistes—since it comes from behind them—they must be lit as if by the reflexion from the water, with 'shadow light' added, in order to get sufficient exposure on artistes and parts of the set not otherwise directly lit. The task which most occupies the cameraman is this achieving of 'balance'—the key light at one end of the scale, the shadow light at the other, and in between the rest of the set. In addition a scene like this one presents special difficulties: water, for instance, is always a problem in the Studio, in particular for the size and rapidity of waves when working with models. Here ripples on the surface of the river in foreground will obviously look like tidal waves when they reach the end of the tank (the dolls'-house end), unless they can undergo a corresponding diminution—which is achieved after long trial and error in the adjustment of the fans. Alterations are made, on Gordon's suggestion, to the perspective continuation of the Quai: Dicky produces brush and paintpot and carries it further up the backing. A new row of street lamps introduced by the Art Department calls for the introduction of new spotlights to simulate their effect on the set . . .

Fifth Week

A quarter-day ahead, we go into the fifth week praying for good weather, for now we have to embark on exteriors. Preparing for the worst, Ralph has shunted his schedule slightly, bringing Louis' Lodgings up before the Paris Exhibition: if we need further weather alternatives besides those provided by the remaining Café scenes, the lodgings will suit the purpose well, whereas a set of the dimensions (and crowd involved) of the Exhibition would be absurdly extravagant to use as a stand-by.

Monday, still in the Studio, will be devoted to the Seine Quai, and Louis' and Maria's Paris taxi scene. On Tuesday, weather permitting, London locations start. 'Morton Street' (Paddington) first, for four days; on Sunday, Chancery Lane and Whitehall (now re-assigned to first unit); leaving still a half day for the Harrow Road (Monday week), and the exterior of Clark's Rehearsal Rooms for another Sunday.

Is it simply the charm of its trick perspectives, its doll-size bridges, or also a certain relief at emerging for a little from Anselmo's Café, which makes the atmosphere of a morning's work on the Seine Quai set distinctly breezier than usual? With so much of the preliminary work already done, it is not long before we are ready to shoot: Gordon puts the finishing touches to his lighting, adjusting it to the needs of the action, and as a final check makes a test shot. Developed and printed, this is back on the floor within twenty minutes, for Gordon's inspection.

The action is relatively simple: first the long shot—Steenie's encounter with the valet, the exchange of money for information, the murder. Then this last is taken in three close-shots, culminating in the pitching of the body into the river. In between set-ups we play a little with our huge (and no doubt fabulously expensive) toy: Thorold and Sid pose gleefully, two cheerful Gullivers, for their photograph to be taken at the end of the set, apparently up to their necks in water; Cyril deserts the sound boom to fish from the side of the Quai; Valentina—interrupting a stills session to visit the set—chortles with delight as the midget cars and buses cross the midget bridge.

In spite of the censors' declared disapproval, we film one shot of Steenie rabbit-punching his victim, and cover with what is apparently a safe alternative —a vicious, and perhaps even more spectacular punch to the kidneys. In both of these, Geoffrey is expertly instructed by Serge's stand-in, here this morning to double the valet's ducking in the Seine. Fortunately this last does not call for more than one take.

Discussing the use and value of a set such as this, Thorold says, 'I think it's a mistake to put out a lot of publicity on the way a scene like this is shot . . . It's much better to let them think we really did go to Paris. Why make their suspension of disbelief more rather than less difficult?'

We move across to Stage 2 before lunch, and embark on further trickery · the Paris taxi scene. On a wheeled, sprung structure in a corner of the stage is the taxi body—front and back seats, roof, steering wheel; behind stands a huge rectangle of wood, which, when stripped, discloses a screen of oiled silk. Onto this a projector at the far end of the stage throws our background—the Rue de Rivoli and the Place de la Concorde taken from the back of a travelling car, some twelve or fifteen years ago. To the side of the taxi, mounted on tracks, rears up an extraordinary contraption: an arc light, supported on a wheeled scaffolding, surmounted by a revolving wheel, from the edges of which hang strips of linen, sprays of withered leaves. As these pass in front of the lamp, and as the whole curious thing is hauled backwards and forwards over the tracks, an irregular succession of shadows falls across the taxi, giving the impression of movement. (Comments from the unit include: 'Our contribution to the Festival' and 'Chinese funeral'.)

Rehearsing the scene after lunch, we are reminded that to-day is a Monday; besides which there are complications of timing an intimate and not unemotional dialogue to business with flowers and cigarettes. The trundling of the edifice annoys Brad, and its wheels have to be changed. A distinguished, grey-haired figure appears on the set, clad in a uniform of somewhat mouldy splendour ('Queuein' all parts,' murmurs Jimmy), and is introduced as General Galbern; Thorold suggests alterations. Finally, just as we are ready to go,

Valentina innocently remarks: 'Shouldn't I have a little pair of white gloves?' The non-provision of gloves doesn't matter, but the discovery, to which it leads, that she has no handbag either, starts something. 'No handbag?' exclaims Thorold, with an outrage reminiscent of Lady Bracknell's. Phil explains that one is never called for in the script; Lily protests that Maria's costume is complete here as designed and ratified: Anthony is summoned and appears hastily with a huge and varied cluster of handbags, from which Valentina makes her choice. We begin. But the scene is evidently reluctant to be taken: the artistes fluff, roses fall out of button-holes, the Chinese Funeral develops a piercing creak. It is something of a wonder that we get it in the can, wild track and all, before the end of the afternoon—which enables us to change back to the Café and anticipate the schedule with another set-up.

Rushes to-day provide us with one of those extraordinary (and therefore entirely typical) mishaps: on the retake of D.15, the second take, which is considerably superior from the actors' point of view, is again marred by a negative blemish. There seems no alternative but to use the inferior take.

To-morrow (D.V.) we start on our four days of location work in Paddington, for the Café exteriors. The Air Ministry forecast at four o'clock (a special service to studios) is favourable, so Ralph and Spike finish the day working out to-morrow's call, arrangements for transport and feeding, as well as an alternative studio call in case the weather turns suddenly nasty. Final orders will be telephoned to the artistes by Ralph at 7.15 to-morrow morning.

Scenes taken: B.63, 63a, 64, 65, 66, 67, 68, 68a, 50, 77, 78. Screen time: 2 minutes 34 seconds.

TUESDAY, APRIL 17TH

Broad sunshine. We have landed miraculously on the first day of summer— no need to ring the Studio to find out if the location is on. At 8.30 there everyone is, cluttering up the Paddington pavement, mystifying the inhabitants with their charabancs, cars and equipment. At first local interest is restrained: the proprietor of the Café regards us with reasonable benevolence from his doorway; a couple of children peek at the camera; housewives with string bags and perambulators stop for a brief look. With the Postman and Penny's stand-in in position, Thorold sites the first shot ('I always start off very self-conscious on these occasions,' he confesses; though he does not look it), while a 'Morton Street' sign is fixed on the wall, and the Café becomes Anselmo's. Jimmy briefs the pedestrian crowd for timing and positions (the women bizarre in ungainly hats and shapeless period costumes), and as the shot is taken two stray dogs nose each other in front of the camera with an aptness which would have taken days to secure had it been specified in the script.

It is all very simple—no lights, no sound (for the first take anyway). One realises how much less formidable picture-making must be in countries where the weather can be relied upon, and post-synching of dialogue is the accepted rule. To-day our luck holds, for the sunshine continues unbroken but for two momentary clouds. The crowds, of course, increase during the morning, and throughout the afternoon the Café looks as though it is being visited by royalty, or on fire. Docile, easily satisfied—what they see can mean almost nothing to them—the people stand and gaze, ask each other what is going on, marvel at the slowness and muddle of it all. Otherwise the life of the street is disrupted remarkably little; traffic moves freely up and down, and we clear the

88

Café in time for them to serve lunches as usual (its liveliest hours of business are anyway after midnight, a spectator tells us). The greengrocer's shop opposite suffers most. Fitted with a false bow window full of chemist's goods, it has to cease operations completely for an hour or so before and after the lunch break, while Thorold and the camera crew rehearse Anselmo and Daly through their scene on the weighing machine. Thorold is immensely tickled to find that Charles weighs exactly the amount specified for Anselmo in the script.

The sunshine, and Thorold's exact knowledge of what he wants, enable the unit to work at high speed. First in the street, then cramped into Daly's shop, then wedged even tighter into the first-floor front window of the Café, the camera-group eats through the schedule with steady absorption. Inessential bodies are better out of the way, or they get trodden on, first literally, then (worse) metaphorically. Even Terry, anxious to consult Thorold about shots scheduled for second-unit shooting to-morrow, finds himself unable to get through. This sunshine is money; we dare not waste a beam of it.

Scenes taken: A.1, 2, 3, 4, 5, 6, 23, D.2, E.56, E.58. *Screen time*: 1 *minute 53 seconds.*

WEDNESDAY, APRIL 18TH

Novel approaches: Serge is sitting in the artistes' car, waiting for his call, when Spike brings a journalist over, introduces him, and leaves them. This is how the interview begins. 'You look very like a friend of mine who is an ice skater. He came over and married an English girl and went back to America.' 'Really?' 'I saw you first in *Les Amants de Verone*. It was a very fine film. I saw it twice.' 'Thank you . . .' Perhaps this is what is known in Schools of Journalism as *Putting Your Subject at His Ease*.

Sun continues.

Scenes shot: D.12, E.44, 47, 49, 59, 65, 71. *2nd Unit*: D.13, E.45, E.64x. B.P. *Plate for D.14. Screen time*: 1 *minute 47 seconds.*

THURSDAY, APRIL 19TH

Last night's forecast being again for clear weather, this morning's call is once more for rendezvous at the location. But at 8.30 the prospect is greyish; and the morning weather report offers hope of scattered sunshine up to mid-day, none in the afternoon. Anxious eyes are cast at the sky, and the possibilities are discussed. Finally, with decision, Ralph gives the order to return to the Studio. Camera, sound, director, make off by car; artistes for the alternative call are summoned by telephone; the rest of the unit troop off to Paddington to return by train. During this retreat, the sun starts breaking through; by the time we are back at the Studio (where the camera is already on the first set-up), the sky is clear and the sunlight is golden.

But Ralph feels no need to be apologetic. 'There's always the risk either way. The question is simply: where do we stand to lose the most? We're well up on schedule now; with a full day of sun we can clear the rest of the Morton Street stuff, and Harrow Road (for Louis' Lodgings) into the bargain. With all that time in hand, why take a chance on the weather which may easily lose us half a day? This way, we know we'll get a full day's work done in the Studio—and we can polish off the rest of the location schedule to-morrow. Or whenever the first clear day comes. We're lucky, in fact, to be *able* to tear back into the Studio. Your headaches really start when you're out, miles from anywhere, and

89

just have to sit and watch the rain pour down . . .' This is undeniably solid sense; still, it is difficult to repress the ironic grimace as throughout the day each visitor to the set reports (with surprise, amusement, commiseration, according to temperament) that it continues to be a lovely day.

Scenes shot: *D.55a, E.62, 62a, 63a, 64, 66, 69. Screen time*: 2 *minutes 4 seconds.*

FRIDAY, APRIL 20TH

Ralph's calculations are correct. To-day dawns fine, and we are all set to clean up the rest of this batch of exteriors. In Morton Street we are left with an assortment of brief arrivals by car, people at windows, watching and being watched—all part of the build-up to the explosion in the Café. 'We are going to need all the cuts we can get in this sequence,' says Thorold, and accordingly helps himself to extra set-ups here and there, which may contribute to the tension.

Late morning, the sun is right for us to start on the Harrow Road material. With our two cameras, we can overlap this with shooting in Paddington, so, leaving Chick's set up in Morton Street (E.1), Thorold, the artistes, and the second camera move across to the Harrow Road. Here we squash into a back bedroom for a location insert into C.39—the camera on the window, looking out over the railway yards, Louis and Maria enter frame, speak the first few lines of the scene just as a train passes outside. From the start, we are menaced by censorship. ('As it is written, the scene has the flavour of an illicit sex affair,' the American censor has commented. 'The scene should not end with the characters sitting on a couch or in any kind of an embrace that would suggest an approximate sex affair.') 'Is it too close to approximate sex if Louis closes the window?' Thorold queries. Phyll has the answer: 'It's all right if she keeps her hat on.'

But for Louis to close the window is more easily suggested than done. The frame is warped, and Serge must heave and strain before it will budge. Then there are the trains: if they are coming out of the station, they pass out of the sunlight, and so are not prominent enough in shot: and if they are speed-ing *into* the station, they are putting out none of that photogenic white smoke. Add to this the chancy timing of entrances and dialogue, and you have all the ingredients of a hysterical hour and a half. Thorold cranes from the window, watching for an approaching express. 'Positions!' The train comes nearer. 'Action!' The artistes walk into shot, speak, and the train passes uselessly by in the background-shadow. The second time, Serge finds the window immovable; in what the Breen Office would no doubt imagine to be an ecstasy of erotic impatience, he hoists himself from the ground in his efforts to move it. 'Props!' On the third take, the train mysteriously fails to appear; on the fifth, what we took to be an express turns out merely a single, comically tubby shunter. This is too much for Valentina, who collapses in the middle of the take, helpless with laughter. 'Darling, I am so sorry . . . I apologise . . .' (These are Valentina's favourite syllables, spoken with such acuteness of self-reproach that they never fail to enchant.) 'I know there's an express arriving at 1.14,' says Thorold, 'because I used to travel up by it.' But in the end we are here till 1.35, leaving off with a score of nine takes, two possibles.

For the rest of the afternoon, two further shots at the Lodgings are dovetailed with the remnants of Morton Street. Gordon superintends C.38 while Thorold shoots from the Café window. Thorold hastens back for E.5, then returns to Morton Street to wind up the day in the last of the sunlight. Thanks to the weather, this completes four and a half days' schedule of work in three days.

Scenes shot: C.38, C.39a, E.1, 5, 61, 61a, 63x, 67, 70, 72, 74, 75, 79. Screen time: 1 minute 23 seconds.

SUNDAY, APRIL 22ND

Sunday is the day for shooting on populated locations, and to-day is reserved for Chancery Lane and Whitehall (Scotland Yard). The first is easy, for the City on a Sunday morning is as open and deserted as a Studio lot. The bus on to which Nora must hop is correctly 1937-type, and carries on its side the Art Department's poster for the serialised life of Galbern in a Sunday newspaper, complete with blow-up of Hugo Schuster's uniformed portrait. Bert Davey, holding the Art Department's brief, regards this with disfavour: 'We haven't been able to make a really good job of it. The bus comes out of London Transport's museum, and they wouldn't give us permission to stick the thing on properly, so we've just had to use transparent tape.' The result is certainly a bit bumpy; but Thorold thinks we can get away with it on a quick cut.

Whitehall after this calm is like a jungle: Ralph's forebodings are amply fulfilled. Direction of sunlight makes it necessary to shoot on Scotland Yard first, and Gordon in addition has to use an arc lamp. So by the time it comes to the pan on Maria and Anselmo as they walk away from Scotland Yard into Whitehall, our presence is well advertised, and the rubbernecks (Ralph's term), the Sunday-morning strollers, are out in full force. Luckily it is not now intended to sweep the whole vista of the street—which would include clothes and vehicles too obviously contemporary. As it is, the right-hand pavement, on which the shot finishes, is at first a solid mass of people, who have to be requested, prayed, threatened to keep moving. Success is only achieved, and the shot taken, at the cost of including Ralph, Spike and Jimmy prominent in foreground—to audiences, of course, as anonymous as any crowd artistes, but to us sticking out like sore thumbs as we imagine the instructions, the imprecations that are issuing invisibly from the corners of their mouths.

Scenes shot: B.2, 5, E.21, 40. Screen time: 1 minute 10 seconds.
Total screen time to date: 63 minutes 50 seconds.

Sixth Week

Good management of exceptional luck (it was not merely the sunshine, but also Thorold's and Gordon's willingness to shoot simultaneously with two units) has put us one and a half days ahead on locations, with still a quarter of a day in hand in the Studio. We return to continue work in the Café (two and a half days), then to move on to Louis' Lodgings for his scene with Maria and the meetings of the London Committee. Next Sunday, if weather continues favourable, will go on the final London street location—for the Rehearsal Rooms exterior.

Further ahead: Ralph has produced a revised schedule to the end of the picture. Minor alterations apart, the chief novelty is the bringing forward of Scotland Yard and the Hospital sequences by nearly a fortnight. This is the direct result of having reversed the shooting order of Louis' Lodgings and the

*Paris Exhibition; as the schedule stands this would leave us no sets to be busy
on while the Exhibition was being dismantled on 3a and 3b. Scotland Yard
and the Hospital, erected cheek to cheek on Stage 2, and using up four days
between them, will provide the answer.*

MONDAY, APRIL 23RD

Half-term reports. Half-way through the schedule, and with the unit now
compactly back in the Studio, this seems the moment to attempt to regain that
bird's-eye view of the production as a whole which is so easily lost in the complexities of day-to-day routine. With most of the first half of the script, and
the bulk of the Café scenes disposed of, the dramatic spine of the film may be
said to be broken. In the second half there are of course scenes equally important but these will be shot with less regard for their script continuity: the Committee scenes in Louis' London Lodgings, and the big set for the Paris
Exhibition; the bomb explosion in the Café; the Garden Party; Maria in
Scotland Yard and in hospital; the scenes in Dublin culminating in the death
of Maria in Phœnix Park. In addition there are the two 'montage' sequences,
hopefully scheduled for the second unit—the girls' journey to Britain, and the
general impression of the Paris Exhibition (stock material, edited with inserts
featuring Maria, Nora and Anselmo).

From a general production point of view, Sid remarks simply that this is
turning out to be one of the smoothest pictures he has worked on. The key is
that 'the director knows what he wants—which has a tonic effect on the unit
as a whole. Everyone becomes that little bit more on their toes. Gordon's a fast
worker too, which helps enormously. Then there's been the weather. That was
really the most incredible luck. Shots you schedule for four and a half days
may very well take you six—to get them in three is quite fantastic. Also, thanks
to our general speed, we've been able to absorb what retakes have been
necessary into our schedule; which means we don't have to keep sets hanging
around until the end of the picture, plus the expense of recalling artistes, etc.
Another great advantage has been that we've shot largely in continuity, which
is of particular benefit to the artistes . . .'

As far as the next half goes, everything seems to be shaping according to
plan. One important change which has recently been decided on is the
abandonment of even the remnants of the Dublin location, 'to save money.
We pared it down so fine that in the end it only consisted of a couple of shots.
Neither is dramatically essential, and if we cut them out, we can save several
hundreds of pounds which we can usefully use in other directions. The Clowns,
for instance, who look as though they are going to turn into quite an expensive
item. Undoubtedly the biggest problem mounting up for us is the post-
synching at the end of the picture—of which there's bound to be a certain
amount. It's difficult to do anything on this while we're shooting; apart from
the fact that Valentina, for instance, is on the floor practically every day, there
are stills sessions, fittings and all the rest of it to be fitted in, which doesn't
leave much time to spare . . .'

Sid's points are echoed pretty consistently by the rest of the unit, from
Muriel's 'Madly, madly smooth (I haven't been in the publicity business for
nothing, dear),' to Ralph's 'Thorold's a dream'. He goes on: 'About this stage
on a picture I always get the feeling I'm in the middle of a long, dark tunnel
—with a pinprick of light in the distance, very far off. But to be honest, I have

92

to admit I'm actually enjoying this one.' Spike sounds the same note: 'As far as artistes go, this is a perfect picture . . . If they're troublesome, they can cost you half an hour a day—always sneaking off the stage, up to their dressing rooms or across the road for a drink in the pub. But these never leave the set. . . . Of course, a lot depends on the cameraman. If he's always promising to be ready in five minutes, and then carries on fiddling for half an hour, they're bound to get unco-operative. Gordon's very good like that, which is a lot of help.' William's verdict is similarly that the picture so far has been 'a walk-over'. 'Not,' he adds, 'because it's a simple job, but because the director knows what he wants.' (This remark is made so often that a report of even five per cent of its occurrences must seem a little repetitious). All the sets are now designed, except for some of the details for the Garden Party. Louis' London Lodgings have replaced the first floor of the Café on Stage 2, and are being finally dressed to-day; on 3a and 3b the Paris Exhibition is under erection, and sets to come—Daly's shop, Dublin Castle, Scotland Yard, the Hospital—are either in the carpenters' shops or taking shape on the drawing board. Terry's Railway Carriage, which will move after all, is also in preparation for the day when the second unit is allowed at last to get its teeth into the Montage.

This last item provides one of the shadows in which might otherwise be a monotonously sunny picture. Asked how he thinks the picture is going, Terry is liable to reply, "Too bloody well'. The speed of shooting, and Valentina's heavy schedule make it difficult to see how the Montage is ever to be squeezed in. 'With a dress change and a hair change for Valentina, she can't just slip across from one stage to another for her second-unit scenes. Ralph has already begun to drop dark hints of postponement to the end of the schedule—in which case it will inevitably be shot by the first unit. . . But I think I've got a B.P. plate to do some time this week, and I'm terribly excited about that.'

Another problem mentioned by Sid is expanded by Steve Dalby, who refreshingly starts by declaring that from his point of view, the picture has not gone terribly well. Partly it is the traditional rivalry between sight and sound: 'You have to accept the fact that if sets fulfil the wants of the photography and the direction, they aren't always ideal for sound . . . On this film we've had certain inconveniences from a sound angle—the hard floors that Thorold wanted so as to be able to manœuvre the camera without tracks, and the fact that he frequently wants the ceiling in camera as well. And then of course we have our three principal artistes speaking accented English, which means that they suffer particularly from any loss of quality. Nor has Valentina been in the best of health; it's a tremendously heavy part, and you must remember that the voice is the first thing to show physical weakness. . . We've fitted wild tracks to quite a lot of the scenes with success, but all wild tracks don't fit, and even they may not be good enough.'

All the same Steve looks forward to the prospect of post-synching with tranquillity. It is not likely to be a very long job (you can post-synch an entire film in four days) and 'It's surprising the improvement you can get with it. When the actors have nothing to worry about except the enunciating of their words, you may get anything up to 100 per cent improvement in audibility.'

This question of sound affects also the editor. Peter remarks with approval that in general the picture is being shot in a straightforward and economical way; as a result everything is cut and assembled up to last Friday's rushes. There is a certain amount of work yet to be done on the Ballet and the

93

musical sequences, and the Bomb scene (D.7) has still to be finalised. 'The procedure is that as soon as a sequence is cut, we run it for Steve, who gives us his views on the dialogue. We don't use any wild tracks until he's been through it line by line and N.G.'d anything he won't pass. Then we look and see what we've got on wild tracks. If that's not good enough, it'll have to be post-synched. After this, comments and suggestions for further re-recording are of course likely to come in from Thorold or Sid or Sir Michael.'

Looking ahead, there is the Paris Exhibition montage to cause slight worry. Together with Terry, Peter has whittled the material down to between 300 and 400 feet of the most usable. 'We've worked out a rough plan, starting with the night shots, which we'll use without any Studio inserts. Then we fade out (we're leaving out the sweeping-up shots, which just aren't good enough) and fade into a day sequence, cutting in glimpses of Maria, Nora and Anselmo . . . I must admit I'm not too happy about the stuff—but then what editor ever is when he has to use material which someone else has already edited?'

From other departments it is impossible to get reactions much less favourable. Like Muriel, Anthony is instinctively aware of the necessity for diplomacy. 'I think it's going frightfully well. I'm awfully thrilled with all the rushes. I think Thorold uses his camera in the most exciting manner.' Appealed to to come off it, he continues, with more apparent honesty: 'For instance, I'm very very thrilled that at this stage of the picture the principal has already worn—or been photographed in—all her outfits; which leaves me free to design the principal clothes for my next picture. Apart from Valentina, Serge has just one suit which he wears all the way, and Audrey has another two costumes to try . . . In all, things have been made easy by the fact that the director and the stars have been extremely reasonable, and ready to compromise where necessary.' For instance? 'Well, Valentina is a good enough trouper to know that if a costume isn't fitted absolutely to the last stitch (perhaps we've just not been able to get her for enough fittings), it isn't really disastrous. Only an idiot or an amateur is perfectionist under all circumstances. You get a ham like —— (don't mention her name) who fusses and refuses to go on the set until the hem of her dress has been stitched to perfection, because she fails to realise that it's not by her clothes that she impresses the audience, but by the quality of her performance.' And how does he find his clothes have come out on the screen? 'Quite well on the whole—the lighting has been very kind to the clothes in general. I'm rather astonished that they even look faintly period . . .' What about the Ballet? 'Put down your pen and I'll tell you . . .'

On the floor we have started winding up the Café sequences—the jig-saw of staccato shots which lead up to the explosion in the cellar.

Scenes shot: E.68, 68a, 68b, 68c, 82, 82a, 83, 82x, 84a, 85a, 84, 86, 87, 88, 89. *Screen time*: 1 *minute* 11 *seconds*.

TUESDAY, APRIL 24TH

An attempt to complete the half-way summary with a report from the director meets with failure: an instant outburst of laughter and, 'What a bloody silly question!' Which is perhaps an answer in itself.

First thing to-day, Thorold inspects yesterday's rushes to clarify his ideas on the sequence and see whether the material shot so far calls for further set-ups unspecified in the script. Shooting starts with retakes of D 19, then resumes the jig-saw—a succession of sharp cuts as the Committee members make for the cellar—Frack is shot down at the door of the Café—the bomb thrown up and kicked back—Maria thrusts herself forward to receive the impact of the explosion. As with the work on location, this sort of shooting is apt to mean little to the unit as a whole: by themselves the shots mostly lack significance. It is their combination and rhythm which is going to build the scene up into excitement. An enormous amount depends on the stimulus of the moment. 'How on earth can you preplan or independent-frame a sequence like this?' Thorold comments 'Everything depends on the way the smoke blows, the way the bomb is thrown, the way a particular artiste wants to react . . .' For the actors such sequences resolve themselves into periods of waiting, then short bursts of activity (rather than acting): a startled look out of camera, a sudden move or cry. You might think this discontinuity would oppress, but the capable technician takes it in his stride. Valentina mimes her reactions to Steenie's appearance, his revolver shot, Frack's death, with no aid but her own imagination. One cannot think the result would be more effective if the events were simultaneous, as they will be on the screen. Early afternoon brings Fracks murder, and Lionel's appropriate exit from the picture. Reflecting on the experience, he remarks that he has learned a lot, 'if only by making mistakes and seeing them on rushes next day. I think I've learned the *tempo* of screen acting'.

Post-script to yesterday: 'We've decided,' says Ralph, 'that the picture is running far too smoothly, so we're going to start re-scheduling.' In fact, the night exteriors (Garden Party and Phœnix Park) are being shifted on a week; since the reversal of the shooting order of Louis' Lodgings and the Paris Exhibition allows insufficient time, as the schedule stands, for striking the Exhibition and building the following sets on Stage 3. By a piece of intricate juggling with sets, stages and shooting order, Ralph manages to give the Construction Department the time and the space they need.

Another advantage is the time gained in the search for clowns. The complications of music-hall bookings are increased, Margaret points out, by the apparent insignificance of the part. 'A big act doesn't like to feel it's just being employed for background. When we used Tessie O'Shea in *The Blue Lamp* she had a personal build-up and a mention by name in the script, which we don't want to have to do here.'

Terry is delighted and surprised to be informed by Ralph that he will be shooting his first day on the Montage this Friday.

Scenes shot: E.83a, 85, 90, 91, 91a, 91b, 92, 92a, 93, 94. (*Retake D.19c, D.19e*). *Screen time*: 44 seconds.

WEDNESDAY, APRIL 25TH

Terry is disappointed but not surprised to be informed by Ralph that he will not be shooting his first day on the Montage on Friday. What has happened is this: Valentina could be free if Thorold would arrange the first unit shooting to suit; but he prefers to take the Committee scenes in continuity, which will keep her engaged. We are, in fact, as Terry appreciated, too well up on schedule for the second unit to be given work which the director would obviously prefer to do himself. It now looks pretty definite that both Montages will be shot by the first unit at the end of the schedule. Terry's reaction? 'I've lost all interest in it, to be quite candid.' And then: 'Well, obviously I haven't, but . . .'

On the floor we dispose of the Café and a few odds and ends (including an extra close-up of Steenie, for cutting in to the Seine Quai sequence) before embarking on the block of scenes in Louis' Lodgings. In the theatre, Valentina and Serge view their location scenes which lead up to, and cut in to, the first of these, then, the mood re-established in their minds, return to the stage to play the bulk of the scene. Towards the end of the afternoon a certain tension develops: a lot of the boys are eager to get away to a football match, and Thorold is aware besides that the London Committee are on call for first thing to-morrow morning. Into the bargain, it is an early night—but we just make it.

Scenes shot: B.63x, 63y, C.39, 40, 40a, 40b, D.22e, E.80, 81. Screen time: 1 minute 53 seconds.

THURSDAY, APRIL 26TH

Professionalism. It is a word which must constantly come to the mind of an observer of activity such as this. Being 'professional' is not simply a matter of being good at one's job; it is even more a question of attitude. Of course the attitude affects the result—but not merely the result of one's own work. Individual brilliance is not the same as professionalism in this sense; it may well cost the whole more than it contributes to it.

Whatever the job, professionals display largely the same characteristics: the instinct for co-operation, an awareness of the problems of others, a constant relation of their part to the whole that must result. Gordon's speed of working, for instance, is part of *his* professionalism. His skill is at the service of the picture, which has to be shot in a certain time. The cameraman cannot, therefore, take time out to refine his perfect satisfaction. 'There's always a bit more fiddling you would like to indulge in, but it just isn't possible. And, to be honest, a lot of it is just cameraman's *chi-chi*—interesting to technicians, but just not noticeable to audiences. I'm not saying you should be content with bad work; there's a difference between a well photographed and a badly photographed picture which people will notice, even if only unconsciously. You just have to accept the necessity for compromise.' So he works briskly and without ostentation. Thorold specifies the set-up, the desired effect; Gordon accepts what is asked for, or if it involves lighting problems which seem out of proportion, suggests alternatives of position or movement; these are usually accepted. Then into routine: building up the lighting, with Tom Chapman at his side to relay instructions to the electricians at the lamps; checking the light-intensity with meter held against faces of stand-ins and actors; calling for an adjustment here, an extra lamp there, an extra touch of make-up. And if a last-minute elaboration by the director calls for a change or an addition in lighting, it will be forthcoming with the same businesslike equability.

Acting is a different craft, but the same considerations can apply. Serge is also a professional ('It's my job'). He is far from regarding the actor as a marionette, to be dangled at the end of a string, to have gestures, inflexions dictated to him; these are things he must do for himself. But, granted this measure of autonomy, he is here to fulfil the function required of him by the director, and as part of an ensemble—never to exploit his personality for its own effect. 'A film,' he likes to say, 'does not belong to the actors, but to the director. The result is his responsibility; he must have the authority too.' In

96

discussions on the scene in hand, he is always tentative in putting forward any suggestions of his own; at rushes, he will state a preference—on grounds of his own performance—for one take over another, only with a prefatory apology for the interference. He will even give it as his opinion that actors should never be allowed to comment on rushes, but one is glad to find human frailty asserting itself on this point every now and then. In Serge's case, this discipline has not come—is not coming, rather—without effort; it is not entirely natural to a temperament as ebullient as his, as critically intelligent. (Off the job, his opinions are inclined to spurt out with compensatory violence.) He still feels himself no more than half way—he would probably say less than that—towards a technique of the forcefulness and simplicity which is his ideal. (When he talks about acting, he will almost certainly mention Gabin's death in *Quai des Brumes*. He speaks of Fonda with awe.)

To-day the second unit really goes into action, though on comparatively unspectacular material. With his cameraman, Lionel Baines, Terry makes two expeditions to Morton Street: in the morning for a shot (additional to the script) of the Café as glimpsed by Maria on her way to Dublin, and in the evening for C.47—the extinction of the Café lights. The latter shot is the more elaborate, involving lamps, generators, etc., and Ralph has applied to the Works Committee for an extension for it; this unfortunately cuts out the possibility of an extra-early start, so the unit is not in position till 9. After redressing the front of the Café, lining up the shot, and three unsatisfactory takes—the sun has moved across to the other side of the street. A return visit will have to be paid for this; the evening shot, though, is taken with success.

In the studio the London Committee assemble, and a solid, a very solid day's work takes us through the first sequence and into the second—the cross-examination of Maria.

Scenes shot: C.47, 50, 51, E.7, 8, 11, 13. (Second Unit: C.50a, 51a, 51b, 51c). Screen time: 4 minutes 19 seconds.

FRIDAY, APRIL 27TH

Actors'-eye view (the Committee reassembles): 'I hope this goes over to three days.' 'I don't—I've got a three-day guarantee anyway, so I'm all for polishing it off in two.' 'It's not like the old days, when no one connected with the money side of a picture ever came near the set.' 'And if anything happened to hold up shooting, it was treated as a tremendous joke.' Reminiscent sighs.

Serge arrives late, having been overcome with nausea in his bath. 'It's all through smoking all those cigarettes for the shot yesterday—inhaling deeply to get a light on the face. And such terrible cigarettes . . .' Valentina also has had her troubles this morning; she has heard a song on the set which she is convinced brings her bad luck. Ten minutes later the carpenters (not in entire ignorance) start it up again, and she appeals in distress to Thorold : 'Forgive me for being hysterical, but some people are superstitious you know. And they do it on purpose.' Spike is despatched, and the singing stops. The scene recommences. 'Miss Brent, I think I know how you feel,' starts Bentley, and the tension breaks in laughter.

As opposed to the Café scenes, this sequence is largely free from 'business,' and progress is accordingly speedy; it is a question, once the playing of the

97

scene, and the placing of the characters, have been established, of hewing the compositions expressive of the required atmosphere out of this raw material on the floor, rather than from the approximations of the script. Rushes are very encouraging; we are reminded once more of the difficulty for most people on the floor, apart from the cameraman, of perceiving quite what is being registered on the celluloid. From the lighting of the set it takes a practised eye to deduce the savage chiaroscuro which is what the audience will see—an effective result dramatically, which must nevertheless disappoint some of the actors, who have been performing so sensitively in what turns out to be pitch blackness.

During the afternoon preparation starts in earnest for next week's big chore: the Paris Exhibition. All week the set has been shaping on Stage 3—hygienic Exhibition buildings, painted scenic backings, false-perspective interiors for the Pavilions. To-day the disputed sprays of artificial leaves are being wired into position, and vividly flowering plants are being bedded into the floor. Between set-ups Thorold works through the sequence with Spike, roughing in camera angles on a reduced set plan provided by the Art Department; from this Spike can work out his schedule, and Muriel, who hovers near, hopes to learn the numbers of crowd likely to be needed each day. 'It's scheduled for four days,' she reminds them, 'but now you say only three. Now how many big days do you want?' Thorold suggests 200 each for the first two days. 'Then I've only got 18 left for the third day—and I've been asked to cut down, you know.' Thorold and Spike take this mildly, in the end agreeing to take 200 the first day, 150 the second, and on the third, when we will shoot the closer shots, the balance. 'I think 200 is too many,' observes William, who materialises as Thorold turns his back. 'I know, dear,' (confidentially), 'but I'm not giving him 200.' 'Well how many are you giving him?' asks the observer. But Muriel's regard is hostile. 'I'm not saying anything more in front of you,' she declares defensively.

Leaving for home, Serge collects his call sheets (for Sunday and Monday) from Jimmy, to gather from them that on Monday we will be retaking the Paris Taxi scene (B.50). He receives the news with incredulity: 'But why?' Jimmy does not know. 'But it's completely stupid! You know—making films is not like making machines. The technicians and the actors must work together. If we are to do the scene again, I must know what for . . .' I try to explain to Serge that Jimmy is obviously as ignorant as he, but again only arouse suspicion. Jimmy complains: 'I wish you wouldn't talk about me behind my back in French to my face.'

Scenes shot: E.6, 8a, 9, 10, 12, 12x, 14, 15, 16, 17, 18, 19, 20, 90a. *Screen time*: 2 *minutes* 17 *seconds*.

SUNDAY, APRIL 29TH

On location in West Street, Cambridge Circus, for the exterior shots after Nora's audition. The set-piece is an immense tracking shot to cover the dialogue between Louis and Maria (telescoping C.36 and 37) as they cross the road from the Rehearsal Rooms, light cigarettes, and talk. Camera movement of this kind is as exciting to take as it is to watch, though considerably more exacting. Before the actors, intimately conversing, there must trundle a whole, pre-occupied cortège: camera and sound boom riding on their hand-drawn dollies; Gordon, keenly watching the light; Thorold, eyeing the action; Phyll, straining to check the dialogue (practically inaudible) against the script; and Spike, strict and wary in command of his extras. And behind all this, the cables which supply the power to keep camera and mike in action must be paid back, out of the way of the backwards-moving procession. We start in adequate sunshine and deserted Sunday-morning streets, but the inevitable snags lengthen the time of shooting: in one take Serge entirely forgets the business with cigarettes; the camera, which is running on the road surface, without benefit of tracks, jolts over a cable; spectators on the opposite side of the road are found to be reflected in the windows of the Ivy Restaurant. By now the usual crowd has assembled and the sun has taken refuge behind clouds: a huge arc light (professional name: a Mole-Richardson Brute) is heaved on to yet another dolly, trained on the actors, and travelled back with us for a seventh and an eighth time. These last two seem both satisfactory. It has taken us over two hours to get them, but for a shot that runs one minute forty-seven seconds you can reckon that as not bad going.

Scenes shot: C.36, 36a, 37. Screen time: 2 minutes 1 second. Total screen time to date: 76 minutes 15 seconds.

Seventh Week

With Sunday's exterior successfully accomplished, we are altogether 2¾ days up—1½ on locations and 1¼ in the Studio. (Last week's Café scenes went quicker than was anticipated, and so did Louis' Lodgings, of which there now remains only one set-up to do.) We have said farewell to Anselmo's Café, and are really embarked on the latter half of the picture.

Next week belongs mostly to the Paris Exhibition, pre-lit on Monday afternoon and shooting till Friday morning, when the first unit will move on to Scotland Yard, while the second unit remains on the Exhibition to shoot material for the Montage. As the film has progressed, Thorold has taken advantage of odd moments here and there to view and comment on the sequences which Peter has been able to put together. Some time this week, he will be able to see the first rough assembly of about half the picture, carrying, apart from the necessary gaps, from the start to the bomb explosion in the Café.

MONDAY, APRIL 30TH

The first set-up to-day polishes off Louis' Lodgings (E.53): on the build-up of this shot, not too luminously described in the script, Thorold comments: 'Cliché No. 66 in the book—detectives searching suspect's room—what on earth is one to do to make that interesting? Cliché No. 66a is of course to have the telephone huge in foreground, and use a wide-angle lens to cover the rest of the room. Well we don't want anything like that, so we do it quite straight and neo-realist: start on a detective examining the fireplace (where they've been burning papers), and pan round with him as he crosses to answer the telephone. Then the detective suggests, 'Wouldn't I use a handkerchief when I pick up the phone, in case of fingerprints?' So we track in on him as he picks it up, to emphasise the handkerchief. Which brings us to a set-up which matches exactly the shot of Maria at the other end of the line—the next cut. Isn't that a perfect little example of how style grows out of subject? It's this sort of thing that Asquith means when he says there are no schools of cinema, only stories which dictate each their own style.'

While Gordon sets up for the retake of B.50, Thorold, with Chic and a viewfinder, starts exploring the Exhibition set. Now all but complete, this looks like nothing so much as an ambitious display at the Ideal Home Exhibition: a sky of rafters and floodlights looks down on white walls and columns, terraces set with tables and large orange umbrellas, a paved garden planted out with shrubs and bright, unnatural-looking flowers. Half-way down the stage, a wooden section, carrying an oddly distorted Royal coat of arms, is being hoisted into the air—a 'foreground cutout' which, when viewed through the camera from one end of the set, will seem to roof buildings sited at the other, giving them the illusion of a greater height than the ceiling of the stage will in fact permit. ('I like these trick shots,' murmurs Dicky—to whom this one is of course the merest child's play—'you can have such fun and games with 'em.')

To the task of filling all this blank space with appropriate crowd, Muriel now applies herself seriously. It is not an exceptional assignment, she explains ('Nothing to *Dance Hall*'), but the problem is complicated by an even larger call at Shepperton Studios, which has started to-day and therefore has the lead on us. Besides, our requirements are to a certain degree specialised. 'There are only 1,030 extras available through the union in all. At least 50 of those are over fifty, and consequently when you're trying to do an unusual call, you discover that your resources are extremely limited   As you know, we're going through a very very bad period in the industry: quite a number of extras have gone out of the business—much as we need crowd artistes, we can never guarantee them a living.' Hopefully, Muriel has broken down her list in about thirty classified groups (ten Smart Young Frenchmen, Man Wearing Indian Headdress, five Elderly Middle-class Frenchwomen), each unit with a number and a pencilled-in name. Whether all of these will be available, however, she cannot know until this evening; for the moment we are entirely dependent on the efforts of the agency. 'The difficult part starts when they begin to tell me what I can't have—then the call is liable to get filled up with totally unsuitable people.'

Meanwhile all that is practicable is done: the time of call has been fixed with Spike, dressing-rooms allotted, feeding arrangements checked. Muriel spends most of the afternoon on the telephone, hectoring the agency. ('Don't dare swing any old Cockneys on me, or I'll murder you'), or being herself hectored by aspirants ('No Martin, we can't use you to-morrow—we had you on the English set.') In the corner her assistant, Vicky, ploughs through the engagement slips—each in effect a one-day contract, filled in with number and fee. Periodically she looks up to check from Muriel: 'Do the Chinamen get extra?' (Coloured artistes, whose opportunities for work are fewer, get a guinea a day more than white.) 'Yes, Low Cow and Chong Choy each get three guineas . . . I may have to give them extra money—they're wearing their own clothes. I'll wait to see them before I decide how much.' 'Do the Arabs get anything?' 'No; they're not real Arabs—they've just got long noses.' As rush hour approaches, Muriel and Vicky fortify themselves with cups of tea, and reminisce over past triumphs: 'Remember *Passport to Pimlico*? We used to be here till ten and eleven every night. One night they locked us in. I was so angry I broke the door down . . .' One can well believe it.

While Gordon has been lighting the set. Thorold has been in the theatre with Peter to view his assembly of everything we have shot so far—an hour and twelve minutes of film. (When one is, so to speak, building a bridge from both ends like this, a long view of progress so far achieved becomes an essential reassurance.) This was followed by a selection of newsreel shots taken at the Paris Exhibition in 1937—somewhat alarming in the hugeness of the area they cover. His return to the floor precipitates something of a drama. During his reconnaissance of the set, he has decided that on all long shots he will use a 25 mm. (wide-angle) instead of a 35 mm. lens—to increase the sense of depth and spaciousness. But, alas, the sequence was planned—and designed—to be shot with a 35, and when the camera position is checked for the first set-up, we discover that the wider angle of vision carries beyond the backing (a painted vista of the Exhibition tailored exactly to the shot as planned) on to the studio wall. William surveys this with gloom. 'The only thing I can suggest is that we hang some drapes—long strips of bunting—on the far side of the backing. We've got some stuff in the store that I think will do.' Thorold comments: 'I wish some of those accountants would come down on the floor once in a while, and see the sort of mess their cheese-paring can land us in.'

Scenes shot: *E.53. B.50 (Retake). Screen time*: *3 seconds.*

TUESDAY, MAY 1ST

At 7.45 it is grey and drizzling as I step off the bus to enter the Studio with three Indian Ladies, one Indian Child and an assortment of (I presume) Smart Middle-aged Frenchwomen, Bodyguards and Gendarmes. In view of the weather, and the hour, it is a surprisingly lively queue that forms up outside the gate, to shuffle slowly past the window from which John is issuing each arrival with his chit for the day's engagement.

Inside the Studio Jimmy directs the flow to their dressing-rooms, where they change, or simply remain till he calls them down to the set. 'If it was a fine day, they'd ooze out all over the Studio,' he comments, looking approvingly at the drizzle outside. 'To-day, thank heaven, they'll just sit quietly until they're wanted. And then, of course, they'll say: "Can't we have tea first?" ' In the steady trickle of extras up the stairs there is not much resemblance to Muriel's three, carefully-timed waves; most of them make straight for the dressing-rooms with the assurance of familiarity, many of them Jimmy can greet personally. 'Hullo Ralph—what are you doing to-day?' 'Gendarme.' 'Why weren't you here at 7.30?' 'Sorry, sir, overslept. Had a hell of a day at Shepperton yesterday. Section leader. I'm absolutely exhausted.' As the crowd thins to an end, the principals start to arrive for make-up, and the unit to seep on to the floor. Muriel, of course, is early in evidence to inspect her charges and report to Spike. 'I was here till ten, and was on the phone to the agency from home till after eleven. We're twenty down on the numbers I asked for, and four have failed to arrive.' Spike is sanguine: 'That's all right. If we have 120 in the crowd I'm not worried.' 'They could have given me more people,' explains Muriel, 'but it would have been Petticoat Lane rather than Montmartre.'

All seems set. The unit is assembled, and Gordon starts to light the first shot—when a snag is revealed. The extra drapes have appeared overnight: they screen the studio wall right enough, but they also (we at once discover) catch the beam from one of the arcs, and cast long shadows on the backing.

William improvises hurriedly: the only remedy is to shift the backing along, and fill in the gap thus left between it and the edge of the British Pavilion with flats. Which takes a little time. 'My name will be mud with the Front Office for the rest of this week,' Thorold muses gloomily, 'but it just can't be helped. It was foolishness ever to think of using a 35 mm. lens on these shots—not on the others. It's a pure convention that once you get on a wide-angle lens you've got to stick on it. That's the only way we ever got any effect of space on our tiny sets in *The Queen of Spades*—we'd bang over on to a 24 mm., and the thing became just that much bigger. But of course you can go just as wrong blowing things out as you can pinching them down—remember the miners' cottages in *How Green Was My Valley?* Ludicrously, vulgarly big . . .'

While we wait, Thorold has the stock material on the Exhibition screened in the theatre; we return to find the set looking even more plainly in need of a wide-angle lens. By 10.45 all is ready, and the crowd, sustained by coffee and cakes, shuffle in in chatty bewilderment ('Isn't it pretty! I wonder where it's supposed to be?'), to be herded and sorted and positioned by Spike and Jimmy. At last the principals can appear, and rehearsal begin in earnest: by lunch time the first shot is in the can, and we can feel that the Exhibition sequence has been begun.

At rushes we see Sunday's tracking shot—unanimously voted a winner. 'Travail extraordinaire de Gordon,' says Serge.

Shots taken: B.22, 24, 26-9, 33. Screen time: 1 minute 12 seconds.

<h3 style="text-align:center">WEDNESDAY, MAY 2ND</h3>

It seems to me there can be few stages of production more trying than shooting on a set like this—of these dimensions, with all this crowd, all this intensity of light. Besides the normal incandescents, the set is flooded (at least while Gordon is building up his lighting, and while shooting is in progress) with the fierce white glare of a battery of arcs. Raise your head to glance or to talk, and you get these in your eyes; be careful—you do not have to look long for your eyes, your head, to develop a sustained, oppressive ache. Then, besides the weariness of light, there is the accumulation of fatigue, from the so many uninvolved, unconcerned, the space-fillers who sit around in heaps, gossiping, reading, flirting, or trying to doze. Somewhere, it is true, a nucleus of activity persists—close shots, say, on Maria, Nora and Anselmo watching the arrival of Galbern—but it is a self-absorbed activity, hard to distinguish through the banks of indifference which surround it.

The long shots are perhaps more fun; at least the crowd can exercise themselves as they stroll chatting across the background, or react more positively in the roles of Galbern's supporters, opponents or bodyguard. Here the burden of strain is shifted decisively on to the director and his assistants. Fingers softly on lips (a characteristic pose) Thorold anxiously measures the timing of the action; crouched over his microphone, Spike bays at the obdurate mass before him: '*Action . . . Now . . . Gendarmes!!!*'

Slowly, however, we penetrate into the sequence, travelling up as we do so from the British Pavilion at one end of the stage to the Café terrace at the other. Progress is quickened in the morning by the importation of an extra camera: while Chick is trained on Anselmo and the girls, Jeff Seaholme shoots the other way, on Galbern at the door of the British Pavilion. By the end of the day Maria has met Louis; for the rest of the sequence we can concentrate on the more intimate, conversational scenes, with fewer crowd.

Shots taken: B.35, 37, 43, 46, 45, 25, 27, 28, 30, 34, 32, 34a. *Screen time*: 1 minute 4 seconds.

THURSDAY, MAY 3RD

Though there are often shots to admire on rushes—an effective set-up, atmospheric lighting, subtle playing—one soon learns to regard them as fragments. It is rare to find one possessing completeness in itself, as does the first in to-day's batch. Rare and exciting. The camera starts on Maria, Anselmo and Nora as they climb down from the chairs on which they have been standing to watch Galbern. In the agitated crowd, Maria is separated from the others by a hard-pressed gendarme; struggling, she finds herself carried along by the mob; she feels a hand reach out to grab her arm; she calls out indignantly, looks up—and the expression on her face changes to one of recognition. So much may be specified in print; what is fascinating to consider, though, are the elements of skill, inspiration and chance which have to conspire for its successful realisation. Three takes have been printed. In the second, the centre of the screen is usurped halfway through the shot by an eye-taking crowd artiste—a splendidly-built Spanish girl, whose appearance here, massive and apparently enjoying the fun, provokes laughter rather than excitement. The third take is marred by no such distraction; the camera follows Valentina faithfully, the crowd jostles, the arm reaches into the frame with the right, surprising timing. It is only in comparison with the first take that one sees the indefinable inadequacy: here the movement *flows*, and emotion builds with it. By a happy accident Valentina stumbles; yet without being lost to sight, or breaking the thread. Swiftly the shot builds to its climax, achieves it, as potent and as self-contained as a line of poetry. (Yet, until you see it on the screen you can never be sure of your effect. Against this take, for instance, Phyll wrote doubtfully: 'Crowd stopped "acting" when Maria got into final position.' On the screen this is not apparent.) Travail extraordinaire de Chic.

This, I suppose, is Film Appreciation—the only final justification for all this analysis, all these lectures, all these books. . . To know how a film is made is not really important, except in so far as it helps us to see and respond to felicities of expression such as this, to make contact with the artist. Without such contact, after all, our fealty to the cinema is a humiliation rather than a source of pride.

Scenes shot: B.22a, 29a, 31, 32a, 38, 39, 40, 40a, 44, 47. *Screen time*: 1 minute 51 seconds.

FRIDAY, MAY 4TH

As if reluctant to let us go, this set proves awkward to the last. The final set-up is on the full complement of actors—Valentina and Serge, Charles, Audrey and Michael (B.48). 'One of those tiresome scenes,' Thorold calls it, 'in which you're trying to get information across to the audience without it being obvious what you're up to. The difficulty is to keep it moving.' Rehearsal starts off lightheartedly, with suggestive eye-play between Serge and Charles ('May I borrow Maria for the afternoon? . . .'), and giggles from Valentina. But—not necessarily as a result—it does not run smoothly: Anselmo's business with a menu card takes too long, keeps Maria and Louis waiting uselessly when they should be eager to go. Valentina suggests the transposition of a line; Charles, who likes his business, resists. More rehearsals. 'This is the sort of stuff for which you've *got* to have actors who are skilled technicians,' murmurs Thorold, as the timing is gradually established. Other members of the unit, though, may be observed to be less tolerant of what seems to them merely a pointless delay. (Odd how these other technicians, who will wait without complaint on the caprices of mechanical apparatus, are yet apt to grudge the actor his occasional minutes of adjustment, to expect performances of quality on penny-in-the-slot terms.)

It is late morning by the time the sequence is completed. As the unit breaks to Stage 2 and the next set (Scotland Yard), we discover that at the other end of the stage, in the British Pavilion Buttery, the second unit is already setting up for its first plunge into the Exhibition montage—Anselmo, Maria and Nora emerging arm-in-arm from the crowd to take a table and enjoy a bottle of champagne. Cut to a close shot of Anselmo and the bottle; the liquid spurts from its mouth; track in to provide an easy link to our stock shots of jetting fountains. Typically, it is the close-shot which gives trouble. Though complaining bitterly that his full quota of electricians has been raided by the first unit, Lionel finally lights the set, and Terry guides his artistes through the action. It is the champagne bottle which refuses to co-operate. The camera has moved in, Valentina and Audrey have departed, Charles sits expectantly eyeing the bottle. With a flourish the waiter extracts the cork: a faint steam arises from the mysterious liquid within. . . Cut and try again. This time the steam is followed by a slow afterbirth of white foam. Laughs from the unit; hard words from the director; in the background the prop men, increasingly desperate, experiment with various exotic combinations of fizz . . . ginger ale . . soda water . . . Coca-Cola. . . . 'Give it a good shake,' they hiss. The waiter obliges; so does Charles. Still the brew refuses to explode. 'I wrote a memo about this five days ago,' Terry fulminates. 'It's the oldest gag in the world; and this is just a bloody waste of time and money.' Frustrated still, after a dozen more attempts, we move on to another fragment—a corner of the set revamped with chairs and tables, Anselmo plunging into a dish of steaming pilaf. In this Nora appears at his side, but the chair opposite must be excluded by the camera angle, for Valentina is on Stage 2, being interviewed by Scotland Yard.

Scenes shot: B.43a, 48, 48a, E.23, 24, 25, 26 (Second Unit B.12, 13, 14.) Screen time: 2 minutes 32 seconds. Total screen time to date: 82 minutes 57 seconds.

Eighth Week

One day ahead in the Studio (last Monday's retake cost us a quarter-day); 1½ on locations. In spite of the initial delay on the Exhibition, we finished and moved to Scotland Yard on schedule. The plan is now for 1½ further days on Scotland Yard; 2½ days on the Hospital; and Friday to be divided between Daly's Landing, Shop and Window.

This week marks the beginning of the end by bringing to an end the contributions of three of our artistes: Megs Jenkins, Charles Goldner and John Ruddock will complete their scenes by Friday evening. The sound and editing departments will start on post-synching.

'To: All Concerned. From: Ralph Hogg. Will you please note that scenes A.25—A.33 are deleted from the script, and that the following sets will NOT therefore be necessary.' And there follow Terry's hard-fought-for sets for the montage, free-wheeling railway carriage and all. Thorold's viewing of the film last Monday, and another look at it on Saturday, has in fact convinced him that the sequence is an unnecessary one, confusing rather than clarifying, adding footage which we can ill-afford, and contributing little to atmosphere. Another result of this viewing is a decision to remake C.40. 'It comes out so drab and joyless. There's far too much talk of principles . . . When you see it in its context in the story, you realise that what is needed here is something emotional: we've got to feel that Maria *loves* Louis, and that's why he's sure he can use her.' This is going to involve rewriting, so Christianna Brand is contacted and set to work on a love scene.

In preparation for this week's shooting of the Hospital sequences, Thorold and Sid have talked, over the week-end, with a specialist in plastic surgery. Their main queries were: how plausible was such a change? What might be done in addition to the make-up already devised for Lena Collins? Was it likely that a surgeon's sketch should be produced in F.19/20? The answers proved encouraging as well as helpful. The procedure is apparently quite plausible, though nothing too drastic should be attempted—the sort of thing liable to leave scars. Shown stills of Valentina as Lena, the expert commented, 'I think that's extremely good.' He discouraged any use of a surgeon's sketch, so that is now removed from the scene. 'You can do a lot of things to change appearance,' he summed up. 'Most of them are fairly simple. What you cannot change are the eyes.'

The Scotland Yard sequence, started on Friday and continuing to-day, has brought Irene Worth back into the picture, after an absence of six months. She approaches Miss Jackson with the same wary caution she extends towards the cinema in general. 'I can't think why I'm playing the part, except that Thorold was so persuasive. What are policewomen like anyway? I saw a couple in Piccadilly last week, and tried to study the way they conducted themselves . But I don't somehow think that's what's needed.'

Scenes shot: E.27, 27a, 28, 29, 29a, 29b, 30, 31, 32, 33, 36. Screen time: 2 minutes 8 seconds.

We embark on the Hospital scenes without, it seems, a great deal of enthusiasm on anybody's part. William has provided a small set, about twenty feet square, utilitarian in design, hospital bedstead, off-white walls. Until yesterday evening, that is, when Gordon gave orders for them to be re-enamelled pure white. This is unconventional, but will be useful for lighting—'Particularly as we'll be working with the ceiling on most of the time, to get these Maria's-eye view shots; so we can't get much light in from the top. With white surfaces we can light the walls and use them as reflectors.' Each time the picture moves on to a new setting, the cameraman must adjust himself to new conditions of working, a crop of new problems to be solved. 'These small sets are infinitely more tiring to work on than the large ones. Once you've lit a huge floor-area— like the Exhibition, for instance—you can move from set-up to set-up with comparatively little shift in lighting. But on a small set, you have to relight every shot.' Accordingly, progress here is appreciably slower.

Thorold is also impatient. 'These little sets are so boring. There's nothing really interesting one can do with them—just get through the action as quickly as possible.' For Valentina, who spends most of the day in bed, it is at least restful, apart from the discomfort of having her left arm tightly trussed in a sling. A result, though, of her long period of inaction, and her Stanislavskian researches into coma, is that when she comes to speak, it is in the scarcely audible whisper of one who has been under morphia for a couple of months. Fireworks (if one can use the word to describe remonstrances so dignified) from Brad produce an increase in volume imperceptible to the ear. A microphone is inserted, held as close to Valentina's lips as the camera will permit. Brad's expression as the scene is played makes it clear that this is still not close enough for him.

Scenes shot: E.22, 34, 35, 37, 38, 39, 42, F.2, 3, 4. Screen time: 1 minute 39 seconds.

WEDNESDAY, MAY 9TH

'Joyce Cary? You mean the actress in Brief Encounter?' Skilled and congenial though the unit is, one cannot pretend it is culturally prodigious; the general reaction to my announcement that we have to-day on the set Britain's most distinguished living novelist is one of incredulity. ('Ever heard of J. B. Priestley?'). There he sits all the same, turning through the book of stills with an odd alternation of abstraction and interest, looking up every now and again to where Valentina lies in her hospital bed, critically noting the dialogue (not his) between Miss Jackson and Maria. 'Now that line, for instance, is too long. There's no need for her to say, "I've told you already, *but you keep forgetting*." It sounds as though she's annoyed with her.' What does a writer feel when confronted with a 'developed,' 'elaborated,' or otherwise altered version of his original? The answer is frank enough: 'If you take a bottle of Burgundy and put 5 per cent sulphuric acid into it, you can't expect it to be Burgundy any more.' All the same, he is pleased with the personification (as evidenced by the stills) of the characters—though his acquaintance with their revised relationships proves rather vague. 'Yes,' Joyce remarks benignly to Valentina, 'Yes, you're quite well cast. She' (pointing to a still of Audrey) 'might very well be your daughter.'

Talking generalities, you find that the novelist's attitude to the cinema is very much what one would expect 'Yes, I'm interested in films: I find them very stimulating. I have a very visual imagination—I like to think in pictures. I have lots of ideas for films. But there just isn't time. In the art I practise now I have complete control; they'll publish anything I write—even the stuff they detest, like my poem. But in the cinema, there's all that fighting all the time. Producers . . . Directors . . . Cameramen. Not to mention the actors. I just haven't got time for it. There've been quite a lot of offers for a book of mine called "The Horse's Mouth," which I suppose might be made. But I don't care what they do with it. I've given the rights to my children, and I'd like the money for them. The people who like my books won't go and see them on the screen, anyway, so what does it matter?' The conviction is strengthened that if the industry is to have the services of good writers, it will have to produce them itself.

Scheduled for further work on the Exhibition montage on Friday, Terry makes spasmodic contact with Thorold between set-ups. Since our newsreel material is generally extremely staccato, with few shots of over 2 metres in length, our glimpses of Anselmo and the girls must be equally short and sharp. Thorold outlines his rough idea of the shape of the sequence, with the new suggestion that we take some hand-held material of our artistes at the Battersea Park funfair: 'The chief principle must be the good old one of "faster-faster-faster".' On Friday, however, Terry will confine himself to Anselmo eating, plus another go at the explosive champagne bottle.

Scenes shot: *F.8, 9, 10, 11, 13, 14, 15, 16. Screen time: 2 minutes 59 seconds.*

THURSDAY, MAY 10TH

A question of some importance has just arisen. On the set this morning Thorold announces that Sir Michael feels uneasy about the end of the film as it is now written and outlines a possible change: 'I think I've got it. The idea came when we discovered that the theatre where we'd been thinking of shooting the Dublin Theatre exterior had its show twice nightly: why shouldn't Nora be appearing on just such a bill? She has this assignation with Louis between performances . . . Instead of ending after Maria's death, we have Miss Jackson taking hold of Nora, telling her that above all she must carry on with her work . . . Dissolve back to the theatre, where we end on Nora again dancing in the Ballet.' But what is to be the emphasis of this new ending; how is it to be shot? 'I'll tell you the exact shots: first Nora in the wings—rubbing her shoes in the sand tray, as we saw her do at the audition, then straight out on to the stage. Cut to the back of the circle, where Miss Jackson and the Irish police inspector are watching: in a mirror behind them we see the reflection of the dancers (we can use some of the stuff we already have for B.P.). Cut to the long track back from the stage which we shot at the Bedford; and we can bring the end-titles up, perhaps, over a close-up of Nora dancing. I think it's a fade-out that ought to satisfy all round: it's relevant to the whole idea of the film; it does away with the rather awful *negation* of the last scene as it's scripted at the moment, and I think it ought to pack a pretty considerable emotional punch.'

Reactions to the news are diverse. William starts quietly to hum 'On with the Motley'; Ralph looks deep for a moment, then hazards 'About £250, I should say,' (apart from this he likes the idea). Spike thinks, 'It's a bit corny, isn't it?' and Jimmy notes impassively that he has never worked on a picture that hasn't had its end changed during shooting. Sid's analysis of the justifications for the change drags us down to fundamentals: 'It's this eternal problem of freedom in an art where expenses are astronomical. You just can't allow yourself absolute liberty, regardless of effect on audiences and box-office. And anyway—need we regard this as a concession? Thorold feels—and I agree with him—that there's almost a moral obligation nowadays not to make films that end in utter defeat, that send their audiences home feeling suicidal. Nora's dancing is a legitimate, positive symbol—she is the justification of Maria's sacrifice of her life . . . Without it the end might be just unbearably frustrating.'

Scenes shot: *F.1 Part 11, F.1 Part 13, F.16b, 17, 18, 19, 20, 20a, 21, 23, 24, 25. Screen time: 2 minutes 44 seconds.*

Two units at work to-day cover four scenes. In the morning Terry goes out to Morton Street for another attempt—this time successful—at F.27; in the Studio, Thorold polishes off the British Pavilion interior (B.23). Scripted as one set-up and previously envisaged as running into two or perhaps three, this is eventually shot from a multiplicity of angles. 'When I saw the Exhibition stuff we'd shot,' Thorold explains to Peter, 'I realised that we'd need to keep the same rhythm here, make it infinitely cutty . . So keep it moving round all the time when you put it together.' In the afternoon the main unit switches to the interior of Daly's shop, while Terry moves back to the remnants of the Exhibition on 3a, for a further try at a champagne bottle, and montage glimpses of Anselmo eating.

In the Production Office the principal task is the scheduling and organising of next week's night locations—one night shared between the exterior of Louis' Lodgings and the exterior of the Dublin Theatre, followed by three in Richmond (alias Phœnix) Park. With the theatre we have hit a snag; the Scala proves after all to be still encumbered with scaffolding, and the London variety house which seemed next suitable has made unreasonable demands. Ralph: 'Here's something *useful* you can put in your book—just because people are making a film, it should not be assumed that they have money to throw down every drain they come to.' For permission to shoot on the outside of the theatre he had, in fact, offered a nominal payment of ten guineas, to which the management (who must have been seeing too many movies) replied, 'Ten guineas be damned; it'll cost you fifty.' Result: Christopher Barry continues to scour for a suitable theatre; Richmond Park must be put forward, and the theatre postponed till Friday.

Our one remaining location—Gunnersbury Park for the exterior of the Garden Party—trembles in the balance. At present we are scheduled for one night out and two days in the Studio. The problem is financial; everyone agrees on the visual advantages of location shooting, but Sid is worried at the expense; also the cost of the Studio reconstruction seems unnecessarily high. After rushes, Sid, Thorold and Gordon confer with William over the proposed plan; Gordon explains that Thorold wants to shoot his exteriors on a 35 mm. lens, and his interiors on a wide-angle (to contract the first, and expand the second). William claims that the use of a 25 mm. lens on Stage 2 will involve a new backing to circle the set. Sid groans: 'There's always this thing about backings, and they always have to be new—and they're fiendishly expensive.' But Gordon is adamant. The final decision on the location is postponed till Tuesday, after a further reconnaissance by Gordon and the Construction Department over the week-end.

Scenes shot: B.23, 23a, 23b, 23c, 23d, 23e, 23f, E.48, 48a, 50. (Second Unit B.15, 16, 17, cuts F.25, 26, 27, retake B.13, E.75). Screen time: 2 minutes 10 seconds.

Total screen time to date: 94 minutes 37 seconds.

Ninth Week

As before: 1½ days ahead on locations, 1 day in the Studio. Scotland Yard overran by ¼ day, but the Hospital scenes went through quicker than expected with the result that we were off them on Thursday evening just the same. Friday's shooting, though not exactly as planned, consumed the equivalent in schedule time.

We proceed to night locations—which the decision to bring the Garden Party completely into the Studio reduces to four nights: Tuesday to Thursday at Richmond (Phœnix Park), Friday halved between Louis' Lodgings (Harrow Road) and the Dublin Theatre stage door—location to be confirmed this week. Also to be finally decided are the Clowns for the Garden Party—one of the most obstinate casting problems we have struck.

TUESDAY, MAY 15TH

Reassembly after Whitsun finds the unit ready for its week (we hope no more) on night locations—a generally unpopular period of production, upsetting to nerves, stomachs and family routines. 'As a man of habit,' says Ralph, 'I hate it.' He has instituted a new routine for his office while this disruption takes place: Spike will work with the unit—7 p.m. to 6 a.m.; John joins shooting after the midnight meal break and works till 11 a.m.; Ralph comes in at 3 in the afternoon, and stands by till 2 in the morning. So the production office remains open for all but the least urgent hours of the twenty-four.

First assignment this evening is the promised conference on the Garden Party. Location or no? A round-table conference assembles to hear Sid's summary of the situation, and his advised decision: 'We've decided,' he starts bluntly, 'to bring it all indoors.' Saturday's reconnaissance by Gordon, Jack Ford and George Speller (Construction) has shown that the financial burden of shooting even part of the sequence at Gunnersbury Park would be too severe for the budget. 'To light the area we'd have to position arcs on the rooftops—which would entail expensive construction work, as they're none too safe. Then the lake is empty. We can have it filled at a cost of 3/- a 1,000 gallons, but as it takes 600,000, it seems scarcely economic. While if we restrict shooting entirely to the Studio, we can help the budget a bit, and feel more justified in a handsome expenditure on the Clowns.'

The arguments appear to be final, and there is no disputing the decision. When discussion starts, however, between Gordon and William on ways and means of simulating Gunnersbury on Stage 2, Thorold breaks in. 'I was just wondering,' he starts, 'whether it wouldn't be better to reconceive the whole thing as not on such an enormous area. Not try to get gigantic distances into it.' William is alarmed: 'But the set is almost built—the plaster work is almost done, and the stage for Nora's dance can't be altered.' Thorold: 'If we think of ourselves in a rich man's house in London . . .' Sid: 'What practical differences are you thinking of?' 'Well, we can have the house at one end of the stage; the floor represents the garden—walled in—perhaps with houses one side—and beyond it a park.'

This new idea catches on rather fast. Gordon is immediately in favour: 'It'll look much more real than the way we're going to try and fake Gunners-

109

bury Park.' Sid asks William if he can do a sketch by to-morrow. William begins to nod: 'Yes, let me think about it . . . I think it's a very good idea. Now Maria can start the sequence coming out of the house.' Thorold: 'I think it's the only honest thing to do. It's useless trying to cheat these grand effects with limited means.' Sid goes on to further points concerning production. The Clowns: it looks as though we will be able to get the Cairolis after all. As they are working all week, it will mean shooting them on a Sunday—with a consequent regrettable bump-up in wages for crowd and technicians. From a Union point of view, though, Sid has found that there is no objection to Sunday shooting. A possible exterior for the Dublin Theatre has been found at Richmond: this can be investigated to-night. The meeting winds up with a discussion on methods of getting the second shot Thorold has envisaged for his new final sequence. Back-project the Ballet in reverse, put a mirror frame round the screen, and stand Miss Jackson in front of it? In which case, how about *her* reflection? Better perhaps to project the Ballet straight on to the B.P. screen; reflect this in a mirror, in front of which will stand Miss Jackson. The second unit can try a test on this next week.

By the time we break, the unit has arrived in force, and is busy embussing, climbing into cars, trailers and lorries, making for Richmond Park. Ralph and Spike start last, but set a speed worthy of the Production Department and arrive first on the location; Spike is dropped off at the park gates, Ralph proceeds to the road-girt copse which is our rendezvous. First arrivals of that astonishing caravanserai which constitutes a film unit on location are the buses—coaches, rather—in which the majority of the unit continue to sit, casting a cold eye on the landscape now beginning to grey into twilight. Gradually these are joined by other varieties of transport: sound van; two camera cars; canteen and jeep; Construction and Props van (with the dolly and tracks); the Paxman; a large hired furniture van (carrying electrical equipment); in addition to such 'props' as Steenie's car, Irish taxi, a Police car, two smaller cars (traffic), and a station wagon. Finally marshalled into order, these stretch down the road beside our location like a circus on the move. A few of the more active members of the unit venture out into the open air. We await the director.

Thorold does not keep us long. Emerging in duffle coat from his car, he calls his staff around him like any brisk and confident military commander. And the martial parallel persists; for as he leads his little company forward to reconnoitre, one is struck at once with memories of exercises carried out in the Army; of those chaotic night patrols (I do not speak of the real thing) in which, weirdly garmented, one stumbled through woods in half-light, interested in anything but the expedition's designed end. But to-night our purposes are less boring: the site has been surveyed, but a location has yet to be pinpointed. We want a tree-trunk, or something of the sort ('William said it was too expensive to make one') for Louis' assignation with Nora, a path leading to it, and a road in the distance, for the car whose headlights must sweep the horizon in F.67. A tree-trunk is found, but its approaches—over several ditches and a long way from the road—prove unsatisfactory. Thorold is off again, and we after him. He finds a clearing, peers this way and that: 'How about this, Gordon?' 'Looks all right to me.' But there, a little further on, lies a sizeable decayed branch, stout enough to sit on. Even better—there is a clear way from the road, and a good view through to the other road beyond, whence the headlamps must flash. 'Props!' And Props appear, to start repairing, with hammer and nails, this opportunely fallen branch.

With Chic and Jeff Seaholme (we have two cameras with us), Thorold carries on with his selection of set-ups, while Gordon and Tom site the lamps round about, and, farther afield, the arcs which will give depth to the background. We are starting on Maria's arrival, her sight of Louis and Nora together, and her approach to them. One camera holds the long shot; the other, trained on Louis and Nora, picks up Maria as she stops in front of them. Nine o'clock brings break ('without cessation of production') for tea and cheese rolls; the artistes arrive. and wisely remain snug in their limousines; the twilight deepens. At ten fifteen the lamps light up, and the darkness is paradoxically intensified; we realise that it is night. Adjustment of lights. It is a quarter past eleven before Serge and Audrey are positioned on their log, and Valentina (in her 'Lena' make-up) on her mark. We have time only to rehearse the action (Valentina's walk over the uneven ground gives her trouble and giggles, but she plunges bravely ahead), and take it on our two cameras, before we must break for food.

To cater at midnight for 93 people (the estimate on the call-sheet is too few by 13) cannot be too simple a matter for a restaurant that usually closes at eleven; but the Globe restaurant in Richmond seems to take it in its stride. ('We didn't know quite what to expect when the gentleman said a film company. We had all the best silver ready, but then Mr. Hogg said just to slap it on and clear everyone out as quick as we could . . .') All the same, the operation takes a full hour and a half—'We'll have to speed that up to-morrow,' says Ralph—and by the time Thorold is back on the location, after inspecting and approving the Richmond theatre on the way, rain is falling.

Thorold, Gordon and Spike confer. Thorold is worried about his artistes: 'What's the use of giving them all chills. just for the sake of a couple of shots we may not be able to use anyway? That sort of thing is false economy.' He is in favour of returning. But Gordon thinks we should stay. 'It's not too heavy, and it may very well clear off. After all we're being paid for it.' So we hang on and hope the rain will stop.

But it does not, and our two authorities—Gordon in the camera car, Thorold with the actors—continue to differ. Periodically, Spike pads across from one camp to the other, carrying contradictory messages. Word comes from Valentina: may she remove her wig? On no account, goes the answer, and Spike orders a blockade on her car: 'Once let Make-up or Hairdressing near her, and she'll have that wig off.' So, for the rest of the night, the 'set' stands empty, spotlights mysteriously illuminating turf and tree-trunks, the steady rainfall flashing in their beams. And around, in the darkness, cigarettes glow intermittently and voices murmur as the unit shelters in silence. in reminiscence or discussion. ('Do you know,' Thorold is remarking improbably to Serge and Geoff Hibbert at half past three, 'that nine-tenths of the tobacco we smoke is grown in Nyasaland?' Serge smiles politely. He does not know where Nyasaland is).

By four, light is coming, and it is obvious that nothing further will be shot. The word is given to pack up for the night, and transport is moving off for Studio and home, when the rain at last peters to a stop.

Scenes shot: F.61, 62a. Screen time: 21 seconds.

The chief drawback to these hours of working is the difficulty of adjustment. Night work rarely goes on long enough for one to get used to it; and how many of us have lives (let alone bodies) that can be organised for a sudden plunge into sleeping through the daytime? Fortunately there is always a certain stimulus in the job in hand: to-night is fine; there seems no threat of rain, and although—to hear them talk—you would think that nobody in the unit has had any sleep at all, we look forward to a full night. A happy innovation: the Props have brought a coke brazier to cheer inactive bodies through the dark hours.

While cables are run out and the lights set up, Thorold gets together with Spike and Phyll in the shooting brake to run through the schedule and plan direction of shots. 'We've got a problem to-night. Gordon wants to do everything in one direction right through. Now to help get the run of the scene I'd like to have at least a close-up on Maria from the reverse angle.' But, appealed to, Gordon stands firm: 'When you start shooting in the other direction, the Brutes all have to go round on the opposite side.' 'Even for close-ups?' 'Yes.' So it is decided to shoot the sequence that way, and Valentina's close-up (F.66) will have to come out of continuity. 'Everything after 71 we'll shoot on the reverse angle.'

Over to the tree-trunk, where, with artistes in position, we re-establish last night's set-up. 'Now Serge, can you remember where exactly you stood up in F.63?' 'Yes . . . It was between Valentina's two lines.' For F.65, with Serge already standing. Thorold wants to start on Louis, and pull back into a three-shot; so we must wait while tracks are laid. This gives Thorold an opportunity to discuss with Serge a point of characterisation. 'I'm afraid Louis may be coming out of this too reasonable—too sympathetic . . . I don't want the audience to go home and say "Louis is right and Maria is a fool".' Serge: 'Yes, I know; but I think perhaps you are attaching too much importance to this question of sympathy. It is *evident* that Louis is wrong.' 'In this scene Louis must be icy cold.' But of this Serge is doubtful: 'I think not cold, but . . .' and he breaks off to describe what he means in the best way an actor can, in gesture and expression. 'C'est tout a fait comme *ça*' (gravity and surprise, hands cutting a straight wedge out of the air) 'and after that—il faut garder le travail avec Nora. And after that, he lets things go.' 'Yes—and for that I'm going to give Nora an extra line. I want Louis to call to Nora, and she replies, "I'm not with you, Louis." And *that's* where you let things go . . . Remember the real dirt of Louis is the way he uses his physical attractiveness for Nora.' By which time the tracks are set up, and we can rehearse. At 10.20 we start shooting.

NOTE.—Good news on the Clowns: the Cairolis are booked, and will be down for shooting on Sunday, May 27th.

Scenes shot: F.62, 63, 65, 67, 68, 69, 70a, 75x. *Screen time*: 1 *minute 2 seconds.*

In one respect the male artistes on this picture have a distinct advantage over the female: they need report at the Studio only very shortly before they will be needed for shooting. But the ladies have still the rituals of hairdressing and make-up to undergo—in these Thorold has asked for a style which reduces both to a minimum, but even that cannot be rushed. To-night, for instance, Serge and Valentina are both wanted on the location by a quarter to ten. Serge can be picked up from his flat at nine-fifteen; but Valentina has to report at the Studio at half-past seven, for transformation into Lena Collins.

Ernie and Barbara are standing by, bottles, brushes, paints, gum at the ready. First, in Barbara's room, Valentina has her hair bound down for the easy accommodation of the blonde wig that comes later; then across to Ernie for make-up. Or rather disguise, for in this case it is nothing less. It takes about fifty minutes and it goes in this order: Clean off. Apply foundation. Fill in new shadows and highlights to give the face its new shape. Apply eye-shadow, nose-shadow, jaw-shading. Powder. Brush and wash off with damp cotton wool (and if you imagine this will bring off the make-up, it does not). Next the eyes, the most vital clue to identification: they are reshaped; the eyebrows are redrawn; false eyelashes are attached; and finally a new line is given to the mouth. As he works, Ernie explains his principles of work, pausing intermittently as he comes to the tricky bits; Valentina conserves her strength for the night. 'This particular make-up has been a wonderful opportunity to prove you can do a complete change of appearance with make-up alone. So many directors think in terms of false noses, built-up features and all the rest of it. And these things really aren't necessary. You can do so much simply by shading; you can create a whole new set of contours for the face— but of course without any of those hard black lines . . .' Ernie talks of the possibilities, the magic of his craft with the intensity of the true enthusiast; and all the time, as he works the soft grey shading into the features, blending it so softly with the foundation that even to the naked eye there is no sense there of application, the new face gradually emerges from under his hands. Standing back, he surveys the result. 'Yes, I think that's quite satisfactory.' 'Darling, it's *beautiful*,' Valentina corrects him. Back now to Barbara for the wig.

What is Ernie's opinion on use of make-up in the film generally, and particularly on Thorold's decision to play as many of the characters as possible (including Maria and Nora) without any at all? 'Well . . . it isn't true, you know, to say that either Valentina or Audrey are appearing without make-up. The only essential difference in this picture is that we're not using a yellow foundation. In fact, as Maria, Valentina is playing without any foundation at all—but she still has at least fifteen minutes with me every morning before she goes on the set. You just can't put someone in front of a film camera without preparation, and expect an unblemished result. And of course to a certain extent this policy on Maria has been dictated by the necessity to create a complete contrast with Lena—where we have to use a heavy foundation to support the changes, shading, etc. And because Valentina is being lit without foundation, we've had to keep to the same principle for the artistes playing with her.' 'But isn't it true that this course has been followed primarily to preserve natural face-textures—not just to make the contrast between Maria and Lena easier to achieve?' Ernie is a bit reluctant to concede all this. 'It's true, yes, that the film calls for a very natural sort of treatment. But you mustn't think of make-up as something that necessarily distorts, or takes away texture. I'm completely opposed to the Hollywood mask type of make-up —the thick layer of foundation, identical eyebrows, overblown mouth. I'm all for keeping make-up natural; but a good foundation, properly applied, will *give* you texture—and on top of that make-up used really properly will give you any effect you want.'

What about men? Here Ernie concedes the point to the neo-realists. 'Personally I prefer them without make-up—unless they're very pale (in which case they're liable to photograph like suet pudding), or very pink (which will come out in blotches). We've done almost nothing on the men in this picture. We've given Charles his moustache, of course, and greyed him a bit, but otherwise his face already has all the character the part needs. And the same with Serge: we've shaded his nose a little, to reduce its breadth, and lightened his hair at the sides to soften its rather harsh natural line—for the rest he plays as he is.'

Valentina returns, displays herself, and is blessed by Ernie and Barbara. Setting out for the location, she looks forward to the night without pleasure. 'It's so cold out there; and that makes it very difficult to play an emotional scene like this . . . Oh, I shall be glad to get back into the Studio!'

Some people enjoy nights, all the same. Take Eileen, the Canteen girl, who gives us tea at ten, and soup at three, as cheerful as a bird. Well, there's the money—three pound six a week isn't much, even with meals thrown in, and these four nights will net her nine pounds fourteen (minus tax: eight pounds sixteen) which is a real windfall. But it isn't just the money. She enjoys the company, and being near the shooting. 'You get to know people much better than in the Studio, and to like them—or dislike them. And at the end of the week you're really sorry to say goodbye.'

Scenes shot: F.52, 53, 64, 66, 67b, 70, 70b. Screen time: 1 minute 30 seconds.

FRIDAY, MAY 18TH

Advice to observers: do not miss a moment. Whatever is scheduled, the two hours you are away will always be the most vital, will always have covered the shots you are most anxious not to miss, and if they say they will send a car to Richmond Station to pick you up—it will not arrive.

So my first sight of the unit comes at half past twelve, as they file into the Globe for food. Thorold collapses rather heavily into his chair. 'I feel like a squeezed orange . . . For God's sake open the window somebody.' After disposing of the three cars (Steenie; Maria; the police) entering the park gates, he has, in fact, gone on to shoot the climax of the sequence in a gulp. Maria's death, Nora's rejection of Louis, his arrest, Miss Jackson leading Nora away—all these are now in the can. 'It's an extraordinary feeling—when you've had a thing inside you so long—getting it out at last. It makes everything seem quite unreal . . . We shot out of a bloody pit in the end.' A pause of exhaustion. 'It's all improvisation . . . I did my damnedest to make that last shot tell—tracking away on Audrey and Irene. If its sufficiently weighty, perhaps we needn't shoot the other Ballet shots for the end. Well, we'll see on Tuesday.'

This good progress has earned us no respite: if we are to be quit of this location to-night we must still cover a long series of approach shots—the cars arriving, Steenie and Nora entering the wood, Maria and the police in pursuit. After break, the lamps are moved and ranged along the road; we start at the beginning (F.56) and work through in sequence, to end with the Inspector's instructions to his men. Shooting up to the verge of daylight, we discover when we switch off the lamps that (it is the converse of the effect when they go on

114

in the evening) it is only they which have given us the illusion of continued darkness: it is already day.

Scenes shot: F.55, 56, 57, 58, 59, 60, 60a, 68a, 70c, 71, 72, 73, 74, 75, 76, 77, 78, 79. Screen time: 2 minutes 12 seconds.
Total screen time to date: 99 minutes 42 seconds.

Tenth Week

As a result of Wednesday's bad weather, we are now only half a day ahead on locations, though still with our day in hand in the Studio. Monday must now go to our last night location, leaving only three working days in the rest of the week. These will be: Wednesday—the Police Office in Dublin Castle; the Theatre Box (for close-ups on Maria during the performance), and an extra close-shot on Miss Jackson in Scotland Yard. On the same day, with both Valentina and Irene in the Studio, the second unit can get their taxi scene, F.28. Thursday: the retake (rewritten) of C.40; and in the afternoon, pre-lighting on the Garden Party set. Friday and Sunday: first two days of the Garden Party.

MONDAY, MAY 21ST

Suddenly you realise: it is a question of days now instead of weeks. The light at the end of Ralph's tunnel is rushing towards us. The diagonal line of coloured-in squares (like the joyful progression of scored-out days on a schoolboy's calendar) now covers over three-quarters of the schedule on the wall of his office; right and left artistes are dropping away; 'Interim Schedule No. 7,' issued to-day 'To All Concerned,' shows that of our eight remaining days, three go to the Garden Party, and the rest on Maria's Dublin scenes, the retake of Louis' Lodgings, and a number of fragments which have been left by the way. This variety is echoed in the sets: Stage 2 is given over completely to the Garden Party—the floor laid with turf, the stage (an elaborately chi-chi affair, with gilt, Janus-headed Caryatids and rambling roses) erected at one end, and a façade of the house going up at the other. William seems doubtfully satisfied with the effect. 'The whole thing was drawn in two days, you realise. If I'd known earlier we were going to do it like this, I'd have made the stage much smaller—this represents a compromise, for use on location and in the studio. It's really too large for this set . . .' Over on 3b, our remaining seven sets stand chock-a-block: the Police Office in Dublin Castle, the Theatre Box, a window in Scotland Yard, a wall of Louis' Lodgings, Daly's stairs and landing, Daly's window, and the Dress Circle bar and corridor in the Dublin Theatre. If all goes according to plan, these will bring us home on Wednesday week-- dead on time.

How, meanwhile, is the picture coming together? Apart from the night locations, Peter's assembly is pretty well up to date, which means that the first half of the film is by now quite closely edited, while the second half has too many gaps for one to be able to get from it anything like a cohesive impression. A major operation getting under way in the cutting-rooms at the moment is the selection of passages in which the dialogue is insufficiently clear, and preparation for post-synching. While, in fact, we have been on nights, some of this has already started in the Studio; for artistes' contracts are beginning to run out, and it is important to get such commitments finished. Last week it was the turn of Anselmo, Penny and Daly; coming to the theatre for rushes this afternoon, we find the doors open and the lights up, as Sid and Mac sit attentive to a flow of parrot-like repetitions from the screen. (Anselmo: 'I don't care .. I don't care .. I don't care'). After each comes a murmur from Sid, and a pencil check from Mac: 'No . . . No . . . That's not bad . . . The first half of that's all right . . . That one's good.' Soon it will be the turn of Valentina and Serge, though Audrey, whose contract expires sooner, and who is likely to be off to France immediately for another picture, must take her priority over them both.

Since we are working to-night, there is naturally no first unit activity in the Studio during the day. In the afternoon though, the second unit may be discovered over on the model stage, testing, with back projection screen and mirror, the Miss Jackson shot for the new end-sequence. Our last night, divided into two, takes us first to the Harrow Road, for exterior shots on Louis' Lodgings; then to Richmond for the meal break, and the Stage Door shots on the Dublin Theatre. The crowds that gather in the Harrow Road are boisterously friendly: Valentina and Serge play their parting on the doorstep to the accompaniment of approving catcalls, and as Valentina walks away down the path, she is greeted with a howl of welcome. This certainly does not worry them—if anything, they seem to enjoy it; but Brad looks despairing, and declares that *not a word* of his guide track will be comprehensible when it comes to post-synching. Richmond, on the other hand, is quiet enough, but Thorold finds himself in need of more angles than he had anticipated, and we are hard pressed for time. Having got through (but only just), we find ourselves again packing up in broad daylight.

Scenes shot: C.43, 45, F.49, 49a, 50, 51. Screen time: 2 minutes 31 seconds.

TUESDAY, MAY 22ND

Day of rest. But for last Friday night's important rushes Thorold, Gordon and Spike come into the Studio late afternoon; also on view is the test shot yesterday by the second unit—which satisfactorily proves that the effect can be obtained. Rushes over, there is a moment's silence. Then Thorold starts to discuss with William more precise details of the mirror shot—a rail for Miss Jackson to lean on, the design of the mirror. From this we presume the new ending is going to be needed. 'If only,' Thorold explains later, 'we'd had a greater length of track out at Richmond with us. We used all we'd got, and just had to let it go at that—and it isn't really enough. Of course we can't tell finally until we've seen the whole sequence cut together, but in the meantime we'll have to play safe and go ahead with the new end . . .'

WEDNESDAY, MAY 23RD

Most of the unit are late for rushes today as a result of a union meeting in the lunch hour to discuss an application for membership by a junior scriptwriter who has been working in the Studio for over three years. The application, which had support from above, is rejected; 'They were trying to swing something on us' seems to be the general feeling in the little knots of discussion which collect on the floor before shooting starts for the afternoon

116

It is very much a part of work in the cinema, this solidarity within the union, this question of the closed shop. The outsider is probably most familiar with the arguments for life, liberty and the pursuit of experience; the official union policy (that the ranks are full, that as long as the present situation of unemployment continues, no recruits can be admitted) appears short-sighted, and bound in the end to result in starvation of talent. It is perhaps an awareness that there is some justice in this view that makes technicians on the whole reluctant to discuss the problem freely and openly. 'But you must,' as Jimmy points out, 'try to look at it from the inside as well. You open the door to one bright, intelligent young man. And within a week you'll have five thousand of them battering to get in. And saying they'll work for less than the minimum wage—and glad to do it for the experience. As it is, there's only fifty per cent employment in the industry; what about the skilled, experienced men, trained for nothing else, who are out of work already?' And there is the other argument: the strong, emotional suspicion of nepotism, of patronage by the privileged which results too often in the employment of ingratiating incompetents in high-level positions. Spike: 'How do you think these people can come in as directors and producers, or as 'assistants to the director,' and make good pictures? Perhaps you can cover up here and there, but by and large, the efficiency of a unit is the efficiency of its director—as you've seen for yourself. Either a unit has confidence in a director or it hasn't; and if they once see he doesn't know what he's about, they're on to him like a knife.'

It is any implied devaluation of technical expertness that these experts, who have worked hard and made sacrifices to achieve their knowledge, most bitterly resent. Spike cites Ealing as an example: 'How else has the Studio succeeded except by training its talent, by building up a group of directors who know what film making really is?' (Most of the Ealing directors and producers worked their way on to the floor through the cutting rooms.) Point out then that this is exactly the channel of development that is now closed. Look around at the hacks who are in steady production still, and ask: does your closed shop keep those down to a minimum, or does it rather prevent a supply of better men to replace them? But the arguments are circular, and therefore endless; since the union apprenticeship scheme came to nothing the only possible entry for the inexperienced seems to be at the top—where they can do most damage Such contradictions are the penalty of insecurity. The fight on the floor, to get the film through on time and on budget, is echoed in the fight of the craftsmen to keep themselves in work, and their families fed.

After a morning in Dublin Castle, the afternoon mostly goes on the close-shots of Maria watching the ballet from a reconstruction of the box at the Bedford. To help work up a little atmosphere, we see the cut version of the ballet before we start shooting; but no playback of the music has been arranged on the floor, so Valentina and Irene are inspired instead by an observer, who whistles selections from the ballet as the cameras turn. Surprisingly, no objections are raised to this by the Musicians' Union.

Scenes shot: F.35, 36a, 39a, 41, 45, 45a, b, 47, 48. *Screen time*: 1 *minute* 2 *seconds*.

THURSDAY, MAY 24TH

To-day we should take the rewrite of C.40, but Valentina is away from the Studio on doctor's orders, and we are left with nothing to shoot except an extra insert which Thorold wants in A.43. However, with the Garden Party to-morrow, there is plenty for Thorold to busy himself with, and he spends the morning on Stage 2, running through the sequence with Chick and planning his set-ups. This is interrupted only by a forty-minute break to view the night location material (assembled in script order but as yet uncut) with Peter. From this it is still not yet possible to be sure whether or not we will need those four extra shots of Nora dancing at the end. 'We'll have to cut it together first, and then make up our minds.'

The last-minute alteration of schedule leaves Serge up in the air. It is decided that rather than waste his day, he had better take the plunge into post-synching—news which he receives without enthusiasm. It is interesting, in fact, to compare the different attitudes towards this necessary practice of Valentina and Serge. By Valentina the chance to post-synch lines which emotion or movement has rendered unclear has always been gratefully seized on. 'Oh, we can post-synch it . . .', not in an off-hand, but in a pleading, caressing tone, has been her constant counter to Brad's repeated appeals for retakes, or adjustment of delivery. 'In Italy we use this so much—to save time, to save money. And sometimes, you know, when there is not time after a picture and I have to go off to do another one quickly, they get another girl to put in my voice. And sometimes this girl has such a beautiful voice—I tell you it improves my performance.' This conviction is not shared by Serge, who indeed at one point of the shooting was driven to serious stages of depression by the suspicion (quite unfounded) that attempts might be made to dub another's voice over his performance. 'I can't post-synch,' he has frequently announced. 'I don't know why—it's terribly difficult for me. Perhaps we can just make wild tracks?' The attitude of the Sound Department towards this diffidence has been that of a kindly nurse: 'Yes . . . yes . . . of course. We'll see. It won't be so bad.'

And, in truth, it isn't; though neither is it a technique to be exercised without a good deal of strain and concentration. The system is as follows: passages of the film in which the words are, for one reason or another, indistinct, are reprinted in short sections. Each of these is joined to itself to form a separate, continuous loop. This is projected on to the screen in the dubbing theatre, in front of which is set a microphone, the artiste concerned, and, by the side, an assistant editor to check for complete synchronisation. Before each speech, the editor has marked three feet or so of the celluloid with a diagonal crayon line—which appears during projection as a line which swiftly traverses the screen, to disappear into the edge of the frame at the exact moment when the character begins to speak. The loop is projected; the artiste watches, refreshing his memory with the timing and intonation of the original. Cued by the crayon-line, he starts to speak, echoing the words issuing from the screen; the sound is switched off, and the artiste rehearses a few times by himself; when he is satisfied with rhythm and feeling, recording can begin.

To-day's session runs without incident or particular worry to anyone except Serge. The lines are mostly short: 'My orders are to save myself, and I obey orders. Come on!' 'The Committee only want to see you before you want to go to Scotland Yard.' 'Seven years . . . a lifetime.' One or two give difficulty, but on most we are content with one take, carrying six or seven versions of the line. Watching the actor at work, limbering up the machine which is himself by repeating the words over and over as he paces the floor, sketching in the action which had supported them, one senses the difficulties of the process: playing cold, weeks after the scene was enacted, without a partner, to a microphone suspended a few feet away, above your head. 'The voice loses its personality,' Serge sighs. 'You know the voice has a personality just as much as a face. If you concentrate on the synchronisation, you lose the feeling . . . You're sure that wasn't too false?' And, reassured: 'Yes, it is false . . . But perhaps not too false.'

By the end of the day Thorold has mapped out the Garden Party completely; Spike and he have agreed on a schedule; and Gordon has been able to pre-light the set as far as he can without the actors. Three set-plans, with camera angles red-inked in, give the assignments for the next three days.

FRIDAY, MAY 25TH

'What a delightful crowd you've got down today!' the Canteen Manager congratulates Spike. 'Real ladies and gentlemen . .' Indeed, you would hardly believe that they are drawn from the same reservoir as, say, our audience at the Bedford Theatre. It is the costume that does it, perhaps; the tails, the evening dresses and the fur capes. In clothes of such elegance—and they are all impersonating Dukes and Duchesses for the day—the crowd acquire unusual habits of courtesy and grace. The tea break is no longer the usual mad scramble: gentlemen bow and ladies take precedence. Subdued, high-toned conversation over the glasses of dry ginger ale keys the atmosphere on the set. The contrast with the last big set—the Paris Exhibition—could not be more complete: all green (grass) and grey (the backings of a night sky), the colour scheme is restful and subdued. The turf is a little damp underfoot but pleasantly soft to the tread. Mercifully, too, the crowd in this sequence is for the most part anchored to its seats; as a result, work proceeds with such calm and orderliness that a visitor from France can only gape at the spectacle. 'In Paris—a set like this—a crowd of this size—they would be raising the roof!'

We start at the beginning. At one extremity of the set is the façade of the house, a striped awning stretching out over a balustraded terrace, steps leading down on to the lawn sprinkled with tables, chairs and exotic lamp standards. At the other end stands the ornate circular stage on which Nora and the Clowns will perform. Up on the terrace, as if a part of the house, is positioned a single flat, carrying window and curtains from the Café living room. In front of this stands Maria, looking down into the street. Overlapping with the scene already shot, Valentina starts: 'You don't think of everything, Louis.' 'Tell me' (Spike reads in for Serge). 'We were not supposed to mix with the guests. I was watching from the terrace . . .' And as the playback fades in with the music for Nora's dance, Audrey starts to pirouette on the stage, the accompanist mimes, and Valentina moves away from the window, camera panning with her, tracking along the terrace as she walks slowly down the steps, till the whole set is held in long shot, the scene established.

From this start, we work through the sequence as chronologically as conditions allow. Two cameras give six set-ups on Nora's dance, with Maria watching in long shot, and the little waitress edging down the steps behind her for a closer look. The Cairolis are not available till Sunday, so the next section can be covered only in reverse angle from the stage—audience reaction to the clowns, Galbern's laughter, Bill's approach and planting of the bomb under cover of asking for a light. During these shots, of course, continuous laughter

119

is necessary, as if to the Cairolis' act: the illusion is effected by Spike, sitting on the stage in a little gilt chair, conducting the amusement of the crowd, raising it, hushing it, detonating it, with expressive sweepings of the arms.

The day finishes on a first shot of the explosion—two cameras still, one on a long, the other on a medium-long shot—as the little waitress hurries forward to Galbern's table and starts clearing away. Spike pre-addresses the crowd: 'Now when the bomb goes off, react just as you would normally if a bomb went off.'

Scenes shot: D.23, 25, 25a, b, c, d, 32, 32a, 38, 46, 48, 50, 50a. Screen time: 1 minute 29 seconds.

Total screen time to date: 104 minutes 44 seconds.

SUNDAY, MAY 27TH

The gates of the Studio are closed, but it is a full call on the Garden Party set, where the Cairoli Brothers have arrived to be our musical clowns. You might think they would be distracted a little by work under studio conditions, with its fragmentation of the act and its largely unresponsive audience; but not a bit of it. In their traditional costumes (Charlie in ill-fitting suit and bulbous crimson nose, Paul in white face, conical cap and brightly spangled satin) they manage even to beguile the jaded crowd: 'If you'd had a few drinks and were feeling cheery, I think they'd be a lovely turn,' one lady remarks. A clown, Charlie explains, must be ready to work under any conditions: 'One day it may be the Albert Hall, and the next just a little crowded room . . . I think perhaps circus people can adapt themselves very easily to the cinema—more than theatre people. They get used to having an audience in front of them; we have to work to people all round us. And always such different kinds of people. Everything you do, you have to do fresh—every time you do it . . .'

With our two cameras, we are trained on the clowns for three-quarters of the day. For the director, it is hard work, for there is no time to spare (Charlie and Paul must return to Blackpool to-night) and the act must be covered from as many different angles as possible without any pre-planning of set-ups. Half-way through the afternoon, we are joined on the set by Valentina (who has spent the day post-synching), and we proceed to the shots immediately following the explosion. We are set up for the fast track with Maria as she runs to help the waitress, when a first rehearsal reveals that Valentina cannot run in her long and voluminious dress: a twenty-minute wait must ensue while it is stitched up. This sets us back, so that when we come to Maria's close-shot there is time for only two takes. 'But Thorold!' Valentina protests, 'It's a very important shot . . . It'll only take two minutes.' 'It's no use, my dear, they won't let me.' For a third go at it we must wait, alas, till to-morrow morning at half past eight.

Scenes shot: D.27, 27a, b, 29, 29a extra cuts D.27/45, 31, 35, 36, 36a, b, 41, 42, 51. Screen time: 2 minutes 32 seconds.

News from Hollywood. The marriage is announced of the actress, Valentina Cortesa, to the actor, Richard Basehart—in London, over Easter week-end—unrevealed till now for personal reasons. Valentina, who has kept her secret well, receives the surprised congratulations of the unit.

Eleventh Week

Still a half day up on locations, lost time last week has brought us down to a mere quarter day up in the Studio. The Garden Party will be through by Monday evening, which leaves, as a solid sequence, only the Dublin Theatre bar, assigned for Wednesday. In between, and leaking over on to Friday, are an assorted collection of scraps—the Taxi shots we missed last week, the two set-ups for the new ending, Daly's landing (Floozie scene), Floozie's window, the postponed retake of Louis' Lodgings.

MONDAY, MAY 28TH

'You can say that the light at the end of the tunnel is now dazzling in its intensity,' says Ralph, not without satisfaction contemplating the schedule for the rest of the week. The Garden Party will be through to-day, which leaves, as a solid sequence, only the Dublin Theatre bar, assigned for Wednesday. In between, and leaking over on to Friday, are an assorted collection of scraps —Taxi and Police-car shots involving back projection, Daly's landing (Floozie scene), Floozie's window, the retake in Louis' Lodgings, new ending. Other signs of imminent break-up are becoming apparent. On 3a, the first set for *His Excellency* is almost ready for shooting (starting Friday), and members of our unit who will be going straight on to it have already been given copies of their new unit list. In the Cutting Rooms, Peter is getting the Phœnix Park sequence into shape as quickly as he can, so that any additional shots that may seem necessary can be done this week, before cast and unit have disintegrated completely. *Secret People* is going off the floor, in fact, not exactly with a whimper, but (to vary the metaphor) in a series of loose ends.

Last day on the Garden Party starts with two further takes on last night's interrupted close-up, and continues on the passages between Maria and Bill, and her reactions to Galbern leaving his table, and the waitress approaching it. Lastly, we turn back for a closer shot of the explosion—'It's vitally important we get this right,' says Thorold, 'if we're to avoid a sensational shot of the waitress wounded and bleeding to death. If we can, I very much want to finish the sequence without showing any more of her at all.' Galbern's table, split already in half, is propped up, wired for the charge, larded with black inflammable, tarry substance. Pamela Harrington, face blackened and dress dishevelled, eyes the preparations nervously, and wishes it were over (the Chorus of *King's Rhapsody*, though less exciting, is less risky). Thorold: 'Now we can only do this once, so let's make it a good one,' and on his 'Ready!' a light is applied to the table-cloth and flames begin to lick about the plates and glasses. ('Oh dear,' whispers Margaret Harper-Nelson at the back, 'I just hate to see them smashing these coffee percolators right and left. They're so expensive'). 'Begin!' The charge explodes in a rush of smoke, the table collapses, flaming, into camera, and Pamela collapses on to her rug. 'Well, that looked all right.'

There is just time left to move on to the model stage, where Valentina and Audrey (who have been post-synching all the afternoon) climb into their taxi, to be driven to the party by Bill.

Scenes shot: D.14, 24, 26, 26a, 28. 30, 33, 34, 37, 38a, 39, 43, 45, 47, 49, 49a. Screen time: 53 seconds.

Arriving on the set this morning to play the Floozie (let's hope the character is graced with a more dignified name on the credits), Grace Draper remarks on the strangeness of thus making a fleeting appearance in a film. 'You realise, I've not met anyone in the picture except the three other people in the scene; yet when you see a film on the screen, you always think of the cast as a unit, like in the theatre . . .' She is, she confesses herself, intimidated by her first screen appearance: chiefly by the unfamiliarity of the whole process, and—echoing the majority of theatre people—the lack of rehearsal. 'It's all over before you know you've started.' On this point Thorold has a comment. 'Very often you find that prolonged rehearsal before a shot takes all the spontaneity out of it. The more you play a scene, the more self-conscious it seems to become. In that respect films are altogether different from the stage.'

Rushes to-day cover the Cairolis' act in full, besides all that was shot yesterday, and last forty minutes. Most eagerly awaited is that final close shot on the explosion; with typical perversity, this appears on the screen only to snap off half-way through—exactly, in fact, at the moment of explosion. Retrieved from the Cutting Room (on a hurried inspection it was imagined that the dead white frame caused by the flame showed the end of a take), this is joined and projected. It looks good enough, but to be sure Thorold makes straight for the Movieola, and splices this set-up to the long-shot—overlapping them, so that the total length of explosion is artificially prolonged. 'The only way to make that sort of effect more striking,' he comments, reporting success, 'is to stretch it. *Vide* Eisenstein.'

After a viewing of the assembly, it has been decided that a few added shots will ease the cutting of the Phœnix Park sequence: close-ups on Louis and Maria at the moment of recognition, on Steenie as he knifes Maria, and an extra shot of Steenie's arrest by the police, as a cover for possible objections by the American censor. Geoff Hibbert cannot be contacted (*Note*: he was in fact at Lord's); so his shots, and Valentina's, are put off till to-morrow. Serge, however, is on call anyway, for the new version of C.40, which we shoot this afternoon. (The scene now comes out shorter by 25 seconds.) For the inserts, a corner of Stage 2, where the turf is still laid and the backing is suitable, has been provided with an artificial tree and a log. Seated here with Audrey, to Spike reading Valentina's lines, Serge replays the look and the movement to cut in to the sequence filmed a fortnight ago in Richmond Park at midnight.

A visitor to the set is carrying a new—yet another—book about how films are made, what they are, are they an art . . . ? Discovering that it is illustrated profusely with pictures of themselves, the unit crowd round to examine it, and delight themselves with quotation. 'It is essential that the Art Director and the Director of Photography work together in harmony.' This gets a special hoot of applause, though Gordon is determined to be fair. 'I suppose that's how films *should* be made,' he comments.

Scenes shot: E.43, 46, 46 (*American version*), 60, 73, 74a, 76 Retake C.40
Screen time: 41 seconds.

WEDNESDAY, MAY 30TH

It is all ceasing to be real. The sensation is perhaps too personal to be strictly in place in an objective account of material progress; and, in some respects, it is demonstrably false. The machine still functions exactly as it has for the last two and a half months: John still issues his call sheets each evening, the unit reassembles at 8.30, production meeting at 11, rushes . . . But departure is in the air; passages are being booked on ships and aeroplanes; Serge enters his dressing room to find his clothes neatly bundled away, the dressing table spread with Mr. Portman's bottles and brushes; Audrey post-synches her last line this afternoon and is off for France this evening—in three or four days she will be acting in another film. It is not like the last night of a play. That is, on the stage side of the curtain, a death, a sudden rending of relationships, and the sad disappearance into limbo of the creation which occasioned them. For though every work of art has a soul, not all are immortal; the soul of a theatrical production dies on the last night of the run. Here also relationships are snapping; but not too painfully, for they have been drawn less tight. The soul of a film is less perishable—it has the endurance of celluloid. What is occurring here is less a death than a transmigration. During the last ten weeks this film has been born, has emerged from the script, has lived and grown, changed and developed. Its body has been the unit, and their work together. Now the metempsychosis has come. Or perhaps it happened before this, and we did not notice that the film (its soul, you may reasonably say) was no longer with us; that it had passed off the floor, into those rolls of celluloid on the Cutting Room shelves, where it began gradually to assert its own nature, mysteriously achieving independence of its creators, a Frankenstein's monster, or a Galatea.

Something of the same feeling is evidenced by Thorold when Irene asks him how he finds the film now he's almost finished it. 'It's almost finished me,' he replies. 'At first, when you start, it's all plain sailing. Every sequence is fresh for you to do what you like with. Then, as you shoot more and more, you have to relate it more and more carefully to what's gone before and after. The whole thing gets tighter and tighter.' The implication is the same: after a time the film takes over.

It has been the Doric Theatre bar all day, with Thorold doubling over to the Model Stage in the morning for the simultaneous shooting of the first shot in the new ending—Nora in the wings, hearing her cue, dancing out on to the stage. And at the end of the day, just time for another of those Taxi shots (F.26).

Scenes shot: F.26, 42, 42a, b, c, d, e, 43, 43a, 80 (new). Screen time: 2 minutes 6 seconds.

THURSDAY, MAY 31ST

Retired into her dressing room in the corner of the Model Stage, Valentina strips from her head for the last time the blonde wig of Lena Collins. She takes a deep breath. 'I made it!' she says.

And so she has. To-day has finished her part and, to all intents and purposes, the film. Steenie's three extra shots started the morning, then an insert on Maria, also for Phœnix Park: camera shooting from Louis' eyeline on to a close-up of her hands, then a quick track forward and pan up to hold a big close-up of her eyes. (A tricky assignment for Herbert on focus.) This, together with the close-up of Louis which we shot on Tuesday, should point his recognition of Maria more effectively than it stands at present. Next, more taxis:

123

Maria and Miss Jackson on the way to Dublin, driving past the rebuilt Café; Maria pursuing Steenie and Nora to Phœnix Park. Finally, two shots on Miss Jackson: leaning over the rail at the back of the theatre, watching Nora dance; and greeting Maria (retake) on her arrival at Scotland Yard. Which brings us to six o'clock and the unit still—to be followed by the unit party.

For this the doors of Stage 1 are thrown open and at the entrance stands a placard: 'Our Secret People (Miss Valentina Cortesa, Mr. Serge Reggiani, Mr. Thorold Dickinson, Mr. Sidney Cole). At Home. Fully Licensed.' From half-past six on, the Stage fills and the party spirit grows. Almost without exception the unit are here—not just the group round and in front of the camera, which is the unit only in the narrowest sense—but workers from all departments which have been feeding the film, directly and indirectly, for the last ten weeks. Even, one is glad to see, the telephone girls, who work such daily miracles of memory and patience, have been remembered.

While we are still in the glass-in-hand, quietly-chatting stage, it is permissible to talk shop a little, and get one or two final comments. Everyone has enjoyed it—that much is obvious and needn't be dwelt on. To finish on time, and slightly under budget, is a rare and rather invigorating experience. It is for the Producer to put these things in a nutshell: 'I'm glad to say the production was very largely a piece of cake as far as I was concerned—which is particularly gratifying in view of the fact that it was an outside subject, not conceived and worked up entirely at Ealing. Of course in a way that was an advantage: it meant we started with a great deal of work already done. But it might have made difficulties. When you're making films in a continuously-running Studio, it's bound to be to a certain extent a factory process. And some subjects will inevitably be more difficult to fit into the mincing machine than others. You might have expected that to be the case on *Secret People*.' And why wasn't it? 'Well I think chiefly because the subject was well prepared in the Director's mind—which is the most important thing of all. The result of that you can see in the day-to-day screen time we got, and those figures are very largely the reason why the film went through so smoothly.'

On finance: 'It did look at first as though the film would be rather more expensive than it should be, and we did have to cut down a little. The main saving of course was on cutting out the French and Irish locations, which really would have been an unjustifiable extravagance. We came off the floor £1,500 under budget . . . That's allowing for future expenses on stock, editing, dubbing, etc. It's true there's a handful of shots still to be taken, but it's without main artistes, except for the funfair stuff Thorold wants to take with Anselmo and Nora for the Exhibition montage. You can say we came off the floor on schedule, I think: officially half a day behind, but then the main unit assimilated a day and a half scheduled for second unit, which cancels that out.'

There remains chiefly the final editing. 'It's all there, I think. It's chiefly a problem now of getting the emphasis right, which is bound to be a question of the editing. As it stands, we've got a picture of about an hour and fifty minutes. By the time it's all tightened. I should think it'll be down to about ninety-five minutes. This doesn't mean we shall lose any scenes, you know. When you start editing, the tendency is to leave everything in. Now it's a question of sharpening the whole thing up—the fascinating stage when you get the dramatic rhythm right. For instance: I feel at the moment that the business of the impact of Brentano's death on Maria doesn't make its full effect. This is really due to the rhythm of the opening; to me, the first sequence should be entirely in the nature of a prologue, so that the first thing you're asked to dwell on is the parcel and Maria's opening of it. You get the impact, in fact, by a lighter touch on the stuff that's gone before.'

That's enough. When it comes to talking about the picture, you can go on for hours, discussing this effect and that, does this scene quite come off, and I like it particularly when . . . But the party is really getting going. Songs have started, and Muriel is jiving with Joe Gitsham (Construction). Here until 10, and continuing in other places until other hours, let joy be unconfined.

Scenes shot: F.28, 54, 81, E.83b, F.70a, F.75z, F.65b. Retake E.24a. Screen time: 54 seconds.

Close of Play

From Phyll's Progress Report for Thursday: Note: The following artistes have now completed their parts in this production barring post-synching: — Miss Valentina Cortesa, M. Serge Reggiani, Miss Irene Worth, Mr. Geoffrey Hibbert. Main shooting on this production now complete. Position: Location —½ day ahead. Studio—1 day behind.

Ralph's comment: 'You may ask, if we're thus only half a day behind, why didn't we finish Thursday midday? Because—apart from extra shots not on the schedule—the first unit took on also another half day of second unit scenes.' My query: *'Why do you say that shooting is completed when we still have shots to do on Friday?'* Ralph: *'Because those scenes do not rate as main shooting.'* My query: *'Who decides what shots are classified as main shooting and what are not?'* Ralph: *'I do.'* Fair enough.

FRIDAY, JUNE 1ST
You do look, my son, in a mov'd sort,
As if you were dismay'd: be cheerful, sir:
Our revels now are ended . . .

But to the sentimentalist (I mean myself), conclusions, and the partings they imply, are always sad. And although the unit reassembles this morning, generally somewhat wan, to dispose of a final scrap or two, the feeling is unmistakable that the shooting of the picture is now over. As if to signalize this, before our actors melt away into the air, Thorold arranges for Valentina and Serge a projection in rough-cut of the entire film up to the explosion in the Café—minus only the Garden Party sequence, which has still to be put into shape. Warning his little audience of the fragmentary nature of what they will see, Thorold announces: 'We promise not to cut our throats for three days. After that, if you still feel like it, you can commit suicide any way you like . . .'

At first, as one might anticipate, it is impossible to regard what is projected as a film at all. Partly this is due to its roughness: scenes missing, sound incomplete, cutting not finalised, adjacent shots not graded for continuity of tone, no music or optical effects. But even more confusing are the multitude

125

of associations which crowd in with every shot, background memories jostling each other as recollection shifts from Stage 2 to Stage 3a, from studio to location, from this dispute to that tension, that laughter. Then gradually, the mind adjusts itself: strangely the film establishes its illusion; still evaluating, we are moved also and excited by these familiar (but cumulatively unfamiliar) scenes played out before us. What a curious experience it is! And how indefinable the sensation with which, after an hour and twenty-five minutes, we detach ourselves from the rain of images, to sit silent for a moment or two, then look up, and at each other, and gasp. (It is almost inconceivable, for one thing, that we have been sitting there for that length of time. The film seems to have dashed by, with never a pause for breath.)

At last it is proper to indulge for a little in the luxury of congratulation. Valentina pays tribute to Serge, Serge to Valentina, both to Thorold. And Thorold replies: 'I'm very proud of you both.' Bemused and exhilarated, we have to be asked to leave the theatre, to be propelled gently through the open doors into the unreal summer outside, where the unit sits smoking and chatting, waiting for their Director.

Which is where we leave them, standing in the sunshine outside the theatre, lively with pleasant sensations of accomplishment. The film, of course, is not yet finished, but this is a milestone far along the way: for the rest, the responsibility will devolve increasingly on Cutting Room and Sound Department. What we have seen this morning has yet to be polished, trimmed and tightened: and the further sequences added to bridge the gaps and bring the story to a close. Then on to that goes the sound track—background noises of talk and music and traffic, dialogue cleanly recorded, music (not a great deal of it) to comment and underline. And ahead lies the ordeal of public exposure . . . But let someone else write a journal about all of that.

On what note, with what movement shall we leave? Resisting the temptation to track slowly back, or to crane traditionally away into the sky, we linger for a moment as our players start to discuss what they have seen. Serge would like fewer close-ups of himself in the latter half of the scene in which Louis gives Maria the bomb; Valentina is worried about the emphasis in the Scotland Yard sequence . . . Thorold and Peter listen politely. Sid, appealed to, suggests nicely that Serge cuts his hair instead of trying to cut the picture. Here, at last, is a suggestion eagerly accepted, and Serge makes off for Ernie Taylor with a cry of relief. And as he turns into Make-Up, he breaks off from our discussion of the film and his showing in it, not ungrateful of reassurances, but refusing to be satisfied with them. 'There is so much still to learn. Not by *learning*, you know, but by experience. By doing it.'

He disappears. The door swings to. Fade-out.

Scenes shot: B.1, E.95. Screen time: 52 seconds.
Total screen time to date: 112 minutes 44 seconds.

Illustrations

Readers will appreciate that to cover every aspect of the making of a film as well as scenes from the film itself, in sixteen pages of illustration, is impossible. These pictures represent only a minimal selection (the most balanced I could manage) from the large number available. I apologise to the many important contributors to the production who have had to be left out.

The name of the photographer responsible for each still will be found in brackets after its reference number (where there is no name the photograph is by the author). I am very grateful to Jack Dooley, head of Ealing Studio's Stills Department and Stills Supervisor on the picture; to Bobby Penn and Roy Gough for the trouble they took to give me what I asked for; to Daniel Farson and the Editor of *Sight and Sound*, for permission to use his pictures; and to John Fletcher, who lent me the camera with which I took the few photographs of my own which are included. All except one of the scenes from the film have been taken directly from the 'frame'—that is to say, they were shot through the camera, and have been selected and enlarged from unused takes.

In many cases I have specified the date on which particular stills were taken; readers may in these cases be interested to refer to the appropriate day in the Diary for further comment.

PLATE I. PREPARATIONS.

1. (Roy Gough). Serge Reggiani tests for Louis—the first day's shooting on the picture, on November 10th, 1950. Nearing the end of a heavy day, the artistes and director are here waiting while the lighting is arranged for the last set-up on Scene B.51. Left to right: Irene Worth, Serge Reggiani, Thorold Dickinson. (Reggiani's beard, grown for his last French picture, is not a permanency. It was decided not to retain it for *Secret People*).

2. (Bobby Penn). The director checks an artiste's height (Michael Allen, for Rodd), to see that he is conveniently scaled to his fellow actors.

3. (Bobby Penn). One of the final script conferences brings together the director and his co-script writer, the producer and the additional dialoguist. Left to right: Wolfgang Wilhelm, Thorold Dickinson, Christianna Brand, Sidney Cole.

4. (Bobby Penn). Unit production manager (Ralph Hogg, right), and the assistant to the studio general manager (Simon Kershaw) together check through the final shooting schedule.

5. (Roy Gough). After playing her test scene for Nora, Audrey Hepburn remains for lighting tests in close-up. These are shot silent, and intended chiefly to give the cameraman opportunity to try his lighting on all angles of the artiste's face. (Gordon Dines—'painting with light'—and Audrey Hepburn).

PLATE 2. THE BALLET—I.

1. (Bobby Penn). The two leading makers of the ballet meet for a first discussion of the score, on February 12th. The composer plays it over on the

piano, while the choreographer listens, visualises it for dance, puts forward her point of view. Left to right: Dock Mathieson, Andrée Howard, Wolfgang Wilhelm, Roberto Gerhard, Sidney Cole, Thorold Dickinson.
2. (Roy Gough). Reconnaissance at the Bedford Theatre, February 23rd. Director and cameraman survey the prospect.
3. (Lawrence Ridley). March 16th. The ballet music is recorded at Denham Studios, under the direction of Ernest Irving, head of Ealing's music department. Left to right: Andrée Howard, Roberto Gerhard, Ernest Irving.
4. (Bobby Penn). March 20th: shooting at the Bedford—in the thick of it. On the crane, the director lines up the long track away from the stage.

PLATE 3. THE BALLET—II.

1. (Bobby Penn). March 19th, morning. The last shot of the ballet sequence is the first to be taken: the camera tracks in on the final *pas de deux;* pan round to include Maria watching from her box; the curtain descends.
2. The shot as it appears in the film. John Field and Audrey Hepburn on stage, Valentina Cortesa in the box.

PLATE 4. ON THE FLOOR—I.

1. (Daniel Farson). On the Exhibition set: the director works out the moves of a scene with his actors. Charles Goldner, Thorold Dickinson, Valentina Cortesa, Serge Reggiani.
2. (Roy Gough). Actors and director: Valentina Cortesa, Angela Fouldes, Thorold Dickinson.
3. (Bobby Penn). The camera group at work on the Exhibition set. Right to left: Herbert Smith (Focus), Chic Waterson (Operator), Gordon Dines (Lighting Cameraman), the director and, from the sound crew, Bobby Healy (assistant boom operator).

PLATE 5. ON THE FLOOR—II.

1. Overhead view of work on the Exhibition set. The camera is lined up on its tracks for the first shot of the sequence (B.22).
2. (Daniel Farson). Right-hand man: Spike Priggen, first assistant, confers with the director.
3. (Bobby Penn). Sound recordist, Arthur Bradburn, checks with his engineers off the set.
4. (Bobby Penn). Recording angel: Phyllis Crocker, continuity.

PLATE 6. TECHNICIANS.

1. Make-up. Charles Goldner and Ernie Taylor inspect Anselmo.
2. (Bobby Penn). In the cutting room. Peter Tanner, editor, marks a cut with his pencil as he runs a scene through on the movieola. Left, Roy Baker, assistant.
3. (Bobby Penn). The art director produces a model of one of his set designs (the Paris Exhibition) for lunch-hour inspection and comment by the unit. Left to right: Ralph Hogg, Gordon Dines, Thorold Dickinson, Sid Cole, William Kellner.
4. (Daniel Farson). Impromptu conference on the floor: editor, first assistant, production manager encircle the director. (Peter Tanner, Spike Priggen, Ralph Hogg, Thorold Dickinson's back).

PLATE 7. ACTORS.

1. (Daniel Farson). Paris Exhibition: Louis meets Maria again (B.40). Serge Reggiani rehearses a close-up to the camera.
2. April 6th: retake of B.51. Valentina Cortesa discusses a point of interpretation with the director.
3. (Bobby Penn). In a corner of the set, the actors run through the scene while waiting for their call. Serge Reggiani and Valentina Cortesa rehearse D.53.
4. (Daniel Farson). Audrey Hepburn relaxes between takes on the Exhibition set.

PLATE 8. A SEQUENCE: LOUIS' PARIS LODGINGS.

Covering the end of B.50, the five set-ups into which B.51 was eventually split, and the beginning of B.53. (A detailed analysis of the editing of this sequence will be found in Appendix One, under the appropriate scene number.) These are the dates on which the various set-ups were shot: 1. (Paris Taxi, retake)—April 30th. 2-3. (Paris Lodgings, retake)—April 6th. 4. (Original scene)—March 30th. 5-8. (Retake)—April 6th. 9. (Vieux Chapeau)—March 28th.

PLATE 9. THREE SCENES.

1 Anselmo and Daly in 'Morton Street'—scene A.6, shot April 17th. Charles Goldner, John Ruddock.
2. (Still by Bobby Penn). Maria and Nora arrive in London, to learn of their father's death. Scene A.45 (March 22nd). Angela Fouldes, Valentina Cortesa.
3 News of Nora's audition. Scene C.21 (April 2nd). Valentina Cortesa, Megs Jenkins, Audrey Hepburn, Serge Reggiani.

PLATE 10. LOCATIONS—I.

1. (Bobby Penn). Inside: shooting from the living room of Anselmo's Café, down into 'Morton Street,' for E.58.
2. (Bobby Penn). Outside: Steenie (Geoffrey Hibbert) has an audience. At the window Louis prepares to throw his cigarette end, under the instructions of the director. Right: first and third assistants stand by.
3. A tracking shot in West Street (Charing Cross Road) for D.36-7; Sunday, April 29th. Left to right: boom operator's leg, Reggiani, Cortesa, Ted Lockhart (pulling back the dolly), Herbert Smith on focus, Gordon Dines watching action through camera, Thorold Dickinson, Phyll Crocker attempting to check the dialogue, and Chic Waterson, camera operator, temporarily dispossessed.

PLATE 11. LOCATIONS—II.

1. Harrow Road location for Louis' London Lodgings: scene C.39, April 20th. The director watches for a train.
2. As above: anticlimax. Spike and Valentina—'Darling, I am so sorry . . .'
3. The scene in the picture.
4. (Bobby Penn). Richmond, for Phœnix Park: May 16th. The unit gets down to work for the night.

PLATE 12. THE ATTEMPT—I.

The four set-ups in which Scene D.7 was eventually shot: April 5th. Valentina Cortesa, Serge Reggiani.
1. Maria: 'Yes, but—what's this? A cigarette case? It's very heavy.'
2. Maria: 'Is it a bomb?'

3. Maria: 'You think it's right to assassinate?'
4. Louis: ' "Resistance to tyrants is obedience to God"—remember?'

PLATE 13. THE ATTEMPT—II.

The attempt on Galbern misfires. Pamela Harrington as the waitress, Valentina Cortesa, and (in still No. 6) Charlie Cairoli.

PLATE 14. THREE SCENES.

1 *Vieux Chapeau*. Valentina Cortesa, Serge Reggiani, Simone Silva, Charles Goldner.
2. Scotland Yard. Maria: 'I had nothing to do with them till yesterday.' (Irene Worth, Reginald Tate, Valentina Cortesa.)
3. Lena and Miss Jackson pass the Café on their way to Dublin. Lena: 'Strange . . . You live in a street for years, and it is nothing. Just a street. And now I remember every single thing . . .'

PLATE 15. TWO SCENES.

1. E.18: The 'London Committee.' Maria is startled as a flashlight suddenly explodes out of the darkness. (An image which will hardly be seen by audiences—for the flash occupies only three or four frames of film, and a fraction of a second of time.) Valentina Cortesa in foreground; at the back, left to right: John Chandos, Serge Reggiani, Geoffrey Hibbert, Michael Ripper.
2. The end of the story. (May 18th—'We shot out of a bloody pit in the end . . .'). Foreground: Audrey Hepburn, Valentina Cortesa. Behind: Serge Reggiani, Joe Linnane, Irene Worth.

PLATE 16. VISITORS AND UNIT.

1. (Bobby Penn). Sir Michael Balcon visits the Garden Party set.
2. (Bobby Penn). Joyce Cary talks with Valentina Cortesa and Thorold Dickinson on the Hospital set.
3 (Bobby Penn). Unit group. Taken on the last day of shooting (May 31st) and in the last quarter-hour of work; result—scramble and many regrettable omissions. Those who do appear are: Front row (left to right)—Ralph Hogg, Gordon Dines, Spike Priggen, Juliana Hadley (companion to Valentina), Valentina Cortesa, Thorold Dickinson, Irene Worth. Behind: Jim Neville (Props), Albert Radford (Painter), Albert Parker (Electrician), Jimmy O'Connolly (3rd Assistant), Daphne Martin (Assistant Hairdresser). Behind Daphne, a quartette of: William Gunner (Stagehand), Steve Willett (Electrician), Frank Bethell (Electrician), Alf Leonard (Rigger). To the right again: Cyril Swern (Boom Operator), Eric Stokl (Sound Camera Operator), Barbara Barnard (Hairdressing Supervisor), Lily Payne (Wardrobe Mistress), Harry Phipps (Props), John Meadows (2nd Assistant), Arthur Bradburn (Sound Mixer). Directly under camera: Ken Westbury (Loading and Clappers). Right of camera, another square quartet: Chic Waterson (Operator), Ted Lockhart (Grips), Herbert Smith (Camera Assistant—incognito), Bobby Healy (Assistant Boom Operator). To the right from Brad: Stan Ford (Electrician), Phyll Crocker (Continuity), Charley Simmons (Electrician), William Kellner (Art Director), Bob Palmer (Electrician), Doc. Matheson (Assistant Musical Director), Peter Tanner (Editor), Alastair McIntyre (1st Assistant Editor), Roy Baker (2nd Assistant Editor).

1

1. PREPARATIONS

Testing
Interviewing
Conferring
Scheduling

2

3

4

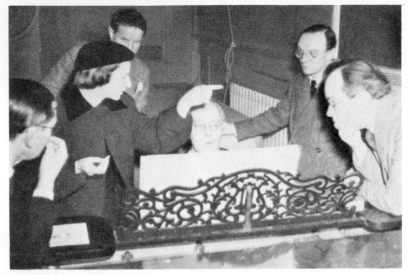

1

2

2. THE BALLET—I

Discussion
Reconnaissance
Music Recording
Shooting

3   4

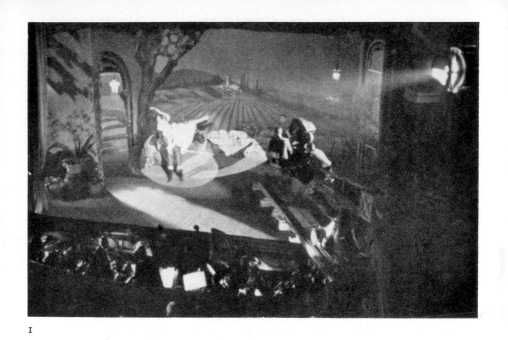

I

3. THE BALLET—II
First take

2

4. ON THE FLOOR—

Director
Actors
Camera Crew

1

2

3

1

5. ON THE FLOOR—II

From above
Assistant
Sound
Continuity

2

4   3

1

6. TECHNICIANS

Make-up
Editing
Design
Planning

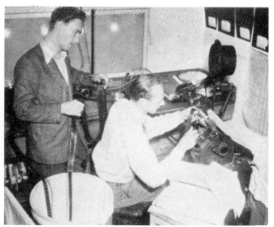

2

3

4

1

7. ACTORS

Act
Discuss
Rehearse
Relax

2

4

3

8. A SEQUENCE

Louis' Paris lodgings
Louis and Maria
(B50 *to* 53)

1

2

3

4

5

6

7

8

9

9. THREE SCENES

Morton Street:
  the story begins
Maria and Nora
Nora's audition

I

3

2

1

10. LOCATIONS—I
Paddington
West Street—
  Charing Cross Road

2

3

1

2

11. LOCATIONS—II

Harrow Road
Richmond Park

3

4

I, 2

3, 4

12.
THE ATTEMPT—I
Louis persuades Maria

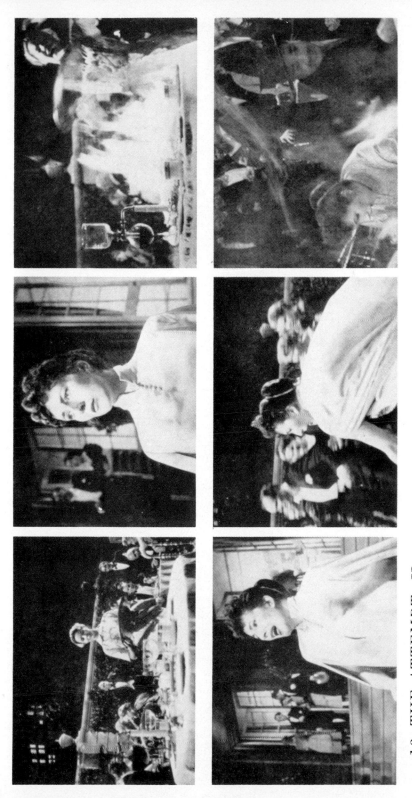

13. THE ATTEMPT—II

The plan misfires

14. THREE SCENES

'Vieux Chapeau'
Scotland Yard
To Dublin

1

2

3

1

15. TWO SCENES
The London Committee
The story ends

2

16. VISITORS

1

2

THE UNIT

Secret People

SHOOTING SCRIPT
BY
THOROLD DICKINSON
AND
WOLFGANG WILHELM

With acknowledgments to
Joyce Cary

Additional dialogue by
Christianna Brand

TO H.T.
who first mentioned the idea

SECRET PEOPLE

MAIN CHARACTERS

ANSELMO
Owner of a café in Paddington, a typical 'Southerner' in spite of long residence in London.

MARIA BRENTANO
Daughter of a Latin democrat who falls victim to his country's new totalitarian government; full of vitality and good humour, she carries her father's ideals with her into exile in London; provoked to act against them, a strong sense of guilt stays with her right through her efforts to atone.

NORA BRENTANO
Maria's sister—younger by nine years; without Maria's ties and preoccupations on account of her youth; artistic and impulsive.

LOUIS BALAN
Maria's father's favourite disciple. Brave but not a martyr; years of underground existence corrupt him to 'an eye for an eye' philosophy; a 'fallen angel'.

STEENIE
His associate; ideologies mean nothing to him; except that he cherishes the one that can best serve his urge to kill; his one loyalty is to Louis.

PENNY
Anselmo's cockney waitress; at her best when chatty and bossing customers; and not when romantically inclined.

FRACK
Unsuccessful journalist and supposed police nark; a social misfit.

INSPECTOR ELIOT
Of the C.I.D. Special Branch, forty years old, athletic, intelligent.

MISS JACKSON
A policewoman of the C.I.D. Special Branch, in her early thirties.

DALY
Owner of the chemist shop opposite Anselmo's café.

RODD
A civilian air pilot.

BENTLEY
Chairman of the London Committee.

SID BURNETT
Theatrical agent.

SONIA DE BLAISE (now: THE HON. MRS. REGINALD KELLICK)
Formerly a musical comedy actress.

GENERAL GALBERN
'Strong Man of the South.'

SEQUENCES

'A' *MARIA*
1930—LONDON

'B' *MARIA AND LOUIS*
1937—LONDON, PARIS

'C' *GALBERN VISITS LONDON*

'D' *A BOMB EXPLODES*

'E' *THE PAY OFF*

'F' *A FRESH START*
1937-38—LONDON, DUBLIN

NOTE

This is the script of *Secret People* as it stood when the film went into production. Before he embarks on it, the reader should be forewarned: a film script is rarely intended as more than a blueprint for the practical guidance of the unit on and off the floor. In this it differs considerably from the text of a play. Writing for readers, producers, actors whom he will never meet, a playwright must communicate in stage directions and comment his desired details of characterisation and atmosphere; in the case of a film, these finer points can be discussed between writer and director, and there would be little point in specifying them in the script. This is doubly so in the case of *Secret People*, for Thorold Dickinson the writer has had no need to put down on paper elaborate instructions for Thorold Dickinson the director. In reading the script, therefore, the layman must expect to find it, from the literary point of view, on the bare side.

In some respects, the reticence is even deliberate. This is a long script, and the degree of sophistication in its shooting depended to a large degree on speed maintained and time in hand. Thus, several scenes eventually covered from a number of angles, and involving quite complex movements of the camera, will be found to have been purposely scripted to a minimum of set-ups, with perhaps no mention of camera movement at all. To be borne in mind also is this particular director's manner of working: in some cases, ideas for composition and movement were certainly present in his mind, though he has not committed them to paper; in others, directions have been left purposely open, to be worked out on the floor, under the stimulus of contact with the actual human and dramatic material.

Scene numbers followed by the word 'Out' refer to scenes removed between the first and the third (which this is) draft shooting scripts. Scenes which were removed during shooting, or which were left on the cutting room floor, will be found listed in Appendix Two, together with other changes and points of difference between the film on paper and the film on celluloid.

Secret People

SHOOTING SCRIPT

SEQUENCE 'A'

FADE IN:

A.1. EXT. MORTON STREET. DAY (LOCATION)

CAMERA STARTS on a small parcel which a POSTMAN carries along in hot sunshine. CAMERA PULLS BACK to show, by the clothes of the passers-by and the types of vehicles, that we are in a London Street (Morton Street) of the Paddington district, and the date is 1930. A Policeman stands on the pavement.
The street links Praed Street with Sussex Gardens; the Edgware Road lies a hundred yards or so to the east.
The CAMERA PANS with the POSTMAN to the front door of Anselmo's café, which stands at a corner beside a narrow alley-way leading to the Mews behind Sussex Gardens. PENNY, the lively Cockney waitress of the café, is scrubbing the floor inside the open doorway. She is about 30 years old and of comfortable size.

A.2 EXT. ANSELMO'S CAFE. DAY (LOCATION OR STUDIO)

POSTMAN. *Parcel, Miss. Name of Brentano.*
PENNY. *Nobody of that name here.*
POSTMAN. *Will you take it?*

A.3 PENNY, POSTMAN (LOCATION OR STUDIO)

CAMERA STARTS ON C.S. on the parcel, showing its label marked: 'Mdlle. Maria Brentano, c/o Anselmo's Café, Morton Street, Paddington, London, W.2. To await arrival.' The label comes from the International Red Cross Society.
PENNY (over). *I dunno. Better ask Mr. Anselmo. He's over at Mr. Daly's.*
CAMERA PANS sharply to a C.S. of PENNY as she points across the road with her scrubbing brush.

A.4 EXT. MORTON STREET. DALY'S SHOP. DAY (LOCATION)

Immediately opposite Anselmo's café is Daly's, the Chemist Shop. The name DALY is printed over the door, which is open and from which voices can be heard. A fat man, ANSELMO, is standing on the scales just inside the door being weighed by DALY, a lean man in a white coat.
Both men are in their early fifties; ANSELMO is fat, voluble and very much of the Mediterranean; DALY is slim and very English. In background, a WOMAN ASSISTANT is busy behind the counter.
ANSELMO. *Da machine is wrong. It is busted.*
DALY. *It's taken you before. Twelve stone ten . . . eleven.*
The POSTMAN enters Daly's shop, past CAMERA.

A.5 INT. DALY'S SHOP. DAY (STUDIO)

SHOOTING ACROSS the shop with no view of the street outside.
POSTMAN (dead pan). *Parcel for you, Mr. Anselmo.*
DALY (sliding the weight on the scales). *. . . twelve . . . thirteen . . .*
ANSELMO. *Just a minute. I no want to weigh da parcel also.*
DALY. *Thirteen stone—five . . . six. You're swelling like a pig.*

ANSELMO. *Den why you sell me dose pills, eh? Dey no good—ab-solute-ly no good!*
POSTMAN (dead pan). *Parcel, Mr. Anselmo.*
ANSELMO (looking at label). *Maria Brentano—nobody of dat name at my café.*
POSTMAN (dead pan). *It says to await arrival, Mr. Anselmo.*
ANSELMO. *I ain't expectin' nobody.* (Suddenly brightening) *Aw, it must be Pietro's daughter.*
DALY (drily). *That makes it quite clear. Thirteen stone ten and a half.*
ANSELMO. *Pietro, 'e was my best frien' at school. 'E teach me English.*
POSTMAN (dead pan). *You'll take it?*
ANSELMO. *Of course!* (frowning to himself) *When she comin'?*
POSTMAN (dead pan). *She 'asn't let me know.*
He goes.
DALY. *Exercise. That's what you want.*
ANSELMO turns and goes towards the door.
ANSELMO. *I run-a da café, don' I? Exercise. I—*

A.6 EXT. MORTON STREET. DAY (LOCATION)
The POLICEMAN is holding up the traffic for schoolchildren to cross. ANSELMO leaves the shop and talks as he crosses the street. CAMERA TRACKING. DALY stands laughing at him until he notices the parcel which ANSELMO has left behind. DALY picks it up and follows ANSELMO.
DALY. *You sit behind a table robbing me at dominoes and gobbling spaghetti.*
ANSELMO (not turning round). *I never play wit' you again! I don' play wit' da bad losers.*
DALY catches up ANSELMO and CAMERA PANS them to the door of Anselmo's café. The POLICEMAN follows.
ANSELMO. *I don' no longer let you rob me for da lousy pills either! I—*
PENNY, on the steps of the café, pours the bucket of water into the gutter.
POLICEMAN. *At it again?*
PENNY. *It's like the wireless, you don't hear it any more.*

A.7 INT. ANSELMO'S CAFE. DAY (STUDIO)
The chairs are still stacked on the tables from the night before. ANSELMO, entering, leaves marks on the clean, damp floor.
PENNY. *All over my nice clean floor.*
ANSELMO (snapping at her). *What shall we do? I'm not Tarzan.*
PENNY (after a pause to inspect him). *You're telling me.*
DALY. *Here you are, Penny girl.*
DALY hands the parcel to PENNY, who walks on through the café carrying her bucket.
DALY (friendly again). *Pietro Brentano—I seem to have heard his name somewhere.*
DALY automatically helps ANSELMO to set the chairs at the tables.
ANSELMO. *Pietro* (mollified). *'E was very good frien' of mine. Teacher of languages. Very fine man. Da last time I 'ear 'e start a big movement against da nationalism and da use of arms.*
DALY (imitating Anselmo's mispronunciation). *Arms?*
ANSELMO. *Arms. Weapons.*
DALY. *Can't be very popular with his new government.*
ANSELMO (ruminating). *No.*
DALY (drily). *He'd better come over and finish teaching you English.*
ANSELMO (incensed again). *Everybody tell me I speak da very good English!*

A.8 INT. ANSELMO'S CAFE. KITCHEN. DAY (STUDIO)
PENNY turns on the radio and puts the parcel on a shelf in the kitchen alongside other letters and packages addressed in care of Anselmo's café. CAMERA PANS to C.S. of a magnificent fatty ham newly cut.
DISSOLVE:

A.9 INSERT. HAM. DAY (STUDIO)
Only the hambone is left.

A.10 INT. ANSELMO'S BEDROOM. DAY (STUDIO)
CAMERA STARTS on ANSELMO, in his shirtsleeves, lying on his bed and patting his stomach. (The room is the first floor back over the café). Anselmo's feet, in boots, are resting on a newspaper of 1930. Beside him, on a table, lies an open box of pills; beyond it a gramophone is playing a worn record of a traditional dance of a Southern European country. A bell (operated from the café below) rings by his bed. He stops the gramophone, knocking over the pills.
ANSELMO (muttering to himself). *Always somet'in'* . . . *Always somet'in'* . .
Penny's footsteps are heard running up the stairs. There is a loud knock.
ANSELMO. *Come in. Who dere?*
PENNY, in a state of great agitation, enters with a letter.
PENNY. *It's me. Penny. I'm sorry, Mr. Anselmo. There's someone to see you.*
ANSELMO. *Let 'em wait.*
PENNY (hands him a letter). *It's urgent.*
ANSELMO. *Always somet'in'. Always somet'in'*!
He restarts the gramophone which plays the same dance record. Then he looks at the envelope and seems to recognise the writing. He opens the letter. PENNY, after a somewhat fearful look at ANSELMO, goes out of the room.
PIETRO'S VOICE (overscene). *'My dear Anselmo, I write to you in great haste and with some diffidence. I could not post this letter to you as all my mail is being censored . . .*

A.11 INSERT OF LETTER (STUDIO)
PIETRO'S VOICE (overscene). *. . . . The two bearers of this letter are my daughters, Maria, whom you will remember as a baby, and my little Eleanora, whom you have not seen. You are the only one I can trust to take care of them as I have been warned that I shall be arrested by the new government any day.*

A.12 ANSELMO (STUDIO)
PIETRO'S VOICE (overscene). *Pray God I may see you all again when this cloud has lifted from our land. Forgive me for giving you this burden without your knowledge or consent. There is nothing else for me to do. Until we meet again, Your old friend, Pietro Brentano.'*
ANSELMO reads the letter with growing alarm and looks at it again, disbelieving his eyes. The record's relentless rhythm and rigidly traditional form gives dramatic emphasis to the letter.
ANSELMO. *Da two bearers*!
He jumps off the bed and rushes out of the bedroom.

A.13 INT. ANSELMO'S LIVING ROOM. DAY (STUDIO)
ANSELMO runs through the living room, dodging the furniture.

A.14 INT. ANSELMO'S CAFE. DAY (STUDIO)
ANSELMO runs out of the living room and stops at the head of the stairs, which lead down to the café. He looks down into the café over (or between) the banisters. There, standing just inside the door like two ill-assorted sentinels, are MARIA, a 19-year-old girl and NORA, her younger sister of 10, both tired and dishevelled. On the floor beside them are two luggage bundles (straw holdalls with straps). The gramophone goes on playing.

A.15 ANSELMO. (STUDIO)
SHOOTING UP from the café stairs. ANSELMO is flabbergasted.
ANSELMO. *Goodness . . . Penny! Where are you?*
PENNY'S VOICE (from kitchen). *Coming, Mr. Anselmo!*

137

A.16 ANSELMO, MARIA, NORA, PENNY. DAY (STUDIO)

SHOOTING PAST MARIA and NORA in foreground on to the stairs and the kitchen behind the bar. As ANSELMO runs down the stairs, PENNY emerges from the kitchen behind the counter with a glass of milk and a cup of tea. She comes along inside the bar and leans over to hand it to the girls, who don't move from their positions. ANSELMO slows up at the foot of the stairs and approaches them cautiously, moving past the few customers present before the evening rush.

ANSELMO. *Maria? Eleanora?*

A.17 MARIA, NORA. (STUDIO)

MARIA (embarrassed). *Yes. You my father's friend Anselmo?*

A.18 ANSELMO. (STUDIO)

He nods.

A.19 NORA. (STUDIO)

She looks up at him with a shy smile.

A.20 ANSELMO. (STUDIO)

He begins to relent. He looks from NORA to MARIA.

A.21 MARIA. (STUDIO)

She looks from ANSELMO to PENNY.

A.22 PENNY, ANSELMO, NORA, MARIA (STUDIO)

CAMERA STARTS ON PENNY, who is very much taken with the two girls. CAMERA TRACKS BACK as ANSELMO takes the glass and cup from PENNY, who is giving them a dazzling smile of encouragement.

He hands the glass of milk to NORA who, exhausted as she is, gives a formal little Continental curtsy, much to Penny's delight. ANSELMO has handed the tea to MARIA. She feels the cup and finds it much too hot. He snatches it back and pours some into the saucer with another encouraging smile. MARIA looks dubiously at it and drinks from the saucer. NORA has finished drinking her milk and hands the empty glass back with another little curtsy. PENNY, in receiving the glass, half-seriously attempts a little curtsy herself, and almost loses balance. ANSELMO roars with laughter; MARIA and PENNY try not to, but can't help laughing, too, and the ice is broken as they all laugh, and from now on, all four are friends.

CAMERA MOVES into TWO-SHOT. MARIA looks upstairs as though tracing the source of the traditional dance music. It seems to bring back all the good of her young life in her own country, and to reassure her.

MARIA. *The music . . . you always play our music?*

ANSELMO. *Sure! To lie down, after good food . . . shut my eyes and listen to—*

He breaks off, seeing her smile fade.

ANSELMO (quietly). *Oh, I'm a big fool . . . Penny, go up, turn it off . . . quick!*

PENNY runs out of shot and is heard going upstairs. ANSELMO stoops down to gather up the girls' luggage, when he stares out of shot.

CAMERA PANS to NORA, who must have collapsed while they talked, and would fall off her chair if ANSELMO were not able to catch her in time. He holds NORA while MARIA kneels by her, rubbing her feet and pulling her worn shoes off.

ANSELMO (to Maria). *Hold her . . .* (he runs to café door).

A.23 EXT. MORTON STREET. DAY (LOCATION)

CAMERA SHOOTING from the doorway of the café, ANSELMO in foreground. He shouts across the road.

ANSELMO. *Daly! Come quick! Daly! In Heaven's name!*

Seeing DALY hurrying out of his shop opposite and running across, ANSELMO turns back into the café.

A.24 INT. ANSELMO'S CAFE. DAY (LOCATION)

MARIA is holding NORA, opening the top of her coat and fanning her with a handkerchief. ANSELMO comes and fusses over them. DALY joins them. Appalled by the child's state, he picks her up, regardless of Maria's reluctance to let a stranger take possession of her sister.

ANSELMO (to Maria). *My friend Mr. Daly, 'e is 'alf a doctor.* (To Daly). *Pietro Brentano's kids . . .*

The gramophone music stops . . .

ANSELMO (continues). *. . . . I told you about him—da man who taught me English.*

DALY (intent on the child). *How on earth could the child get into this state?*

MARIA (haunted). *We been travelling a long time . . .*

N.B. Scenes A.25-33 are symbolic close shots with explanatory sound effects and no dialogue. There are no optical links.

A.25 EXT. DOOR TO CONTINENTAL RAILWAY CARRIAGE. NIGHT (STUDIO)

A CLOSE TWO-SHOT of MARIA and NORA, their clothes and luggage clean and tidy, being pushed on to a train. Judging by the brutal noise coming from offscreen, all the noisier after the quiet of the café, this is one detail of a scene of despair: the ruthless herding together of many fugitives on the platform. UNIFORMED ARMS push MARIA and NORA up to, and through, the dirty carriage door behind an AGED MAN and WOMAN.

A.26 MARIA, NORA. DAY (STUDIO)

The deafening clanging of train couplings as the same carriage stops dead. In CLOSE SHOT another pair of UNIFORMED ARMS pulls the carriage door open. MARIA and NORA, travel-worn and unwashed, are revealed in the carriage. The ARMS pull them down, NORA hanging on to MARIA, who is loaded with their cases and bundles. They nearly fall down on to the platform, which is offscreen.

A.27 EXT. CONTINENTAL RAILWAY SIDING. NIGHT (STUDIO)

(Possible travelling matte shot.)

On a noisy railway siding in CLOSE SHOT an unscreened acetylene lamp burning with a nasty hiss illuminates a desk on which a pair of hands, sticking out of the cuffs of a uniform, roughly fingers Maria's and Nora's passport. The two girls, in profile, are facing the MAN BEHIND THE DESK. MARIA, one arm round her exhausted sister's shoulder, tries to argue with the man, only to shut up when his hand closes to a fist and comes crashing down on the table. CAMERA PANS DOWN as a foot, in jackboots, kicks against their luggage and bundles. Maria's hand opens one of their cases. On top are their travelling provisions, and the kick has smashed a screw-top glass bottle whose contents, milk, are flowing over the clothes at the bottom of the case. A pair of child's ballet shoes are prominent.

A.28 INT. CONTINENTAL GOODS TRUCK. DAY (STUDIO)

In the corner of a goods truck, MARIA and NORA are herded together with other exiles heard offscreen, MARIA half-sitting to allow NORA more space for stretching out. The train starts with a jerk and NORA wakes up, her tired, frightened eyes looking up to MARIA.

A.29 INT. CONTINENTAL GOODS TRUCK. EXT. RAILWAY PLATFORM. DAY (STUDIO)

The doors of the truck slide open and CAMERA SHOOTS DOWN on to the platform. In shot foreground, Maria's hands holding two tin bowls and stretching out towards a Red Cross trolley which is rolled into shot. It is filled with bubbling thick soup. A white-coated RED CROSS WORKER ladles soup into Maria's tin cups.

A.30 INT. CONTINENTAL GOODS TRUCK. NIGHT (STUDIO)

Night in the same goods truck. NORA is asleep at last, MARIA is stiff with sitting so that NORA can lie comfortably. A shaft of light falls upon them as the heavy, sliding door of the truck is rolled back. NORA wakes up to stare at an ANGLED FACE with foreign forage-cap which shouts up to MARIA and other exiles. Timid hands offering passports enter the shot . . .

A.31 INT. CONTINENTAL GOODS SHED. DAY (STUDIO)

In a goods shed, MARIA, the sleeping NORA in one arm, opens her bundles which are on a ramp. UNIFORMED ARMS search them, one of them producing a pair of children's ballet shoes, another a photo album. A snapshot of a coastline with a fort is torn out, a large photo of a young man (LOUIS BALAN) is ignored. There is the sound of the loading and unloading of heavy consignments—the din is frightful.

A.32 ANOTHER DESK IN THE GOODS SHED. NIGHT (STUDIO)

At another desk, another PAIR OF HANDS with uniform cuffs turns over the pages of the photo album from which more snapshots are missing. The photo of the young man (LOUIS) is still there. A THIRD HAND passes a gramophone record across. The pair of hands takes it, holds it for a moment's examination, then breaks it across the desk's edge.

A.33 EXT. CHANNEL STEAMER. SIDE OF DECKHOUSE. DAY (STUDIO— TRAVELLING MATTE)

MARIA and NORA are seated against the deckhouse, their luggage beside them, their bodies moving with the rolling of the ship. There is the sound of big waves smashing against the hull. As a particularly big wave is heard, the image is lifted on the screen with the impact.

A.34 INT. ANSELMO'S LIVING ROOM. DAY (STUDIO)

The Camera's movement in the previous shot is linked to this shot by the CAMERA PANNING DOWN on to the couch. In absolute silence DALY is bending over the exhausted NORA, who is lying on the couch, wrapped in a blanket.

DALY (after a pause). *She'll be all right. In a day or two. You poor kids . . .*
CAMERA PANS UP. ANSELMO is looking at the luggage which MARIA has opened.
ANSELMO. *Dey lost everything. Look, Daly.*
DALY (turning to Maria). *I'll give you both a sedative.* (to Anselmo). *And then a good tonic . . . and plenty of milk. They need building up.*

A.35 ANSELMO, MARIA, DALY

ANSELMO is looking at the torn album of photographs. He points to the photograph of the young man (LOUIS BALAN).
ANSELMO. *This your boy friend?*
MARIA fingers a ring on her right hand.
MARIA. *Yes; Louis.*
ANSELMO. *You have this Louis. Why Pietro let you travel alone? Why Louis not come with you?*
MARIA (quite shocked).*Oh, no: my father needs him.*
ANSELMO. *He works for your father, eh?*
MARIA. *Oh, yes. My father is too well known. He knew the police would get him. He sent Louis into hiding to carry on the work. When we left home, father was waiting . . .*
ANSELMO. *That's Pietro for you!*
DALY, realising that MARIA has had enough, takes ANSELMO with him to the door. ANSELMO follows him, a look of extreme worry on his face as though expecting bad news.

A.36 INT. ANSELMO'S CAFE. DAY (STUDIO)

As the door closes behind them, ANSELMO faces DALY.
ANSELMO (anxiously). *What de matter? . . . Nora?*
DALY. *No. She'll be all right. It's high time we left them alone for a while.*

ANSELMO (relieved). *Sure, sure.* (Shouts down into café), *Penny, you come and help Maria! I take over downstairs.*
PENNY (coming up to them). *O.K. Pot of tea for two number three, jam sponge twice number five.*
PENNY enters the living room, while ANSELMO *hurries downstairs.*

A.37 ANSELMO, DALY, FRACK, PENNY (STUDIO)

ANSELMO and DALY come down the stairs into the café.
ANSELMO. *Thanks a lot, Daly.* (suddenly) *What am I going to do wid 'em?*
DALY (confidently). *You're doing it already . . . keep them, help them to settle down.*
They reach the counter where ANSELMO raises the flap and goes behind. He begins to make a small pot of tea. FRACK, an oily, ingratiating individual, is sitting quietly at the counter with a cup of tea and an evening paper.
ANSELMO. *Yes . . . you t'ink? How dey fit into da life of a café? I don' know . .*
DALY. *Two more for you to boss. I'll send over the sedative in a few minutes.*
He leaves the café. At the end of the counter near the door TWO CUSTOMERS are seated over cups of tea. One passes a betting slip to the other, FRACK watching. ANSELMO also sees them in the act as he carries the tea towards table number three.
ANSELMO (to two customers). *I've seen you before. I don' want to lose customers* (he points to a anti-betting notice on the wall behind the counter) *but this is a respectable place—eh?* (he nods his head).
FIRST CUSTOMER. *O.K. Guv'nor.*
The TWO CUSTOMERS leave. ANSELMO returns from the tables and goes behind the counter, where FRACK sniffs with a look of enquiry towards the kitchen.

A.38 ANSELMO, MARIA (STUDIO)

CAMERA IS SHOOTING along the counter towards kitchen, taking in the stairs. ANSELMO smells something burning. As he hurries into the kitchen, he calls in the direction of the stairs.
ANSELMO. *Penny—you dere?*
MARIA comes to the head of the stairs. She is beginning to lose some of her sadness.
MARIA. *Gone up—above—top?—My English! Gone up for bedding.*
MARIA sniffs the air and runs downstairs. ANSELMO reacts.
ANSELMO. *Something burning. In 'ere.*
ANSELMO dashes into the kitchen. MARIA follows him.

A.39 INT. ANSELMO'S CAFE. KITCHEN. DAY (STUDIO)

CAMERA IS SHOOTING back into the café. ANSELMO and MARIA rush in.
MARIA. *I do it, I do it!*
She opens the oven and handles the dish quite confidently. ANSELMO fusses around but MARIA does all the work.
ANSELMO. *Can you?*
MARIA. *I can cook! Go on, go back there; I do this.*
FRACK is leaning over the counter, watching. ANSELMO shakes his head and smiles with relief. He goes out.

A.40 INT. ANSELMO'S CAFE. DAY (STUDIO)

CAMERA SHOOTING towards kitchen. ANSELMO comes from the kitchen and addresses FRACK, who is still peering along the counter into the kitchen, intent on watching MARIA.
ANSELMO. *Cup o' tea, Mr. Frack?*
FRACK. *And why not? You didn't tell me you had a new waitress, Anselmo.*
ANSELMO. *Daughter of an old frien'.*
FRACK. *Foreign by the looks of her.*
ANSELMO. *She only just come. She not work 'ere.*

141

MARIA is at the table just inside the kitchen door.
MARIA. *Not work? I want to work.*
ANSELMO serves the cup of tea.
FRACK. *You'll have to go to the police first.*
MARIA (frightened). *Police? Why police?*
ANSELMO. *You have to register as an alien. You can't get a labour permit without.*
MARIA. *Always the police!*
ANSELMO. *Dey won't eat you—not in this country. Dey our friends.*
FRACK. *As long as you keep out of trouble.*
MARIA. *I must make money for Nora and me.*

A.41 INT. ANSELMO'S CAFE. KITCHEN. DAY (STUDIO)
ANSELMO comes back into kitchen to join MARIA, turning his back on FRACK.
ANSELMO. *Maria, forget da money. You need permission to stay 'ere.*
MARIA. *I get permission. Not for long—only until my father is free.*
FRACK leans over the counter in background.
FRACK. *They put 'er old man in quod?*
ANSELMO (anxiously). *You t'ink da new governments, dey come and go like leaves on da trees? You are young, optimist! But you must face facts. Your father, he not popular wit' da new government. General Galbern . . .*
MARIA. *General Galbern not touch him, he not dare. Too many people they love my father. My father works only for peace.*

A.42 PENNY, ANSELMO, MARIA (STUDIO)
A wider angle. PENNY enters and sees Maria's work on the cooking.
PENNY (gratefully). *Well, I never. I forgot all about it.*
She lifts down the parcel.
PENNY (to Maria). *This came a few days ago. It's for you.*
Eagerly MARIA tears the parcel open, CAMERA TRACKS IN to show that it contains a few of her father's belongings: fountain-pen, watch, family photo of them all in happier times, rosary, two sets of thick-lensed spectacles and a book entitled 'Mahatma Gandhi'.

A.43 ANSELMO, MARIA, PENNY (STUDIO)
A wider angle. MARIA, reading the note, breaks down. ANSELMO sends PENNY out into the café.
ANSELMO. *You and Nora stay with me. No man can be like Pietro, but I try. You can no go back, Maria.*
MARIA. *They killed him. Galbern killed him. My father—he hated violence and destruction.* (she takes up the pen) *He used to say, 'This is my sword!' And now they have killed him.* (more composed) *Nora—she must not know; not yet.*
ANSELMO. *My poor child, how can you . .* (i.e. keep up such a pretence with her).
MARIA. *Oh, I will pretend. I can be strong . . . But Louis—what happen to Louis?*
ANSELMO. *You will hear soon from him. Go upstairs now and lie down, my poor one. Dis is your home now.*
Taking the parcel with her, MARIA precedes ANSELMO out into the café.

A.44 INT. ANSELMO'S CAFE. DAY (STUDIO)
SHOOTING BACK towards kitchen. MARIA crosses to the stairs, followed solicitously by ANSELMO. FRACK is still lingering at the counter.
ANSELMO (continuing). *We go get a labour permit to-morrow.*
FRACK (insinuating). *A girl like you can get on without a permit. Without work, for that matter.*
MARIA, lost in grief, simply doesn't hear him, but ANSELMO does. He sends MARIA on her way and then rounds on FRACK.

ANSELMO. *Mr. Frack, if you speak like dat to her again, you no longer come to my café.*

FRACK (dangerously). *Just a minute, Anselmo. Didn't I see you give a glass of liquor to old Carlo the other night?*

ANSELMO. *It was 'is seventy birthday. I did no' ask for payment.*

FRACK. *Even so—you haven't a drink licence. Good-bye. See you to-night, maybe . . . see you any time I like.*

CAMERA PANS with FRACK as he passes PENNY on his way to the door.

PENNY. *What you need is a second-class hearse.*

FRACK (reaching the door). *That's a nice thing to say.*

A.45 INT. ANSELMO'S LIVING ROOM. DAY (STUDIO)

Carrying the parcel, MARIA opens the living room door quietly and makes for NORA in her improvised bed. The curtains of the room are drawn. The sight of Louis' photo arrests her. She looks at it and at the rosary, and lowers her head devoutly. Her field of vision fills with the label and its red crosses and next, as her glance strays, with Nora's improvised bed. MARIA enters shot, smiling now as she looks down at little NORA, who is fast asleep. Nora's ballet shoes are neatly placed on her little pile of belongings.

FADE OUT:

(END OF SEQUENCE 'A')

SEQUENCE 'B'

FADE IN:

B.1 INSERT AS IN SOLICITOR'S OFFICE. DAY (STUDIO)

MARIA'S VOICE (in good English). *I, Maria Brent, swear by Almighty God that I will be faithful and bear true allegiance to His Majesty, King George the Sixth, His Heirs and Successors, according to law.*

On a table in the office of a Commissioner for Oaths, the Royal Arms form the heading to a Certificate of Naturalisation. It bears the name of 'Maria Brent, formerly Maria Brentano'. Maria's hand, bearing Louis' ring, begins to sign the document, which is dated 1937 (June).

CAMERA PANS to Nora's Certificate lying close by, made out in the name of 'Eleanora Brent, formerly Eleanora Brentano'.

NORA'S VOICE (free of accent). *I, Eleanora Brent, swear by Almighty God that I will be faithful and bear true allegiance to His Majesty, King George the Sixth, His Heirs and Successors, according to law.*

B.2. EXT. CHANCERY LANE. SIDE STREET. DAY (LOCATION)

From a doorway plastered with nameplates, ANSELMO, MARIA and NORA emerge into a typical Chancery Lane side street full of the offices of Solicitors and Commissioners for Oaths. The girls are now 26 and 17 years old, respectively. NORA has grown into a gay wisp of a girl. ANSELMO pauses to give each girl a quick kiss.

ANSELMO. *Now you are British. You feel different, Nora?*

NORA. *I'll say! No more labour permits! Maria, I'll rush round and tell Mr. Burnett.*

ANSELMO. *What Burnett cares? He's only an agent.*

MARIA. *It'll make a difference, getting her jobs.*

A bus is approaching a request stop a few yards away and NORA hails it.

NORA. *He says I might get some cabaret work in the autumn.*

ANSELMO. *Cabaret work? What for?*

CAMERA PANS after NORA as she goes gaily skimming after the bus. As she jumps on, she calls back.

NORA. *Money! For more classes! For more cabaret work!*
MARIA. *And meanwhile she'll miss to-day's class! What a child!*
NORA is climbing to the top deck of the bus. As it pulls away we notice on the side of the bus, a poster advertising a Sunday paper's serial on the life of 'General Galbern, Strong Man of the South'. There is also a photo of him, smiling, bemedalled, martial to the tips of his moustache. NORA is waving out of the window exactly above Galbern's head.
The bus drives out of shot.

B.3 AND B.4 OUT:

B.5 ANSELMO, MARIA. DAY (LOCATION)
MARIA, her eyes on the poster, looks after the bus.
ANSELMO. *Ah, you don't 'ave to worry about 'im any more. Come and 'ave a drink.*
MARIA (her pleasure gone). *I've got my baking to do.*

B.6 INT. ANSELMO'S CAFE. DAY (STUDIO)
SHOOTING TOWARDS the kitchen. The café is crowded, for it is lunch time. CAMERA STARTS on a tray of eclairs which MARIA is carrying from the kitchen to the counter.
PENNY. *You've been working overtime! Now then, one at a time.*
MARIA. *My word, that kitchen's hot.*
ANSELMO. *Iced lemonade.*
He hands it to her.
HAIRDRESSER. *'Ere, let me buy that for 'er.*
ANSELMO. *It's on da house.*
HAIRDRESSER. *Smashing cook you are, Miss Brentano, if I may say so.*
ANSELMO. *No more Brentano. Brent's the name. Maria is British now—like me.*
DALY. *We can take it.*
A SHOE SHOP GIRL. *Now, isn't that nice?*
HAIRDRESSER. *We've got her for keeps, eh?*
They all shake hands with MARIA across the counter. MARIA is shyly delighted.
ANSELMO. *I don't know what I do wit'out 'er.*
MARIA smiles at him and retires to the kitchen.
PENNY (calling after her). *Two spaghetti meat sauce.*

B.7 INT. ANSELMO'S CAFE. KITCHEN. DAY (STUDIO)
MARIA goes to the stove and ladles out the spaghetti and meat sauce. ANSELMO enters to fetch piles of sandwiches from the refrigerator.
ANSELMO (aware of Maria's preoccupation). *Somet'ing on your mind, Maria. Why you not tell me?*
MARIA. *No, no. It's just . . . Everything's behindhand to-day.*
ANSELMO. *It's that picture of Galbern upset you—no?* (calls) *Awright, I come . .*
ANSELMO goes out with plates piled with sandwiches. CAMERA REMAINS on MARIA, who wipes her face and drinks her lemonade thirstily.
ANSELMO (offscreen). *Awright, awright! I prepare it for you special. You see!*
ANSELMO re-enters and sees MARIA.
ANSELMO. *It don' make me feel good, the way you go on working.*
MARIA. *I look after myself.*
ANSELMO. *No. You wrong. You look after Nora. You look after me. You look after the café. Then you look after Nora some more. What time have you left for yourself? Now, Maria—you have something on your mind; you tell me, eh?*
MARIA. *Oh, uncle—you've done everything for us . . . We owe you so much . . .*
ANSELMO. *No. You wrong again. You pay with your work. All the time the business improves. But you do too much; I feel guilty. So now you tell me— what is on your mind? It's da picture?*
PENNY (off). *Thick soup twice.*

144

MARIA. *No, no; but it's true, it set me thinking.*
ANSELMO. *Of your father?*
MARIA (eagerly). *He didn't mean me to do this—all my life. Uncle—Nora will soon be earning her own living. If I could find you someone, I could train her to take my place—then I could get a job where I could use my—my mind; I could teach perhaps, teach languages, or work on a paper or for a writer . . .*
ANSELMO. *But, Maria—you have been happy here?*
MARIA. *Oh, yes—happy. But my mind is getting lazy, I am forgetting my father, I am forgetting all he worked for. You're not angry?*
ANSELMO. *Angry? You speak like Pietro's daughter, you make me very proud. But you will not leave us, Maria, you don't want to go away?*
MARIA. *Oh, no, no.*
ANSELMO. *That's good. You and Nora stay here, live here wit' me; but soon you find a nice feller and settle down, eh?*
MARIA (brushing it off, laughing). *Nobody wants to settle down with me!*
ANSELMO. *Oh—oh! Plenty, I know. Maria—you should have a home of your own, a fine woman like you. 'Ave a husband and kids, eh?*
MARIA. *Now uncle! . . . (i.e. let's not have this all over again).*
ANSELMO. *Seven years you keep your love for a photograph! But, Maria—the photograph don't write: no flowers, no kisses, no fun wit' a photograph. No news of your Louis; but you know what happened to your father.*
MARIA is silent ANSELMO having said his piece, changes to liveliness.
ANSELMO. *Aw, listen. I been t'inking. Take your mind off! You know what da English like to do when dey take a 'oliday? Dey get da heck out of da country! You like dat, eh?*
MARIA *Oh—un-cle! . . . But what about the café?*
ANSELMO. *Penny manage. She get someone in. Just for da weekend.*
MARIA. *Oh! Where shall we go?*
ANSELMO who has been working up to it, pulls a prospectus, colourfully illustrated, out of his overall pocket. The prospectus advertises the 1937 Paris World Exhibition.
ANSELMO. *Dere! To Paris!*

B.8 INT. PASSPORT PHOTO STUDIO. DAY (STUDIO)
ANSELMO poses a little self-consciously. Effect of iris opening and closing as for time exposure.

B.9. MARIA. DAY (STUDIO)
MARIA poses, wistful and a little bewildered. Effect of iris opening and closing as for time exposure.

B.10. NORA. DAY (STUDIO)
NORA poses, eager and excited. Effect of iris opening and closing as for time exposure.

B.11. INSERTS. THREE PASSPORT PHOTOGRAPHS. DAY (STUDIO)
CAMERA ZIP PANS from photograph to photograph, revealing three dreadful reproductions of the facial expressions seen in B.8, B.9 and B.10.

B.12 to B.20 EXT. PARIS EXHIBITION MONTAGE. NIGHT AND DAY (STOCK AND STUDIO)
Sequence establishing the Parish Exhibition of 1937. To be worked out with existing material interspersed with shots of the three visitors.
The Paris World Exhibition at night, in a blaze of fireworks and illuminated fountains (Stock Shots, B.P.s, existing newsreel shots, etc.)
ANSELMO, MARIA and NORA are enjoying the sights . . .
An impression of the quiet of dawn in the Exhibition—the cleaning up of the night before.

145

L

Then the great show bursts into life again; stock shots of the rivalry of the pavilions, culminating in the antagonism of the Nazi and Communist statues opposing each other; of pottery-making, folk-dancing, weaving, land cultivation and other traditional crafts in the grounds and gardens of sundry pavilions. Public address loudspeakers are giving information in several languages (French, English, German, Spanish, Italian).

Whenever we see ANSELMO, he seems to be eating something different in the restaurants of the various countries. The two girls are secretly amused by his appetite.

B.21 EXT. SWISS PAVILION. DAY (STUDIO)

Anselmo's feet give him trouble. He is trying to drag the girls away from a demonstration of toy-making in the Swiss Pavilion grounds.

ANSELMO. *Have you not 'ad enough? I could sleep on a bed of nails!*

NORA. *Then let's go back to the Indian Pavilion.*

MARIA (laughing). *You're eating too much, uncle.*

ANSELMO (trance-like). *Ah, da shupchick carnatche in da Turkish restaurant, it was a dream—butterfly wings melting on your lips . . .*

NORA. *And the Madras curry at the Indian cooking lesson.*

MARIA. *And the fogosz in oil in the Hungarian Pavilion.*

NORA. *And the bottle of Tokay.*

ANSELMO (closing his eyes in rapture). *It was sweet and mild, like da Lacrima Christi.* (yawns). *I'd like a nice cup of tea now.* (more lively). *A cup of tea in da British Pavilion! Just da t'ing—after all, we are a British family!*

Two typical English visitors—a GUARDS TYPE and his FIANCEE—also watching the toy-making demonstration, look at them queerly.

B.22 EXT. BRITISH PAVILION. BUTTERY. DAY (STUDIO)

We get a glimpse of the outside of the British Pavilion Buttery just as an ex-serviceman COMMISSIONAIRE, in the typical uniform, shows three men (FRENCH SECURITY OFFICER, TWO BODYGUARDS) into the building.

CAMERA PULLS BACK to include STEENIE, a thin, hatchet-faced man, who is sitting at a table, smoking.

ANSELMO, MARIA and NORA enter and settle at a table nearer the Pavilion entrance. In doing so, they obscure Steenie's view of it, and he shifts a little in order to regain it.

Passing Anselmo's table, hands in the pockets of the trousers of his morning suit, is the British Pavilion MANAGER. The COMMISSIONAIRE comes out of the Pavilion entrance and makes for him.

STEENIE, throwing his half-smoked cigarette away, quickly puts a new one into his mouth and gets up.

While the COMMISSIONAIRE addresses the MANAGER, within earshot of Anselmo's table, STEENIE strolls over to them. Coming to a halt behind NORA and facing MARIA and ANSELMO, he strikes a match on the match-box holder on their table and lights his cigarette, standing quite still while he does so.

ANSELMO and MARIA react in obvious dislike at his rudeness.

COMMISSIONAIRE (to Manager). *Gentleman from the French Security Police to see you, sir. He's got two other gents with him.*

He accompanies the MANAGER to the Pavilion entrance.

STEENIE, ignoring Anselmo's and Maria's glances of dislike, moves off, out of shot, flicking the burnt-out match carelessly behind him so that it falls on, or near, MARIA.

ANSELMO (making a fist). *If I was not in a foreign country I would learn dis fellow a t'ing or two!*

MARIA puts a soothing hand on his fist.

MARIA (smiling). *'Teach,' uncle . . . teach!*

146

B.23 INT. BRITISH PAVILION. RECEPTION ROOM. DAY (STUDIO)

Standing in the room are a smallish, rotund official of the French Sureté, SECURITY OFFICER and TWO BODYGUARDS, tall, hook-nosed, martial-looking chaps who are in smart morning dress and quite obviously feeling very lost and uncomfortable in civilian dress. The MANAGER enters to them.

The four men are standing by a coffee table in the foreground. There are several modern armchairs round the table. When they sit, they put their hats on the table. The MANAGER offers cigarettes, the SECURITY OFFICER accepts, but the TWO BODYGUARDS refuse.

MANAGER. *Please sit down, gentlemen. Well . . . Who is the distinguished visitor this time?*

The French Official—a trifle flustered, opens his mouth, but before he can speak—

CHIEF BODYGUARD. *General Galbern presents his compliments, sir. His Excellency is passing through Paris and wishes to visit the British Pavilion.*

MANAGER (concealing his displeasure). *A great—pleasure. Oh, yes.*

SECOND BODYGUARD. *In ten minutes' time, sir.*

MANAGER. *Oh, dear, I'd like to tidy up the place a bit first.*

SECURITY OFFICER. *Please, monsieur. No unusual preparations. We don't want to—*

CHIEF BODYGUARD. *His Excellency has twelve minutes to spare. Ten minutes for the exhibits and two minutes for your greeting.*

MANAGER. *Two minutes is hardly enough for everything I'd like to say to His Excellency.*

CHIEF BODYGUARD. *You will warn your staff.*

MANAGER. *Oh, they're pretty spry. They know the ropes.*

CHIEF BODYGUARD. *No ropes. No public at all. It is our rule to close all buildings to the public for His Excellency's visits.*

SECURITY OFFICER (piqued). *Your rule? You seem to forget that you are in France, and . . .*

MANAGER (quickly). *My dear fellow, we couldn't do that. Infringing the catering licence, and so forth. There'd be an awful row.*

CHIEF BODYGUARD. *It is our rule.*

MANAGER. *Too late to get on to the Foreign Office now. I say, you couldn't drive the General round a bit while we sort this out?* (the Bodyguards look outraged) *No?*

SECURITY OFFICER. *You needn't be afraid of the public in this Pavilion, I assure you.*

CHIEF BODYGUARD. *His Excellency is never afraid.*

MANAGER. *Of course not, gentlemen. The less fuss, the less—I mean—just a private visit. Ten minutes. Most honoured.* (to himself) *Blimey ——*

SECURITY OFFICER. *Quite private.*

CHIEF BODYGUARD. *His Excellency is travelling incognito.*

B.24 EXT. BRITISH PAVILION. MAIN DOOR. DAY (STUDIO)

Three camions, packed with uniformed FRENCH POLICEMEN, draw up. They jump down and line the way up to the pavilion steps. Their arrival at once attracts the curiosity of exhibition visitors who are streaming towards the British Pavilion.

B.25 EXT. BRITISH PAVILION. BUTTERY. DAY (STUDIO)

On the pavement opposite the entrance to the British Pavilion, ANSELMO, MARIA and NORA pay their bill. The sound of motor cars and of the commotion outside the pavilion attracts their attention. They stand on their chairs and watch.

B.26 EXT. BRITISH PAVILION. MAIN DOOR. DAY (STUDIO)

Outside the main entrance, ordinary visitors press in behind two lines of French Policemen who are keeping a narrow passage free for the distinguished visitor (GENERAL GALBERN). The latter is as yet not visible, since he is surrounded by numerous BODYGUARDS, amongst whom we can just single out the TWO TALL FELLOWS (Bodyguards) we met in the Manager's office.

B.27 THE TWO BODYGUARDS. DAY (STUDIO)

The haughty manner of the TWO BODYGUARDS has gone. They are scared that something untoward may happen and their eyes never rest. If it hadn't been for them, the Pavilion MANAGER could never get through the bodyguard who are clustered around GALBERN like workers round a Queen Bee.

B.28 MANAGER, GALBERN. DAY (STUDIO)

The MANAGER shakes hands with GALBERN, who is an imposing man in a morning cutaway suit. The GENERAL smiles, nods, smiles, his eyes roving around for signs of any trouble. He talks to the MANAGER, who addresses him with formal courtesy.

B.29 GROUP SHOT. DAY (STUDIO)

PRESSMEN take photos, typical PLAIN CLOTHES MEN are searching the curious, seething crowd of ordinary visitors. A group of the General's COMPATRIOTS, led by a CHEER LEADER, stage a 'spontaneous' demonstration, shouting:
DEMONSTRATORS. *Gal-bern! Gal-bern! Galbern!*
The loudspeakers, ironically enough, radiate with insistent gaiety the music of Anselmo's favourite dance.

B.30 EXT. BRITISH PAVILION. BUTTERY. DAY (STUDIO)

ANSELMO, MARIA and NORA, standing on their chairs, watch the General's party.

B.31 EXT. BRITISH PAVILION. MAIN DOOR. DAY (STUDIO)

GALBERN, with the MANAGER at his elbow, looks towards them (Anselmo, Maria and Nora) before turning to enter the Pavilion.

B.32 EXT. BRITISH PAVILION. BUTTERY. DAY (STUDIO)

ANSELMO realises Maria's state of emotion and holds her arm. MARIA, in turn, puts her arm around the shoulders of NORA—it is an instinctive gesture of protection.
NORA. *Is he the man who killed father?*
MARIA. *Hush!*

B.33 EXT. BRITISH PAVILION. BUTTERY AND MAIN DOOR. DAY (STUDIO)

STEENIE is pushed towards them by the crowd of DEMONSTRATORS.

B.34 STEENIE, DEMONSTRATORS. DAY (STUDIO)

(From Anselmo's and Maria's point of view).
The DEMONSTRATORS jostle STEENIE.

B.35 ANSELMO, MARIA, NORA, DEMONSTRATORS. DAY (STUDIO)

MARIA and ANSELMO look after STEENIE, who moves with the DEMONSTRATORS. NORA is still staring after the General.
ANSELMO. *Come on, Maria, Nora!*
Maria's eyes return once more to the man responsible for her father's fate. She cannot take her eyes off him. ANSELMO has to drag her and NORA out. They leave, all their pleasure and excitement gone.

B.36 OUT:

B.37 EXT. BRITISH PAVILION AND TERRACE OF CAFE. DAY (STUDIO)

The crowd, attracted by the visit of the notorious Galbern, compels ANSELMO, MARIA and NORA to make a detour on their way.
This brings them towards the raised terrace of an outdoor café just beyond the British Pavilion, crowded with people wanting to get a view of General Galbern on his return.
As they reach the end of the terrace, a pair of hands appears over the low railings of the terrace and seizes one of Maria's hands—

Her free hand tries to sweep them aside, but it is seized, too. MARIA looks up angry and bewildered.

MARIA. *What . . . Let go of me!*

Suddenly her features grow rigid; she can no longer move.

B.38 EXT. TERRACE OF CAFE. DAY (STUDIO)

The man holding her, leaning down from the terrace above her, is LOUIS BALAN.

LOUIS. *Maria!*

B.29 MARIA. DAY (STUDIO)

Maria's eyes never leave him and she allows him to pull her up over the low wall, until she is standing before him.

B.40 MARIA, LOUIS, RODD, STEENIE. DAY (STUDIO)

MARIA and LOUIS stand on the terrace, facing one another, forgetful of the crowd, the music, the loudspeakers around them in this unexpected reunion.

LOUIS. *Maria!*

MARIA. *Louis! Is it you? Oh, Louis!*

LOUIS takes her hands, remembering them. He notices the traces of manual labour.

LOUIS. *Your lovely hands—my poor Maria!*

MARIA. *I'm a working woman. I've got Nora to bring up.*

LOUIS (smiling). *But your eyes will never change, Maria.*

MARIA ignores her awareness that he has changed.

MARIA (loyally). *And you, you haven't changed, Louis.*

LOUIS smiles and shakes his head.

LOUIS. *I wonder you could recognise me. Seven years—a lifetime!*

MARIA. *What is a lifetime—if we have not changed.*

B.41 & B.42 OUT:

B.43 NORA, ANSELMO, MARIA, LOUIS, STEENIE, RODD. DAY (STUDIO)

NORA and ANSELMO are fighting their way from behind the statue up to the terrace and push their way through towards them. As they approach MARIA turns to them.

MARIA. *Look who I've found!*

NORA looks puzzled.

LOUIS. *Why should they know me?*

NORA. *The photograph! It's Louis, uncle. It's Louis!*

ANSELMO. *The photograph! Louis! I am Anselmo Porri, uncle by adoption.*

LOUIS (still holding Maria's hands) *How do you do. And you must be Nora. I used to buy you ice cream! Remember me?*

NORA. *I remember the ice cream! Oh, this is lovely.*

ANSELMO looks in the direction of the table by LOUIS and recognises ——

B.44 THE GROUP. DAY (STUDIO)

STEENIE. The two men at Louis' table exchange glances in reaction to Nora's unrestrained voice. RODD strolls up, while STEENIE goes without a word. ANSELMO, recognising him, stares after him.

LOUIS. *This is Rodd Saunders. He flies stuff over for the exhibition.*

ANSELMO shakes RODD warmly by the hand.

ANSELMO. *I am pleased to meet you!*

LOUIS, once or twice, looks sharply at the nearest loudspeaker which keeps up the music of the dance. NORA, who is talking animatedly to RODD, pulls ANSELMO over to them so that MARIA and LOUIS can be more by themselves.

B.45 EXT. BRITISH PAVILION AND TERRACE OF CAFE. DAY (STUDIO)

MARIA, prominent in foreground of shot, is, against her will, compelled to look at the British Pavilion entrance, prominent in background, where GENERAL GALBERN is making his departure. Wanting to spare her the sight, LOUIS steps in front of her but MARIA looks over his shoulder.

MARIA. *He changed our lives, Louis.*

At this moment the loudspeaker music of the dance is broken off. Instead, we hear from it the sound of a scuffle and, almost in an instant, another voice.

LOUDSPEAKER VOICE. *A bas Galberni! Assassin! Galbern is a murderer!* (same in Italian, Spanish: repeat *ad lib* until, after another scuffle, the loudspeaker is switched off).

Louis' expression makes it clear that he had been waiting for this. He exchanges a glance of understanding with RODD.

B.46 EXT. BRITISH PAVILION. MAIN DOOR AND BUTTERY. DAY (STUDIO)

General Galbern's departure is a very hurried one. The police are pushing crowds of demonstrators and counter-demonstrators out of the way to allow his fleet of cars passage.

B.47 EXT. TERRACE OF CAFE. DAY (STUDIO)

The clamour dies down, MARIA having looked after Galbern's car with blazing eyes, turn back to LOUIS. She finds his eyes on her. The expression in them tells her everything.

MARIA. *Louis! That's some of your work, isn't it?*

LOUIS. *Window dressing, we call it.*

MARIA. *What do you mean?*

LOUIS. *It keeps the public on their toes.* (with irony) *It tickles Galbern's vanity; but that can't be helped.*

His gesture tells her to be silent. Of the other group only NORA, who stands with her back to MARIA, has heard what he said. She looks at LOUIS with admiration.

B.48 ANSELMO, RODD, NORA, MARIA, LOUIS. DAY (STUDIO)

ANSELMO speaks to RODD and LOUIS as they move towards the table.

ANSELMO. *Dis your table? Let's have somet'in.*

NORA. *Uncle! You'll explode.*

LOUIS looks at his watch.

LOUIS (hesitantly). *Maria . . .*

ANSELMO reads his thoughts.

ANSELMO. *Yes, Take 'er, take 'er. But bring 'er back safe. We 'ave to go home to London to-morrow.*

LOUIS. *Rodd, you show Nora around.*

NORA. *I want to do a parachute jump.*

MARIA (alarmed, yet smiling). *You won't let her?*

RODD. *What, me? I never could stand heights!*

ANSELMO. *I take my siesta. And we all meet 'ere for dinner.*

NORA thrusts an enormous menu card at him.

ANSELMO. *Perfect. Now I 'ave a nice lunch.*

RODD. *What about the "Vieux Chapeau", Louis?*

NORA. *What's that? Dancing?*

RODD nods his head.

LOUIS. *We'll meet there about ten o'clock. After dinner—*

LOUIS touches MARIA'S arm; she gives him a friendly look. He links his arm in hers. It is as if seven years have fallen away.

They move out of shot as ANSELMO speaks.

ANSELMO. *You got a friend with you, Mr. Rodd?*

RODD. *No.*

ANSELMO. *I t'ought I saw someone—*

RODD. *Oh, that was just a chap who had some business with Louis. No one special*

ANSELMO shrugs his shoulders.

B.49 OUT:

B.50 INT. FRENCH TAXI. DAY (B.P.)

As the taxi drives off, LOUIS takes a packet of cigarettes from his pocket, removes two, lights them both in his mouth, and hands her one with a smile. It is an old custom. While he is dealing with the cigarettes, MARIA takes two of a spray of white roses and puts one in his buttonhole and one in hers. They kiss and sit back, smoking.

LOUIS, *Mind if we go back to my lodgings? I have to be on tap for messages.*

MARIA. *You're still carrying on with father's work?*

LOUIS. *I do what I can. Officially, for a living, I'm a journalist. Oh, it's a very small living. On a very small paper.*

MARIA. *Isn't your life dangerous, Louis?*

LOUIS. *I'm not allowed to take risks.*

MARIA. *But who gives you orders?*

LOUIS. *I am a small cog in a big wheel, Maria. I have trained myself. I have become—I think—an expert.*

MARIA. *And all this long time—have you thought of me, Louis? Sometimes?*

LOUIS. *Always.*

MARIA. *You never wrote to me.*

LOUIS. *I was afraid to implicate you. Everything is watched. We haven't been living in public, you know.*

MARIA (anxiously). *Will you have to go back?*

LOUIS. *Some day. Don't let's worry about it now.*

B.51 INT. LOUIS' LODGINGS IN PARIS. DAY (STUDIO)

LOUIS is cooking at a gas-stove in a tiny primitive kitchen, opening off a bed-sitting room.

LOUIS. *The professional touch! You never saw such a dish of prawns. I could earn my living as a chef.*

MARIA. *I do earn my living as a chef!*

LOUIS is staggered.

LOUIS. *You cook for a living?*

MARIA (laughing). *I never stop! I cook all the specialities for Anselmo's café.*

LOUIS. *Oh, Maria. And here am I showing off to you about my prawns.*

MARIA is very gay.

MARIA. *It's been wonderful—watching you do everything all wrong. And so pleased with yourself.*

LOUIS. *But the effect!*

The telephone rings.

MARIA. *There's your phone call. Tell him you're busy all day.*

LOUIS goes behind her. He kisses the nape of her neck. CAMERA TRACKS BACK before him.

LOUIS goes to the telephone on the dresser in the main room.

LOUIS. *Gregor speaking. I'm just back from it. Yes, it came over very well. Well—he didn't enjoy it. He's left already? Ah—yes, to-night at eleven. It's all arranged. I understand. Yes—very well. I've got it quite clear.*

MARIA is serving up the dish of fried prawns. She indicates to LOUIS 'to hurry', and carries the dish past him.

LOUIS. *Good-bye.*

On the table, which MARIA has made look attractive in spite of battered crocks, are the roses in a jug of water. The salad is on the dresser beyond the telephone.

MARIA. *Bring the salad, Gregor. How long is it since anyone called you Louis?*

LOUIS forces himself back into the mood of the day.

LOUIS. *Not since the last time we mixed a salad.*

He tastes the salad dressing appreciatively.

151

MARIA. *With Marco interfering all the time. Do you still see Marco?*
LOUIS answers abruptly, not wishing to pursue the subject.
LOUIS. *No. I don't see him.*
MARIA (with an amused smile). *Dear Marco! He was such a charming person.*
LOUIS. *No.*
MARIA. *Ah—I wondered how he would fit in with your hard life . . .*
LOUIS. *He didn't fit in. He's dead, Maria.*
MARIA. *He's dead? Marco?*
LOUIS. *Don't let's talk about that life, Maria. We have such a short time.*
MARIA. *I wonder . . . I might stay on for a little while.*
LOUIS. *I have to leave Paris to-morrow. That's what the telephone call was about.*
MARIA. *Perhaps you will come to London some day?*
LOUIS. *I don't know. I am not my own master. Let's just enjoy to-day. We must have it to remember. We must have a wonderful day.*
They kiss.
B.52 OUT:
B.53 INT. "VIEUX CHAPEAU". NIGHT (STUDIO)
MARIA and LOUIS are dancing to a foxtrot.
MARIA. *What a wonderful day!*
LOUIS (smiling). *What a terrible partner! I've forgotten how to dance.*
MARIA. *I don't want any better partner, Louis.*
LOUIS. *Let's ask them to play a tango?*
MARIA. *A tango! Of course. You remember our tangos, Louis?*
LOUIS. *I remember.*
As they pass the band, LOUIS addresses the BAND LEADER.
LOUIS. *Monsieur! Un tango, s'il vous plaît?*
BAND LEADER. *Oui, bien sur. Avec plaisir.*
The Band changes to a tango. The LEADER bows towards MARIA.
MARIA. *Now Louis is in his element.*
By the side of a column, in its shadow, someone stands watching them. It is STEENIE. He looks at his wrist-watch and then in Louis' direction.
B.54 LOUIS, MARIA, DANCERS. NIGHT (STUDIO)
LOUIS looks over Maria's shoulders at his wrist-watch and then surreptitiously about him. Then he recognises someone.
B.55 STEENIE. NIGHT (STUDIO)
STEENIE, watching him, points at his wrist-watch.
B.56 LOUIS, MARIA, BAND AND LEADER, STEENIE, PHOTOGRAPHER, DANCERS. NIGHT (STUDIO)
LOUIS' concentration thus centred, he becomes obviously *distrait* and almost forgets to dance. MARIA is teasingly reproachful.
MARIA. *Louis! Remember me?*
LOUIS starts back to awareness.
LOUIS. *I'm sorry, Maria. Come, I'll get you a drink.*
MARIA. *No, no, but you must keep your mind on your dancing.*
He gives in but dances past the Band, giving a slight nod to STEENIE. MARIA is smiling her thanks to the BAND LEADER and notices nothing else. When LOUIS and MARIA have danced past him, STEENIE checks his watch.
A flashlight PHOTOGRAPHER takes a souvenir photo of a group at a table.
B.57 LOUIS, MARIA, STEENIE, MEMBERS OF BAND, DANCERS. NIGHT (STUDIO)
LOUIS, turning MARIA in the dance, sees STEENIE move towards the exit, then pays attention to MARIA again.

152

B.58 ANSELMO, GIRL STUDENT, BAR GIRL, STEENIE, DANCERS, CROWD IN BAR. NIGHT (STUDIO)

ANSELMO, arm in arm with an attractive STUDENT GIRL, walks off the dance floor towards the bar. About to order a drink, someone passes them on his way out. ANSELMO recognises the man as STEENIE. The BAR GIRL waits for his order. The GIRL STUDENT waits, too.

STUDENT GIRL. *Tiens, papa!*

ANSELMO (coming to). *Pardon, ma petite. Qu'est-ce qu'on prend?*

B.59 INT. CAFE ON STREET CORNER. NIGHT (STUDIO)

CAMERA SHOOTING out towards street. The large awning is brightly lit, cobbled surface of street less brightly. Darkness beyond. TWO MEN and a WOMAN are sitting at a table in foreground. They nudge each other as STEENIE walks past, lit from the café. He nods to them as he goes.

B.60 INT. "VIEUX CHAPEAU". NIGHT (STUDIO)

MARIA in LOUIS' arms, dancing . . . He stops dancing.

LOUIS. *Will you forgive me, Maria?*

MARIA. *You have to go now?*

LOUIS. *For a short while. I shan't be long.*

RODD (cutting in). *May I?*

He sweeps MARIA away before she can answer.

LOUIS moves away. MARIA looks after him, over RODD's shoulder, as he passes the bar.

B.61 ANSELMO, GIRL STUDENT, BARMAID, LOUIS, CLOAKROOM ATTENDANT, DANCERS, CUSTOMERS AT BAR. NIGHT (STUDIO)

CAMERA SHOOTING ACROSS bar, with ANSELMO and GIRL in foreground. ANSELMO and the STUDENT GIRL are sipping their brandies and playing poker dice with the BAR-MAID. ANSELMO notices LOUIS leaving. Again he grows pensive.

BARMAID. *C'est à ton tour, papa.*

ANSELMO, shaking the dice, throws them, still looking after LOUIS, who passes the cloakroom without claiming his hat, which the ATTENDANT has ready for him.

B.62 EXT. CAFE ON STREET CORNER. NIGHT (STUDIO)

CAMERA SHOOTING from café out towards street. Some heavy lorries are passing along the street; only their wheels are visible in the light from the café. LOUIS enters and sits down at the table with the TWO MEN and the WOMAN.

WOMAN. *He went by some time ago. What is keeping him?*

LOUIS. *Steenie doesn't waste time.*

B.63 EXT. QUAY ON THE SEINE. NIGHT (STUDIO)

CAMERA SHOOTING on to the quay under a road bridge crossing the Seine, with Notre Dame in background. STEENIE is standing with a cynical YOUNG MAN (VALET) of the Mediterranean type. He has the dark clothes and regular features of a valet in a well-to-do establishment. His face is sweaty and has an alcoholic air. He is holding a sheet of paper with typewriting on it in one hand, and is holding out the other hand for money. STEENIE reluctantly pays him in hundred franc notes.

The VALET watches them, then lets STEENIE take the document, thrusts the notes unsteadily into his pocket, raises his hat insolently and walks away, lurching and steadying himself against the wall of the archway that supports the bridge. As he stands there he begins singing.

STEENIE watches him. The heavy lorries are heard rumbling up over the bridge. The VALET turns, sees STEENIE and waves him away.

B.64 STEENIE, VALET. NIGHT (STUDIO)

STEENIE goes to the VALET, pulls him upright on his feet and lets him go. The VALET loses his balance, staggers and turns on STEENIE aggressively. STEENIE pushes

153

him towards the edge of the quay, looks up and down the river, sees nothing and hears only the lorries.

B.65 STEENIE. NIGHT (STUDIO)

A CLOSE UP of Steenie's face with an expression of complete competence.

B.66 STEENIE, VALET. NIGHT (STUDIO)

A CLOSE UP of the outer edge of Steenie's hand hitting the valet's neck from behind.

B.67 STEENIE, VALET. NIGHT (STUDIO)

As the body slumps, Steenie's hand pulls a bundle of bank notes out of the man's pocket. In the background below is the river.

B.68 STEENIE, VALET. NIGHT (STUDIO)

Steenie's face is in the picture and he pushes the body from him. A loud splash as the body hits the water comes above the sound of the lorries travelling over the bridge.

DISSOLVE:

B.69 INT. CAFE ON STREET CORNER. NIGHT (STUDIO)

STEENIE is sitting with LOUIS and the others outside the bistro. LOUIS is fingering the paper money. The TWO MEN make quiet comments to each other in French.

> WOMAN (apprehensively). *It's a favourite place for fishing. They may find the body.*
> STEENIE (hurt). *What would you have done? He was noisy drunk. He might have blabbed.*
> LOUIS (to both of them, with authority). *That's enough. This is what we needed.*
> WOMAN. *But he was our only contact at the Embassy!*
> LOUIS. *I'm sorry. You'll have to find somebody else, someone more reliable.* (to Steenie) *You'd better have this cash back. You leave for London to-morrow morning. Via Newhaven.*
> STEENIE. *What'll I do when I get there?*
> LOUIS. *You'll be met at the station.* (turns to the woman) *Will you warn the London committee?*
> WOMAN. *Of course.*
> LOUIS. *So long, Steenie. Don't talk in your sleep. And keep your hands in your pockets till I tell you to use them.*

STEENIE goes.

> LOUIS (looking at folded sheet). *If this is true, Galbern will be in London three days. And no public functions . . . But there's a private party on the third evening; that's our chance. Evening dress, dinner and cabaret.*
> SECOND MAN. *It'll be very exclusive.*
> LOUIS. *We'll get in somehow. We must.*
> WOMAN. *You'll have to get into England first.*
> LOUIS. *That's a simple matter.*

B.70 INT. "VIEUX CHAPEAU". NIGHT (STUDIO)

CAMERA STARTS on a CLOSE UP of RODD, in civil pilot's uniform, dancing with NORA in the "Vieux Chapeau". Now and then NORA, completely carried away by the atmosphere, dances away from RODD only to drift back into his arms. The other dancers comment on her skill with undisguised admiration.

> FRENCH GIRL (dancing, to her partner). *Elle s'y connait, la petite anglaise.*

B.71 RODD, NORA, MARIA, ANSELMO, STUDENT GIRL, LOUIS, DANCERS. NIGHT (STUDIO)

CAMERA STARTS on MARIA, who is alone at a table, as RODD and NORA dance past. MARIA is laughing as ANSELMO and his STUDENT GIRL, carrying glasses and a magnum of champagne, manage to pass NORA and RODD two filled glasses. This done, ANSELMO

154

looks round for MARIA. Seeing her alone, he makes for her, followed by the STUDENT
GIRL.
We travel closer to them while they are drinking. When quite close we see ANSELMO
looking out of shot. For a moment, his exuberance gives way to thoughtfulness . . .
LOUIS enters shot. He appears preoccupied. The STUDENT GIRL puts another glass
down and, filling it, winks at ANSELMO meaning 'They want to be alone'. They
leave.
LOUIS takes the glass of champagne which MARIA hands him. MARIA drinks and LOUIS
takes her hand.
> MARIA (concerned). *Is something wrong?*
> LOUIS. *Not really.*
> MARIA. *My poor Louis.*
In the background other dancers are leaving the floor to give NORA and RODD more
space. Some start clapping rhythmically and all the others join in. RODD leaves the
floor to let NORA dance on alone in an improvisation of her own, dictated by her
happy mood.

B.72 LOUIS, MARIA, NORA. NIGHT (STUDIO)

LOUIS and MARIA are watching NORA. Maria's hand is in his. He is smiling at NORA
as she dances past. The smile dies—returns once more.
> LOUIS. *Well—look at our Nora! She's good.*
> MARIA. *They're right—she'd do well in cabaret.*
LOUIS catches at the last word, which fits in with something he has heard earlier
to-night.
> LOUIS. *Cabaret? Is she a professional?*
> MARIA. *Oh, yes. It's her whole life. 'My dancing . . .' 'My classes . . .' 'My
> agent . . .'*
MARIA watches NORA dancing. After a pause—
> LOUIS (casually). *She has an agent?*
> MARIA. *Yes, A man called Sid Burnett. He's very go-ahead.*
LOUIS registers the name. MARIA continues to watch NORA. There is a bright flash
of a photographer's bulb. LOUIS jumps and makes a rapid movement of his head.
The blurred image freezes to a still photo . . .

(END OF SEQUENCE 'B')

SEQUENCE 'C'

C.1 INT. ANSELMO'S LIVING ROOM. DAY (STUDIO)

The still photograph taken in the Cabaret fills the screen. ANSELMO, PENNY, MARIA
are heard laughing. CAMERA PULLS BACK as Maria's finger points at the blurred
image of LOUIS.
> MARIA (laughing). *And that's Louis! He nearly jumped out of his skin.*
> PENNY. *What a shame!* (looking at Louis' photo on the wall). *Has he changed
> much?*
> MARIA. *It's seven years. But that's the only difference.*
ANSELMO, in background, a little dubious . . . The café bell rings. PENNY snatches
up a pirate cap.
> PENNY. *I'll go.* (hurries out). *Thanks for the present.*

C.2 MARIA, ANSELMO (STUDIO)

> MARIA. *It was a wonderful week-end, uncle.*
His eyes look away from her.
> MARIA. *You liked Louis, didn't you?*
> ANSELMO (pretending surprise). *What you say? Of course I liked him! Why*

not? (after a glance at Nora) *Young Rodd, he was a nice fellow.*
MARIA (smiling). *All Louis' friends must be nice.*
ANSELMO. *Dat ot'er fellow wasn't so nice.*
MARIA. *Which fellow?*
ANSELMO. *Da man who took a match at our table.*
MARIA (startled). *That man. What's he got to do with Louis?*
ANSELMO. *I don' know. But he was dere, wit' Rodd on da terrace. He sneak away, but he was dere. And he was also in da "Vieux Chapeau". He and Louis, dey make signs wit' da eyes.*
MARIA. *Oh, nonsense, uncle!*

C.3 ANSELMO, MARIA, PENNY (STUDIO)
PENNY runs into the room, carrying a bunch of white roses which she hands to MARIA, smiling breathlessly.
MARIA. *For me? Who sent them?*
PENNY. *Who brought them, you mean. He's here!*
MARIA. *Louis!*
MARIA rushes out.
PENNY. *Hasn't wasted any time, has he?*
ANSELMO. *He must have flown here.*

C.4 INT. ANSELMO'S CAFE. DAY (STUDIO)
CAMERA SHOOTING from the window. FRACK, seated at a table in the foreground, is trying to converse with LOUIS. LOUIS is uneasy and pays no attention.
FRACK. *There's never any grumbling here since Maria came. Anselmo's got a tidy sum tucked away, you can bet! Why, he was only telling me the other day . .*
LOUIS rises from his seat as he sees MARIA coming down the stairs. She stops by the kitchen door as LOUIS comes up to her.

C.5 INT. ANSELMO'S CAFE. KITCHEN. DAY (STUDIO)
CAMERA SHOOTING from kitchen towards café as MARIA welcomes LOUIS with a delighted smile and leads him into the kitchen. Once inside, they take each other's hands, MARIA closing the door. Then they embrace.
PENNY (off). *Look what they brought me! A Pirate's cap—Paris.*
FRACK (off). *You going to wear that in bed?*
PENNY (off). *You'll never know!*
FRACK (off). *Where's the skull and crossbones?*
PENNY (off). *Keeping 'em for the stew.*
Meanwhile, at the end of the embrace ——
LOUIS. *I couldn't wait.*
MARIA (delightedly). *You'll stay?*
LOUIS. *A few days.*
They look at each other and then embrace. The telephone rings upstairs. MARIA ignores it. LOUIS looks up in the direction of the sound.

C.6 to C.17 OUT:
C.18 INT. ANSELMO'S CAFE. DAY (STUDIO)
CAMERA SHOOTING TOWARDS Public Telephone on first floor landing as NORA answers the phone. She listens with growing excitement. ANSELMO comes downstairs from the second floor.
NORA (into telephone). *Yes, of course . . . But me? Oh, thank you, Mr. Burnett. Yes, I can, right away. All right, I'll bring her. Yes, we'll be there in no time . . .*
She bangs down the receiver and rushes into the living-room.

C.19 INT. LIVING-ROOM AND BEDROOM. DAY (STUDIO)
NORA runs through the living-room into the bedroom (which was formerly Anselmo's) pulls open a cupboard, takes out her practice dress and dancing shoes and stuffs them into a small suitcase. ANSELMO follows her.

156

ANSELMO. *What now? What you doing?*
NORA. *Mr. Burnett rang up. An audition.*
ANSELMO. *Audition? What audition?*
NORA. *Oh, I can't tell you now . . . For a solo. Something terrific. Good-bye.*
She hurries out and is heard running downstairs.
ANSELMO. *Well, all right. Good luck, Nora. Don't get run over now, take care . . .*

C.20 INT. ANSELMO'S CAFE. DAY (STUDIO)
CAMERA SHOOTING on stairs from behind counter. NORA enters café looking around for
MARIA.
PENNY. Now *what's the excitement?*
NORA. *Where's Maria?*
PENNY. *In there.*
NORA looks at the kitchen door, opens it.

C.21 INT. ANSELMO'S CAFE. KITCHEN. DAY (STUDIO)
NORA enters kitchen. LOUIS is there with MARIA.
NORA. *Ma—Louis!*
MARIA enjoys her sister's surprise. NORA hugs them both, but she is a tiny bit
deflated because she wants Maria's help and now LOUIS is here.
NORA. *Mr. Burnett's rung up . . . And he thinks he's got a job for me, a cabaret
turn at some terrific party. I've got to go and do an audition for Mrs.—Mrs.
Reginald Kellick or some such name. It's all being got up in a terrific rush.
They're having two singers from Covent Garden—and Pantorello the Clown! And
me! If I'm available. Oh, gosh, it's—it's . . .*
MARIA (laughing at her). *It's terrific!*
NORA. *Yes, but—Maria, Mr. Burnett wants you to come with me and help me
through, and we must go now, this minute.*
MARIA. *Oh, Louis . . . ?*
LOUIS. *Of course you must go.*
NORA. *Only for an hour. Maria, be quick, darling!*
LOUIS. *I'm so glad, Nora. Good luck!*
MARIA. *Meet us afterwards?*
NORA (to Louis). *Oh, yes. 21 Smith Street. An hour from now.*
PENNY enters from behind the counter with coffee for LOUIS.
PENNY. *O.K. Maria. We can manage.* (to Louis) *I've made it specially.*
MARIA goes, unfastening her overall.
LOUIS (tasting coffee). *London girl makes good coffee! What a headline!*
PENNY (thrilled). *Oh, Mr. Louis!*
NORA. *Get us a taxi, Penny!*
PENNY. *Taxi, indeed. Get it yourself, my lady! I'm not Maria.* (weakening). *Oh,
all right, just this once.*
She runs out through the café into the street, leaving NORA and LOUIS alone.
LOUIS. *Am I going to be allowed some of Maria's time?*
NORA. *When I've done with her. You're not on holiday, are you?*
LOUIS. *No.*
NORA. *What have you come to write about?*
LOUIS. *Would you like me to write about you?*
NORA. *Why not? I'll let you have a lot more of Maria's time if you do. There's
something up, isn't there?*
LOUIS. *One thing at a time. You dance well this afternoon—then maybe I will
see.*
NORA. *Oh! Louis. I'm sure I'm going to be sick.*

C.22 INT. ANSELMO'S CAFE. DAY (STUDIO)
CAMERA, SHOOTING from alley side of café, starts on MARIA hurrying downstairs,

followed by ANSELMO, who still registers a certain amount of shock, having heard of Louis' arrival.

MARIA. *Nora—have you got your music?*

NORA indicates the portfolio under her arm with a triumphant little laugh.

MARIA (also laughing). *It's a miracle!*

LOUIS. *Good luck, Nora!*

PENNY. *Goodbye, ducks: set 'em alight!*

MARIA waves to LOUIS. PENNY continues with her work, leaving ANSELMO and LOUIS near the kitchen.

C.23 ANSELMO AND LOUIS (STUDIO)

LOUIS turns to ANSELMO.

LOUIS. *Well, sir, none the worse for the trip, I hope.*

He shakes Anselmo's hand.

ANSELMO (haltingly). *You come quick, very quick. I am glad to see you. So you are a journalist now, Maria tell me, Mr. Balan.*

LOUIS (nodding). *Louis to you.*

ANSELMO (feeling his way). *You very busy?*

LOUIS. *Yes. Plenty happening.*

ANSELMO. *Maria—she is a fine young woman, but—I t'ink she is love wit' you still. Don't get her mixed up in anything, eh? No politics.*

LOUIS. *Maria and I understand one another.*

ANSELMO. *It is good. I trust you.*

LOUIS. *Her father did.*

ANSELMO grips his hand firmly. LOUIS, having finished his coffee, walks to the door, CAMERA PANNING, ANSELMO follows.

LOUIS (to Penny). *How much for the coffee?*

PENNY. *It's on the house, Mr. Louis!*

ANSELMO. *Dat's right—it's on da house.*

DISSOLVE:

C.24 INT. CLARK'S REHEARSAL ROOMS. DAY (STUDIO)

At the far end of a large, bare room with a low ceiling, NORA, in a practice costume, is getting ready to dance. MARIA is holding Nora's coat and briefing the PIANIST, who sits studying the music at a tinny upright. A door opening and voices from behind CAMERA cause the group to turn sharply and look.

C.25 SONIA DE BLAISE, SID BURNETT (STUDIO)

SID BURNETT, a theatrical agent of 32, leads the way into the rehearsal room, followed by THE HON. MRS. REGINALD KELLICK (SONIA DE BLAISE), a former musical comedy actress now married into the peerage. She is in a smart summer outfit with an elaborate hat, and a large string of pearls. She pauses inside the room and surveys the scene.

BURNETT. *This is the—er—rehearsal room. I'm afraid it's not very nice in here, but—er . . .*

SONIA. *My dear, I'm only too thankful to see the girl anywhere. Can you imagine!—three days' notice—a party on this scale!* (curiously) *You didn't waste any time, producing your candidate.*

BURNETT (smugly). *A little bird told me. If you'd care to take a seat . . .?*

SONIA. *You'll have to lead the way. I can't see a yard.*

They advance towards two lonely plain chairs in the middle of the room.

C.26 BURNETT, SONIA (STUDIO)

Reaching the chairs, BURNETT flicks one chair with a handkerchief.

BURNETT. *Allow me, Mrs.—er . . .*

SONIA. *Oh, good heavens, a little dust won't kill me.* (she sits down and peers through the gloom). *Who's the other gal?*

SONIA has taken out her lorgnette and looks at the group. In the background, a mysterious head can be seen framed in the glass panel of the door leading into the rehearsal room—a head of someone outside looking in. SONIA and BURNETT mutter in undertones while the PIANIST strums a few light chords.

    BURNETT. *Her sister; come to give her moral support.*

    SONIA. *Really? I didn't get much of that when I was starting on the stage.*

She giggles reminiscently, then goes straight on.

    SONIA (continuing). *Let's hope she can dance—can't they start?*

    BURNETT (calling). *Start, please, Miss Brent.*

The music begins in earnest.

C.27 SONIA (STUDIO)

    SONIA (to herself). *The last one was so embarrassing . . .*

C.28 NORA (STUDIO)

NORA gulps and picks up her music cue. She swirls away into the dance, CAMERA TRACKING BACK with her . . .

C.29 MARIA (STUDIO)

Pride and anxiety mingled in Maria's face as she watches her sister.

C.30 SONIA AND BURNETT (STUDIO)

The face of SONIA is immobile behind her lorgnette. BURNETT glances to see her reaction. Seeing none, he glances back anxiously at the dance.

C.31 GROUP SHOT (STUDIO)

NORA is dancing with her heart and soul, oblivious of her small, odd audience.

C.32 INT. CORRIDOR OUTSIDE CLARK'S REHEARSAL ROOMS. DAY (STUDIO)

SHOOTING THROUGH the glass panel into the rehearsal room from outside. LOUIS is a big head in foreground, peering through the panel at the dance which can be distantly seen. Without taking his eyes off the panel, he lights a cigarette.

C.33 INT. CLARK'S REHEARSAL ROOMS, DAY (STUDIO)

Without taking her eyes off NORA, SONIA addresses BURNETT.

    SONIA (impressed). *She's really rather enchanting, you know.*

C.34 BURNETT, SONIA (STUDIO)

    BURNETT (pleased). *Well—I've thought so myself ever since I found her. She's—er—just back from Paris, actually.*

    SONIA. *Paris? Is she? Well, of course, Doris Welbury does love it if she can discover some little, unknown dancer . . .*

    BURNETT. *You mean, if you can discover . . .*

    SONIA (still looking at Nora). *I merely advise her, Mr. Burnett. Tell the child to stop. She can finish the dance at Lady Welbury's party. It's a deal.*

She puts up her lorgnette and rises.

    BURNETT (to Nora). *O.K. That'll do.*

The music stops.

    SONIA (shouting to Nora). *Very pretty—thank you, my dear. I hear you've just done a season in Paris?*

NORA opens her mouth to explain, but SONIA, without waiting for an answer, is sweeping off towards the exit.

    SONIA (continues to Burnett). *Ring me about nine in the morning and we'll settle the details. Now I must fly. I've an appointment with my masseur, and he's so fierce if I'm late.*

She sweeps out, followed by BURNETT—leaving NORA and MARIA standing rather bewildered.

C.35 INT. CORRIDOR OUTSIDE CLARK'S REHEARSAL ROOMS. DAY (STUDIO)

SONIA sweeps out, not noticing LOUIS, who makes himself unobtrusive. She disappears up the stairs. When she is out of sight, CAMERA PANS to LOUIS and BURNETT, who converse quietly just outside the glass panelled door.

LOUIS. *I'm very grateful.*

BURNETT. *Always glad to oblige a gentleman of the Press.*

LOUIS. *And Maria goes too?*

BURNETT. *Yes, I'll fix that.*

LOUIS. *You won't mention my name?*

BURNETT. *Not a word. Don't worry.*

LOUIS walks off swiftly up the stairs and away. BURNETT stands there for a moment. Then, with a bewildered shrug, he pushes open the glass-panelled door and calls into the rehearsal room to NORA and MARIA.

BURNETT. *It's in the bag, girls. See you upstairs when you're ready.*

Then he goes off in a leisurely manner up the stairs.

In the rehearsal room, NORA makes a great gesture of excitement and spins round in a circle, snatching up her coat and scarf, etc.

C.36 EXT. SOHO STREET OUTSIDE REHEARSAL ROOMS. DAY (LOCATION)

In C.U., LOUIS comes out of a public house and walks over to MARIA, who runs to meet him with delight.

LOUIS. *I don't have to ask . . .*

MARIA. *She's got the job. Isn't it lovely?*

LOUIS. *I'm so glad.*

MARIA. *Nora's thrilled. And it may be the beginning, at last.*

LOUIS. *Now what? Are you hungry? Or shall we have a drink to celebrate?*

MARIA. *Let's just walk a little. It's so nice to have you here with me. Must you really go back, day after to-morrow?*

LOUIS. *It looks like it.*

MARIA. *Then this is our only evening together. To-morrow . . .* (she breaks off).

LOUIS. *You have something to do to-morrow?*

MARIA. *I'll have to go with Nora, Louis. Mr. Burnett wants me to look after her. There's the music and her costume—and a thousand things.*

LOUIS. *Of course. Don't worry. We've a few hours to-night anyway. And then I've someone to see.*

MARIA. *Tell me about yourself, Louis. How are you working now? I have lost touch so much with everything.*

C.37 EXT. SOHO STREET. DAY (LOCATION)

As MARIA speaks, she takes the arm of LOUIS and they begin to walk. There are very few people about. Someone goes by. LOUIS lights two cigarettes and gives one to her. LOUIS is thinking hard. He answers obliquely.

LOUIS. *Has Anselmo said anything to you—about me?*

MARIA. *Yes, he has. He's worried.*

LOUIS. *I think he knows my writing is only a cover.*

MARIA. *We saw a man outside the British Pavilion. He thought you knew the man.*

LOUIS. *Well—what if I did?*

MARIA. *We didn't like the look of him. Anselmo swears he saw him later: at the café and again at the night club.*

LOUIS. *We have to use all sorts of people, Maria.*

MARIA. *But there was never anyone like that in father's time.*

LOUIS. *We didn't need them then.* (with emphasis) *You say you hate Galbern, Maria, you talk so much about your father's work; but what do you do?*

MARIA. *It's true—I've got lazy, I've forgotten. Of course we talk and argue.*

160

LOUIS (lightly). *No. It doesn't add up at all. Are you serious when you say you want to work with us again?*
MARIA. *I'd like to work with you, Louis.*
CAMERA PANS as they turn into a side street.

C.38 EXT. FOLEY STREET. EVENING (LOCATION)

MARIA and LOUIS stroll along the street by the railway cutting near Royal Oak Bridge. Street lights are just coming on. They go up the few steps to the front door of one of the houses there, now very much come down in the world.
LOUIS opens the front door with his key. They enter. CAMERA PANS up the front of the house to the first floor.

C.39 INT. LOUIS' LONDON LODGINGS. EVENING (STUDIO)

On the first floor landing, LOUIS unlocks the door to a flat. Inside, he switches on the light. It has no shade. MARIA covers her eyes. LOUIS switches it off again and helps her out of her coat. She looks around her. The room, in semi-darkness, is very barely furnished.
MARIA. *Who lives here?*
LOUIS. *A man I know. He's away on a story.*

C.40 MARIA AND LOUIS (STUDIO)

MARIA takes it as it is meant. She sits down on the couch and gestures to him to sit down beside her. They kiss.
A train rushes past.
MARIA (in a turmoil). *You have a strange life. Never in a home of your own. How often I've—anguished over you, Louis, thinking of you always in hiding, always hunted, always in danger.*
LOUIS. *You wouldn't want me to give it up?*
MARIA (quite gaily). *Who—me? I'm in it with you.*
LOUIS (seriously). *It's a—dedication, Maria. We are a society, we have rules; you must abide by our rules. You must trust us.*
MARIA. *I trust you.*
LOUIS. *That's not quite the same thing.*
MARIA. *Yes, it is. My father trusted you; you're carrying on his work. And now —so am I.* (she is serious, but happy). *This is my—dedication.*
LOUIS (sombrely). *To selflessness: and to danger. This is a war, just like any other.*
MARIA. *But in war it doesn't matter what you do to win. That goes against everything my father stood for.*
LOUIS. *Your father was almost the first casualty; there have been so many since.*
MARIA. *Yes. It was what he always said. Once you shed blood, it flows on and on.* (she suddenly cries out passionately) *Louis! Don't go back!*
Another train . . . .

C.41 INT. ANSELMO'S BEDROOM. NIGHT (STUDIO)

In the bedroom next to the living-room above the café, NORA is just slipping into bed. ANSELMO switches off the light.
ANSELMO. *I am so glad you got da job. Sleep well.*
He gives her a kiss. When he goes, NORA opens her eyes.
NORA. *Uncle . . .*
ANSELMO. *I am in da middle of a game of dominoes.*
NORA. *Can you keep a secret? I went round with Sid to sign the contract. When I thanked him, he said something—it slipped out and he asked me not to tell anyone—not even Maria. You know what he said? 'Always glad to oblige a gentleman of the Press'.*
ANSELMO (thunderstruck). *Louis? He mean Louis?*

NORA. *Wasn't it sweet of him? He must have looked up Sid Burnett first thing after coming to London. Just to please me; and make Maria happy.*
ANSELMO (to reassure NORA). *Yeah. Dat's it. To make Maria happy.*
NORA. *Promise not a word?*
ANSELMO (grimly) *Promise; not a word.*
He goes out, shutting the door behind him. He is disturbed.

C.42 INT. ANSELMO'S CAFE. NIGHT (STUDIO)
There are very few customers. DALY is sitting at a table, looking down at an unfinished game of dominoes. PENNY is standing by him. ANSELMO is heard coming downstairs.
PENNY. *Of course, he looks much older than his photo. But his eyes—I can't get 'em out of my mind.*
DALY. *You women.* (to Anselmo) *Your turn.*
ANSELMO sits down.
ANSELMO (absently). *My turn.*

C.43 INT. LOBBY OF LOUIS' LONDON LODGINGS. NIGHT (STUDIO OR LOCATION)
MARIA and LOUIS are in the house doorway. LOUIS is in shirt-sleeves. (N.B. But with coat on for American version.) MARIA opens her handbag, takes out a fountain pen, gives it to LOUIS.
LOUIS (kissing her) *Goodnight.*
MARIA. *I want you to have this now, Louis. My father's pen. 'This is my sword,' he used to say. It was the only weapon he knew.*
LOUIS. *A relic from another world.*
He looks down at the pen with a bitter smile.
LOUIS (raising her hand and kissing it, glancing back towards the house). *Forgive me, Maria. I must go. To-morrow?* (i.e. we shall meet to-morrow?)
He watches her as she goes down into the street, then shuts the front door quietly.

C.44 INT. LOBBY OF LOUIS' LONDON LODGINGS. NIGHT (STUDIO OR LOCATION)
At the end of the hall a door opens. A man in shirtsleeves looks at LOUIS. We recognise him by his voice.
RODD. *That you, Louis?*
LOUIS. *Hullo, Rodd.*
RODD (with a hint of reproach). *The committee are waiting.*
LOUIS (coming nearer, fingering the pen). *O.K. I'm ready.*

C.45 EXT. FOLEY STREET. NIGHT (LOCATION)
MARIA walks along Foley Street, through the cooling wind. Another train goes by. She crosses the railway bridge. A free taxi passes her, slowing up a little. She ignores it, walks on . . .

C.46 INT. ANSELMO'S CAFE. NIGHT (STUDIO)
PENNY is ready to go home. The clock shows eleven. DALY and ANSELMO are still facing one another across their game of dominoes.
DALY. *That's three games he's lost, Penny. You're witness.*
ANSELMO. *I don' care, it don' matter.*
DALY. *Say that again.*
ANSELMO. *You heard.*
PENNY. *Proper old misery to-night.*
ANSELMO. *Shut up and go home.*
PENNY (hurt). *Mr. Anselmo!*
DALY. *Leave him be.*
PENNY. *I can take a hint!*

162

She pulls off her cap and apron, slings them behind the counter, gets her pirate cap and coat from the kitchen and stalks out, followed by DALY.

ANSELMO. *I am sorry, Penny.*

PENNY (softening). *Never mind. We all get the nasties. Happy dreams.*

She and DALY go out. ANSELMO, alone, gathers up the dominoes.

C.47 EXT. MORTON STREET. ANSELMO'S CAFE. NIGHT (LOCATION)
The lights in the café are extinguished.

C.48 INT. ANSELMO'S CAFE. FIRST FLOOR LANDING. NIGHT (STUDIO)
MARIA quietly comes up the stairs to the first floor landing.

ANSELMO'S VOICE. *Maria?*

He comes down the stairs towards her, still fully dressed.

ANSELMO (anxiously) *Had a good evening?*

MARIA. *Yes, thank you, uncle.*

MARIA turns her back on him abruptly.

ANSELMO. *Something wrong?*

MARIA (bravely). *Louis is leaving. The day after to-morrow.*

ANSELMO relaxes. MARIA kisses his cheek.

MARIA. *I must get some sleep. I'm going with Nora to-morrow night.*

ANSELMO. *Good! Splendid!*

MARIA. *And uncle—what do you think! Louis is giving me a dress to wear— isn't he sweet? Goodnight.*

ANSELMO, anxious again, watches her enter the living-room. He goes back upstairs.

C.49 INT. ANSELMO'S BEDROOM. NIGHT (STUDIO)
MARIA is undressing in darkness.

NORA. *We'll have to borrow a dress for you, Maria.*

MARIA (laughing). *I shall wear a dress of my own, thank you, Miss! Nora!— Louis is giving me a dress!*

NORA. *Well! When I was the woman in his life, he only gave me ice cream.*

MARIA (scrambling into bed). *He's not so cold with me, dear! And, Nora!— he's going to arrange for a private car to take us there.*

NORA. *Oh, Maria—how sweet! Fancy thinking of that!*

MARIA. *Well—to sleep now.*

NORA. *I'm much too excited.*

A door bangs.

NORA. *Uncle can't sleep either.*

C.50 INT. LOUIS' LONDON LODGINGS. NIGHT (STUDIO)
LOUIS is lying smoking in his shirtsleeves in the foreground, on the couch to which he took MARIA. The CAMERA DRIFTS BACK to reveal the room is occupied by half-a-dozen men and women about Louis' age. STEENIE is in a corner, rather impatiently sitting next to RODD.

BENTLEY, the chairman (who is not clearly seen, being in shadow), is speaking to JOHN, a bespectacled, youngish man of considerable intelligence. BENTLEY has a deep, bass voice.

BENTLEY. *You've not got cold feet, have you?*

JOHN. *I'm just reminding you. Here in England we've not had to go as far as this before. We've always operated within the law. And within the sanction of public opinion.*

BILL, a spare, good-looking, cynical type, interjects.

BILL. *Pretty near the edge ——*

JOHN. *In other countries our members have had to behave differently. In some, they've been driven underground already.*

BILL. *By people like Galbern.*

BENTLEY. *What are you driving at, John?*

163

CHARLIE, a frank, cockney lowbrow.
CHARLIE. *He's gone yellow.*
JOHN. *This one action, attacking Galbern, whether it succeeds or fails* ——
CHARLIE. *It won't fail.*
JOHN. *Very well, even if it succeeds, it'll certainly put us outside public opinion in this country. We shall lose every scrap of real sympathy we have built up for ourselves. We shall have to cut down our programme for a time, at least.*
BENTLEY. *But surely it's worth all that to get rid of Galbern? There'll be a rising against his government. It'll shake others.*
JOHN. *I agree that* ——
BILL. *Plenty of people in this country will thank us for it.*
JOHN. *They may be glad it's done. But they won't welcome us with open arms for doing it.*
BILL. *Only because they're too darn sentimental.*
CHARLIE (to John). *You're wasting our time.*
BENTLEY. *John's a perfect right to state his point of view.*
CHARLIE. *It'll be too late soon.*
JOHN (with a winning smile). *It's all happened so suddenly. I just don't want us to be stampeded into an action we may regret later. If everyone decides it's worth it, well and good.*
CHARLIE. *The rest of us decided that long ago. Let's get on with it.*
BENTLEY. *Agreed?* (they assent). *Sorry to keep you waiting, Gregor.*

C.51 C.S. LOUIS TO GROUP SHOT (STUDIO)
CAMERA STARTS on LOUIS as he sits forward to face the committee. CAMERA PULLS BACK into GROUP SHOT FROM DIFFERENT ANGLE.
LOUIS. *Must get agreement first.*
BENTLEY is still in shadow.
BENTLEY. *How can we help? You're the expert.*
LOUIS. *I've decided to divide the responsibility. A carrier to take in the bomb* and *an agent to place it.*
CHARLIE. *But why?*
LOUIS. *Because it's safer for the agent; the only evidence against him is during the time that he's setting the bomb.*
BENTLEY. *Steenie's the agent. Have you found a carrier?*
LOUIS. *I'm pretty sure I can guarantee the carrier. But Steenie can't be the agent.*
CHARLIE. *Why not? That's what he's here for.*
LOUIS. *Steenie was seen with me in Paris—after he . . . had been a little careless.*
STEENIE. *But, look here, Gregor—*
LOUIS. *It's too much of a risk.* (Coldly) *These are my instructions. To finish the job clean with no trouble for the organisation.*
BENTLEY. *Of course. We'll have to find someone else.*
LOUIS. *I've other work for Steenie. He won't be idle.*

FADE OUT:
(END OF SEQUENCE 'C')

SEQUENCE 'D'

FADE IN:
D.1 INT. ANSELMO'S LIVING-ROOM. DAY (STUDIO)
CAMERA STARTS on bedroom door, SHOOTING from living-room, as the café bell rings. PENNY hurries out of the girls' bedroom, closing the door after her, and in her action releasing and shutting off again a confused murmur of voices. PENNY runs across the room, which is disordered with open cardboard boxes and lids, tissue

164

paper, cleaning materials, old stockings, etc; the windows are open, for it is a sunny afternoon. She flings open the door to the living quarters, which gives on to the landing where the public telephone is installed.

PENNY. *Coming!*

ANSELMO'S VOICE (downstairs). *De car's here.*

CAMERA PANNING, PENNY runs back across the room and looks out of the window.

D.2 EXT. MORTON STREET. DAY. (LOCATION)

CAMERA SHOOTING DOWN into street. Sure enough there is a very neat, closed, four-seater at the café door. LOUIS gets out carrying a parcel. PENNY waves down to LOUIS.

PENNY. *Yuhoo! They're just ready.* (under her breath) *I hope!*

D.3 INT. ANSELMO'S LIVING ROOM. DAY (STUDIO)

PENNY runs back to the bedroom door, flings it open.

PENNY. *The car's here.*

The murmur in the room rises to a crescendo of reaction.

NORA'S VOICE (off). *He's early. He'll have to wait.*

PENNY turns round, shuts the door, runs across the room again and looks down over the banisters as LOUIS comes up the stairs. It is noticeable that he is pre-occupied and not sharing Penny's mood.

LOUIS. *Where's Maria?*

PENNY (comfortably). *Just you sit down for a minute. They won't be long.*

LOUIS (firmly). *Please tell Maria.*

PENNY. *All right, all right. Aren't you impatient.*

She turns and crosses the room to the bedroom door and knocks.

PENNY. *Mr. Louis' here.*

There is no reply. To fill in time, she turns to LOUIS.

PENNY. *She's looking ever so lovely in your dress.*

LOUIS looks at his watch, still preoccupied. The bedroom door opens and DALY comes out, carrying a small, empty medicine glass.

LOUIS. *Something wrong?*

DALY (bowing slightly). *Just a mild sedative.*

He smiles to PENNY, who nervously smiles back as DALY goes out of the living-room door and down the stairs.

D.4 LOUIS, PENNY, SHOE GIRL ASSISTANT, WOMAN, MALE HAIRDRESSER, MANICURIST (STUDIO)

The bedroom door opens a second time, and out comes the SHOE SHOP GIRL from the local shoe shop. She is carrying half-a-dozen boxes of shoes.

N.B. (She and others still to appear in this scene have been established as regular customers.)

SHOE SHOP GIRL. *Bye-bye, Penny.*

PENNY. *Bye, ducks, thanks ever so.* (she turns confidentially to Louis) *They're letting us have 'em at cost.*

As she speaks, another WOMAN (SCARF SALESWOMAN) walks out of the bedroom, ignoring both of them, with a pile of head scarves on her arm which she puts in one of the cardboard boxes on the table.

SCARF SALESWOMAN (as she sweeps out). *Good-afternoon.*

PENNY. *You've got time for a cup of coffee, haven't you? It's all ready.*

SCARF SALESWOMAN (exits). *Oh, thank you.*

PENNY. *She's got a nerve. Thirty bob for a bit of net and a few sequins.*

As she speaks, the MALE HAIRDRESSER from down the street comes out with the MANICURIST, who gazes at LOUIS.

MALE HAIRDRESSER. *Mr. Balan, I shouldn't wonder. Pleased to meet you.* (shaking hands) (to Manicurist) *Run along, Gladys.* (to Louis) *You've started something, Mr. Balan. Maria'll never be the same again.*

165

The bell rings from the café, violently.

PENNY. *Blimey, this place is getting like a fire station.*

HAIRDRESSER. *Come on, Penny, let's go and have a nice cuppa.*

They go to the door. The HAIRDRESSER suddenly turns round in astonishment.

HAIRDRESSER. *You ought to have a dinner jacket on, old man. You can't go out with them like that.*

PENNY. *He's not going.*

HAIRDRESSER. *Well, if you ain't asking for trouble.*

He throws back his head in total incomprehension. They go, shutting the door behind them.

D.5 LOUIS, MARIA'S SHADOW. (STUDIO)

LOUIS watches them go, then begins to open a small parcel which he has brought. Inside is a cardboard box. As he bends over it, the bedroom door opens quietly offscreen, and the early evening sunshine from the bedroom window falls across him, followed by Maria's shadow. LOUIS spins round, and a look of intense admiration comes into his eyes.

D.6 MARIA, LOUIS (STUDIO)

MARIA stands framed in the doorway with the sun streaming past her, lighting her hair, her shoulders, and her simple and very becoming white gown. Her face is quite beautiful in the half shadow of the living-room. She slips forward, closing the door behind her, smiling at LOUIS.

LOUIS. *Maria!*

MARIA stands smiling at him. LOUIS rises.

LOUIS. *I've never seen you look so lovely!*

MARIA. *You've never seen me in such a lovely dress.*

She offers her lips to him. They kiss.

MARIA. *If only you could come, too.*

LOUIS. *I'll be here when you come back.*

He picks up the cardboard box, opens it, revealing a white brocade bag, embroidered in gold.

D.7 MARIA, LOUIS (STUDIO)

MARIA. *Oh, Louis! How lovely!*

She takes the new bag and begins to open it.

LOUIS. *Wait, Maria. I've something to tell you.*

But MARIA has already opened it and discovered a silver case inside.

MARIA. *Yes, but—what's this? A cigarette case? It's very heavy.*

She opens it, looks inside and pulls out the silver case which she weighs in her hand.

LOUIS. *It's light for the job.*

MARIA. *The job?*

LOUIS. *Maria. Galbern will be there to-night.*

MARIA. *Galbern? At the party?* (half laughing) *Is it a bomb?*

LOUIS (deadly serious). *Yes. It is. Maria, we're counting on you. No one will suspect you of carrying it in. That's all we ask you to do. You'll give it to one of our men. He'll use a password, 'Curious tracery'. Are you listening?*

MARIA (rigid). *I heard you.*

LOUIS. *It's quite safe until the pin's removed. Then it takes sixty seconds.*

NORA (off). *Maria!*

MARIA. *Why did you have to ask me at the last minute?*

LOUIS. *It's our rule—you might have talked. Even in your sleep.*

NORA (off). *Maria! It's time to go.*

MARIA. *There's no time to think—*

LOUIS (at door, confidently). *She's nearly ready, Nora.*

MARIA (bitter, almost laughing). *Nearly ready—how can you treat me like this?*

166

You of all people—father believed in you more than anyone.
LOUIS. *I've never let him down—this is a fight, Maria. Galbern killed your father. He murdered him. He's murdered hundreds of people. You don't understand what I've been through these seven years. You must trust me.*
MARIA. *I want to trust you, Louis. Who else have I?*
LOUIS. *Then help us, Maria—believe in me! We've been waiting years for a chance like this.*
MARIA. *But it's murder. Father never would have allowed murder.*
LOUIS. *There was no fight then. We were all alive. Maria, you've got a lot to learn. You've been so sheltered all this time. You told me you wanted to help.*
MARIA (slowly). *You think it's right to assassinate?*
LOUIS. *To free a whole people? Yes, I do. 'Resistance to tyrants is obedience to God' . . . Remember? I don't ask you to plant the bomb—only to carry it in. Our man has the responsibility. He'll make contact with you by admiring your handbag.*
MARIA. *Who is he?*
LOUIS. *It's better for you not to know.* (he pauses) *Maria, you don't think I could ask you to do this, if I didn't know it was right?*
MARIA (looking at the bag, but not touching it). *Curious tracery . . .*
LOUIS. *That's the password.* (he points at the bag) *It is curious, you know, quite exquisite.*
MARIA. *How you've changed, Louis. Why do you talk like that?*
LOUIS. *To keep you calm. You must behave as if you're accustomed to these things.*

D.8 NORA, LOUIS, MARIA (STUDIO)

From the street, the sound of the car's horn. NORA throws open the bedroom door and lifts her suitcase into the living-room.
NORA. *Look out, you two. I'm ready. Hullo, Louis. Doesn't she look lovely?*
MARIA goes into the bedroom, leaving the new bag behind. LOUIS eyes NORA with admiration and picks up her suitcase.
LOUIS. *You both look lovely Don't tell me you needed a sedative.*
NORA. *Poor old Daly and his sedatives!* (she gives him a quick kiss) *Thank you, darling.*
LOUIS. *Who—me? What for?*
NORA. *For getting me the audition.*
LOUIS (quickly). *How did you know?*
NORA (imitating Burnett). *'Always glad to oblige a gentleman of the Press.'*
LOUIS (rapidly). *Keep it to yourself.*
NORA. *Of course I will.*
LOUIS. *I don't want Maria to know.*
NORA (impressed). *I wouldn't let you down, Louis—not for anything in the world.*
He smiles at her. She shows a little awkward embarrassment.
The car's horn sounds again, impatiently. PENNY hurries into the room.
PENNY. *Come on! What are you all waiting for? Maria!*
MARIA, wearing a sequin head scarf and a simple evening cloak, re-enters.
NORA. *Here we go.*
NORA takes Maria's hand to lead her towards the landing and stairs. PENNY hurries downstairs again ahead of them. MARIA, following, throws one glance back at LOUIS, who picks up the handbag she forgot to take. He follows with handbag and suitcase, apparently unmoved by the reproach and misery in her eyes.

D.9 INT. ANSELMO'S CAFE. DAY (STUDIO)

The café hums with excited voices. NORA and MARIA descend the stairs, followed by LOUIS with handbag and suitcase.

The crowd by the counter look admiringly at the two girls. PENNY and ANSELMO stare, lost in admiration. PENNY, rushing round the counter towards NORA, pushes her way through to kiss her.

MARIA, still holding Nora's hand, looks absent and distraught. ANSELMO, looking at MARIA, grows anxious—

HAIRDRESSER. *Nora, darling, you must give me a photograph with your signature.*
MANICURIST. *For the window display!*

The SCARF WOMAN tries to press some business cards into Maria's and Nora's hands.

SCARF WOMAN *If anyone asks you, give them a card—there'll be ten per cent in it for you, my dear.*
OTHER VOICES (repeat ad. lib.). *Good luck, Nora.*

The HAIRDRESSER ushers them towards the street door. The car hooter sounds again. NORA at last makes progress towards the door, MARIA follows. Now she comes in for comments.

VOICES. *E bella! Lucky Anselmo! Fancy having the likes of them planted on him!*
LOUIS (fighting his way through). *Excuse me . . .*

The HAIRDRESSER is holding the café door open.

D.10 EXT. MORTON STREET. ANSELMO'S CAFE. DAY (LOCATION)

The DRIVER (BILL) of the car is getting out of his seat to open the near door. He is neatly dressed in black with a chauffeur's cap and long, white summer overall. His back is to CAMERA.

D.11 EXT. MORTON STREET. ANSELMO'S CAFE. DAY (STUDIO)

ANSELMO, coming up to the doorway, kisses NORA. He is too moved to speak. She smiles at him, reassuringly. All ·around them, enthusiastic shouts and good wishes.

ANSELMO (to Maria). *I know she'll be a success.* (Maria nods) *You all right?*
MARIA (feeling Louis close behind her). *Yes, uncle.*

D.12 EXT. MORTON STREET. ANSELMO'S CAFE. DAY (LOCATION)

MARIA slips past ANSELMO and, with LOUIS, makes for the car. LOUIS gives MARIA the handbag. She takes it and enters the car quickly. LOUIS hands Nora's case to the DRIVER (BILL) who, back to CAMERA, shuts the door and then climbs into the front seat.

D.13 EXT. MORTON STREET. ANSELMO'S CAFE. DAY (LOCATION)

SHOOTING from inside the car towards the café. There is LOUIS, and all around him well-wishers who have come out of the café. Their eyes, radiant and encouraging, are on MARIA and NORA. Louis' eyes are on MARIA alone.

The car jerks ahead. All eyes and faces disappear. CAMERA MOVES to include driving mirror. There is now only one pair of eyes—those of the DRIVER (BILL), visible in the mirror.

D.14 INT. BILL'S CAR. DAY (B.P.)

A front shot of these eyes, as they begin to concentrate on the road ahead. We have seen the face before—it is that of BILL, the tough, intelligent-looking man from the Foley Street meeting.

D.15 INT. ANSELMO'S LIVING-ROOM. NIGHT (STUDIO)

The clock in Anselmo's living-room at 10.45 p.m. ticking away—the lights are lit. ANSELMO is sitting huddled, staring forward, distraught. CAMERA DRIFTS BACK. LOUIS is in the background by the window. He has just told ANSELMO about the attempt on Galbern's life.

ANSELMO. *Why you drag me into this—why you no leave me be?*
LOUIS. *You dragged yourself into it. There are two kinds of people we don't fear; those who know, and those who don't know. Being suspicious, you put*

yourself half way. That was dangerous. Now you know everything, we shall treat you as one of us. You know what that means.

He looks at his wrist-watch, then out of the window.

ANSELMO. *You make Maria break da law. A criminal! You-you! Sheltering behind a woman—what kind of a man are you? Maria doing your dirty work.*

LOUIS. *Maria took the opportunity. That's all.*

ANSELMO suddenly makes a decisive movement towards the door. LOUIS is after him at once, walks close behind him.

LOUIS. *Remember. You must help us to protect her.*

D.16 INT. ANSELMO'S CAFE. NIGHT (STUDIO)

ANSELMO, at the top of the stairs, stops dead, his eyes staring downstairs. LOUIS is behind him.

LOUIS. *You never forget a face—do you?*

D.17 INT. ANSELMO'S CAFE. NIGHT (STUDIO)

CAMERA SHOOTING down from their viewpoint on the landing. STEENIE is seated at the far end of the counter. FRACK is seated two stools nearer the stairs.

D.18 ANSELMO AND LOUIS (STUDIO)

ANSELMO and LOUIS at the top of stairs. (As D.16)

LOUIS (to Anselmo). *He's one of our best men—(gently pushing him on) This man Frack all right?*

ANSELMO (quietly). *'E is a customer. 'E talk big. 'E think 'e know everything.*

LOUIS. *We better get him out of here.*

D.19 INT. ANSELMO'S CAFE. NIGHT (STUDIO)

CAMERA SHOOTING from viewpoint of window. In the foreground, STEENIE has his eyes on FRACK, who sips at his cup of tea, ignoring Steenie's staring. In the background, LOUIS and ANSELMO descend the stairs.

The clock by the staircase shows a few minutes to eleven. A YOUNG COUPLE, in the corner by the side door, are the only other customers.

STEENIE (his eyes on Frack). *Another ginger.*

PENNY (behind the counter). *I hope you're insured.*

She opens a ginger beer, ANSELMO has joined her behind the counter.

FRACK. *Good-evening, Mr. Balan.*

LOUIS. *Good-evening.*

STEENIE silently draws Louis' attention to FRACK. LOUIS sits on the stool between STEENIE and FRACK and glances at the clock.

FRACK (sarcastically—indicating Steenie). *Another journalist, Mr. Balan? What does he do—edit the children's page?*

LOUIS. *Just a friend, Mr. Frack. (to Penny) One portion of pie and a coffee, please, Penny.*

STEENIE. *That's it—a friend.*

FRACK. *Thank you—nicely put.*

STEENIE (muttering). *Nark . . .*

LOUIS (polite). *Have something, Mr. Frack?*

FRACK. *Very kind of you, Mr. Balan. Anything interesting lately—inside information? Paris is such a hotbed of intrigue.*

STEENIE almost chokes over his drink. PENNY returns from the table by the side door, the YOUNG COUPLE having paid and left.

LOUIS (bringing out flask). *Try my cough medicine. Penny—some ginger beer for Mr. Frack.*

FRACK *Well, really, Mr. Balan, I'd as soon have some solids.*

Louis' eyes are on ANSELMO, who, on the customers' side of the counter, pretends to read an evening paper. Behind him, the clock is ticking away.

169

STEENIE (muttering to Louis). *Get rid of him.*
PENNY brings the drink.
LOUIS. *Some pie for Mr. Frack, Penny. A large piece.*
LOUIS pours liquor from his flask into the ginger beer.
FRACK. *Funnily enough, I could knock off a piece of your pie, Penny.*
He tries to pinch her. PENNY, recoiling, puts a plate of fruit pie in front of FRACK,
who is taking a long drink.
STEENIE. *Leave 'er alone, or someone'll knock you off, you old—*
PENNY (breaking in—to Frack). *Custard?*
FRACK, laughing, nods to PENNY and almost finishes the gin and ginger.
LOUIS pours a lot more gin into his glass.
FRACK. *Like to put a rope round my neck, Mr. . . . ?*
STEENIE. *No, it wouldn't hurt enough.*
FRACK takes another long drink.
FRACK. *Ha, ha, ha! . . . that's a good one, too.* (genially) *Look here, I'm on the
straight with friends.*
STEENIE (muttering). *Wot do they 'ave to 'ave. Flat feet?*
LOUIS adds more gin to Frack's drink. FRACK grins at STEENIE, then turns to LOUIS.
FRACK. *Steady on, old man . . . this dump hasn't got a licence.*
STEENIE. *Gosh, you being funny?*
He looks at FRACK furiously. LOUIS glances at STEENIE sharply. A further glance
at the clock is followed by a jerk of his head as if to say 'Go'. STEENIE steps off
his stool, goes towards the side door.
FRACK (who has watched everything). *Eleven o'clock. The journalist's most
critical hour . . . waiting for the news to break that'll make to-morrow's head-
lines.* (to Louis) *Expecting anything?*
LOUIS. *Yes.* (looking at Anselmo) *The 'Café Anselmo' to shut.*
ANSELMO gets up.
FRACK (drinking). *What a headline!* (drinking again) *To you, Steenie boy—*
STEENIE. *I'll be seeing you—*
STEENIE moves on towards the side door and out of sight, as though making for
the toilet.
ANSELMO (to Frack). *Please, time to go.*
PENNY. *One and three, please.*
LOUIS. *I'll settle for him.*
ANSELMO manoeuvres FRACK towards the front door.
FRACK (laughing drunkenly). *Steenie boy, you'll be the death o' me!*
ANSELMO pushes him out, shuts the door, turns round the OPEN/CLOSED sign. After
another glance from LOUIS he switches off most of the lights.
There is a noise. They turn in the direction of the side door.

D.20 MARIA, NORA, STEENIE (STUDIO)

CAMERA SHOOTING towards foot of stairs and side door as the latter opens and two
women are seen in cloaks, silhouetted against the glass of the door. They turn
towards the light and are seen to be MARIA and NORA, clinging together. NORA is
carrying her suitcase. MARIA sees STEENIE, who is standing in the toilet doorway.
She stops and then goes on upstairs. NORA follows her.

D.21 LOUIS, PENNY, ANSELMO, STEENIE (STUDIO)

CAMERA SHOOTING from the direction of the street door. LOUIS gets up. ANSELMO
makes a gesture of helpless despair.
LOUIS. *Is that you, Maria?*
But she has gone. LOUIS and PENNY exchange glances.
PENNY (following). *You not coming, Mr. Anselmo?*
ANSELMO (looking at Steenie). *In a minute.*
STEENIE (to Anselmo). *I'll help you clear away.*
PENNY, carrying a tray of tea, follows LOUIS upstairs.

D.22-23 INT. ANSELMO'S LIVING-ROOM. NIGHT (STUDIO)

CAMERA SHOOTING from doorway of living-room towards window. NORA is standing with cloak open, still in her dance costume. She is very pale, but controlled. Her suitcase is in the middle of the floor. There is a faint resemblance to the scene of the girls' arrival seven years before.

MARIA turns her back, looks towards the window.

LOUIS. *Hullo—you're back early!*

NORA. *Something horrible happened. There was an explosion . . .* (she breaks down).

LOUIS is concerned only to get MARIA alone.

PENNY. *An explosion?*

NORA. *Oh, it was terrible . . .*

LOUIS looks at PENNY as he speaks.

LOUIS. *Go with Penny, Nora. She'll look after you.*

PENNY takes NORA out. The moment they have gone, LOUIS whips round with an entire change of attitude. He is triumphant.

LOUIS (to Maria). *It worked.*

MARIA, at the window, keeps her back to him. She is making a great effort to control her horror and repugnance.

MARIA (bitterly). *You don't think of everything, Louis.*

LOUIS. *Tell me.*

MARIA turns into profile. She will not look at LOUIS. Beyond her head is the street with walkers and loiterers lit by the street lamps. Her voice is resentful, like that of someone compelled to speak.

MARIA. *We were not supposed to mix with the guests. I was watching from the terrace.*

As MARIA speaks, the street beyond and below her, becomes less and less distinct. At the same time, the CAMERA DRIFTS CLOSER to her. Then, as MARIA begins walking away, the background, growing more and more distinct, becomes the scene of the garden entertainment which she is describing.

MARIA'S VOICE. *During Nora's dance, I went down for a closer look.*

MARIA begins to walk, no longer in the living-room but down into the garden, away diagonally from the CAMERA until she is in full length on the screen in her white dress.

MARIA passes waiters and waitresses as she goes.

D.24 EXT. GARDEN PARTY. NIGHT (LOCATION)

An eager little WAITRESS takes courage from the movements of MARIA and goes forward with her, carrying an empty tray.

D.25 NORA (LOCATION)

In the distance, NORA is dancing on the stage. Her dance quickly finishes.

D.26 BILL AND MARIA (LOCATION)

During the applause, BILL, the chauffeur, in evening-dress, comes up to MARIA.

BILL. *Good-evening. What a beautiful bag. Have you a light?*

D.27 CLOWN, GUESTS (LOCATION)

The next turn begins—a musical CLOWN.

D.28 MARIA AND BILL (LOCATION)

Maria's eyes are on the CLOWN, refusing to acknowledge Bill's presence.

BILL (uncertain). *Have you a light? Curious tracery . . .*

MARIA, immobile, her face set, looks past him towards the CLOWN. BILL falters. Suddenly a vulgar burst of laughter, in a man's voice, very prolonged and sickeningly demonstrative. MARIA looks sideways.

D.29 GENERAL GALBERN, DISTINGUISHED MAN, CHIEF BODYGUARD, GUESTS. (LOCATION)

CAMERA SHOOTING from Maria's eyeline (sideways). She sees several yards away, GALBERN sitting at a table. The tails of his coat sweeping the lawn as he rocks on his chair, convulsed with laughter. A DISTINGUISHED-LOOKING MAN and the CHIEF BODYGUARD share his table. (The BODYGUARD is the one we saw in Paris.)

D.30 MARIA, BILL (LOCATION)

Maria's reaction is instantaneous. She opens her bag and BILL, relaxing, takes the silver cigarette case. MARIA strikes her cigarette lighter, her eyes still on GALBERN. BILL lights his cigarette.

BILL. *Thank you very much.*

D.31 CLOWN (LOCATION)

CAMERA SHOOTING from backs of guests on to the stage, where the CLOWN is performing one of his important gags.

D.32 BILL, GALBERN, GUESTS (LOCATION)

CAMERA SHOOTING from stage angle towards GUESTS where BILL is seen approaching Galbern's table.

'D.33 MARIA (LOCATION)

MARIA looks after BILL uncertainly again.

D.34 MARIA, BILL, GALBERN, GUESTS (LOCATION)

MARIA walks away, keeping an eye on Bill's movements, while the GUESTS are kept in constant laughter by the brilliant clowning.

D.35 CLOWN (LOCATION)

CAMERA SHOOTING towards stage, where the CLOWN is performing one of his important gags.

D.36 GUESTS INCLUDING PRINCIPALS (LOCATION)

At the end of the act, the GUESTS are deservedly enthusiastic. They rise to their feet and applaud

D.37 WAITRESS (LOCATION)

The eager little WAITRESS cranes her head forward excitedly to watch.

D.38 BILL, GENERAL GALBERN, DISTINGUISHED MAN, CHIEF BODY-GUARD, GUESTS (LOCATION)

BILL pauses by General Galbern's table.

D.39 MARIA, GUESTS (LOCATION)

MARIA moves on closer to the performers' dais, applauding. She begins to count the seconds under her breath.

D.40 BILL, GUESTS (LOCATION)

BILL strolls away towards the corner of the house.

D.41 CLOWN AND GUESTS (LOCATION)

(As D.36) The GUESTS sit down as the CLOWN begins an encore number.

D.42 CLOWN (LOCATION)

CAMERA SHOOTING towards stage, where the CLOWN commences to perform one of his shorter gags.

D.43 MARIA (LOCATION)

MARIA is still counting. She has to hold on to a chair.

D.44 BILL, GUESTS (LOCATION)

BILL passes behind the end of the house.

D.45 MARIA (LOCATION)

MARIA moves on again, deliberately counting. She hears applause as the CLOWN (off) again reaches a conclusion. Then she hears a voice.

VOICE. *One moment, Lady Venner. May I introduce General Galbern?*

MARIA turns quickly.

D.46 GALBERN, DISTINGUISHED MAN, CHIEF BODYGUARD, ELDERLY WOMAN (LOCATION)

The GENERAL and the TWO MEN with him leave their table and go to an ELDERLY WOMAN.

D.47 MARIA (LOCATION)

MARIA stares at the unoccupied table, as though relieved.

D.48 HEAD WAITER AND WAITRESS (LOCATION)

The HEAD WAITER makes a gesture and the little WAITRESS steps forward to tidy up the table.

D.49 MARIA (LOCATION)

MARIA grows rigid; only her mouth opens as if to scream.

D.50 WAITRESS, MEN GUESTS (LOCATION)

There is an explosion under the table. The WAITRESS, falling, screams horribly. A MAN in evening dress falls by her. The other GUESTS, mostly men, seem stunned.

D.51 MARIA, WAITRESS, CLOWN, GUESTS (LOCATION)

MARIA hurries, stumbling, forward. She kneels and tends the WAITRESS, resting her head on her knees. The CLOWN joins her, seizes the cloth from a nearby table and tears it to make a bandage. Others bend down to help.

D.52 INT. ANSELMO'S LIVING ROOM. NIGHT (STUDIO)

CAMERA SHOOTING from viewpoint of window where MARIA is standing.

MARIA. *She was frightfully injured.*
LOUIS (reflectively). *That was a good idea . . .*
MARIA. *Idea?*
LOUIS. *Using first aid. A perfect cover.*

D.53 MARIA, LOUIS (STUDIO)

CAMERA SHOOTING towards window where MARIA is standing. She turns her gaze from the window to LOUIS.

LOUIS. *Don't worry about Galbern. We'll get him. Steenie'll get him.*
MARIA. *Steenie? That man downstairs?*
LOUIS. *Yes.*
MARIA. *Oh, no, Louis—no more of it!*
LOUIS. *Hush, Maria, calm down. You've had a shock.*
MARIA. *That girl died in my arms.* (shivering) *She didn't want to die. She was frightened to die.*
LOUIS. *It wasn't your fault.*
MARIA. *Yes, it was. Mine and yours. We murdered her. You and I. I've got her blood on me now.*

D.54 MARIA, LOUIS (STUDIO)

Maria's control begins to go though she tries hard to hold herself in.

LOUIS. *Maria . . .*
MARIA. *I don't blame you for tricking me into this. Yes—tricking me. That's your job. But I am Pietro Brentano's daughter. He died sooner than have the Steenies work for him. I've failed him. I have killed all that we lived for.*
LOUIS. *For God's sake, Maria—keep your head.* ('For God's sake' must be deleted for U.S.A.)

He moves forward as though to touch her, but she avoids or refuses his touch.
MARIA. *You send your Steenie back to where he came from. I won't have any more murder.*

D.55 LOUIS, MARIA, PENNY (STUDIO)
CAMERA SHOOTING towards window, but taking in viewpoint of bedroom door, which opens and PENNY, putting in her head, calls.
PENNY. *Maria.*
MARIA indicates a parcel on the table beside her.
MARIA. *Take this away and burn it.*
PENNY. *What, your lovely dress?*
LOUIS (quickly). *I'll take care of that.*
PENNY. *What's wrong with it?*
He snatches the dress from the bewildered PENNY and nods to her to look after MARIA.
LOUIS. *It's got blood on it.*
PENNY. *It'll clean, dear.*
MARIA looks at LOUIS. LOUIS looks at her in silence, takes the dress and goes.

D.56 OUT:
FADE OUT:

(END OF SEQUENCE 'D')

SEQUENCE 'E'

FADE IN:

E.1 EXT. MORTON STREET. ANSELMO'S CAFE. DAY (LOCATION)
Early morning. CAMERA SHOOTING towards Anselmo's café as CHARLIE, one of the London Committee, is strolling in the street, watching the café.

E.2 INT. ANSELMO'S CAFE. FIRST FLOOR LANDING. DAY (STUDIO)
The telephone on the landing rings. ANSELMO emerges from the doorway straight out of bed, unshaven, in pyjamas, and comes to answer it, yawning horribly.
ANSELMO. *Hullo!* (yawn) *Dis Anselmo's café. Maria Brent? She not up yet. Can I take a message?* (horrified) *Scotland Yard? She did? You are? You want her to—? Ooh! Sure. She will be pleased! Yes, I tell her. T'ank you very much. Good-bye.*
ANSELMO replaces the receiver, scratches his head and walks into the living-room.

E.3 INT. ANSELMO'S LIVING-ROOM. DAY (STUDIO)
ANSELMO crosses to knock on Maria's bedroom door. He glances across the room as he goes and then does a double 'takem.'

E.4 MARIA AND ANSELMO (STUDIO)
MARIA is sitting in an armchair near the window wrapped in a blanket, half asleep and looking towards the floor. Her hair is dishevelled. She looks up haggard and distraught.
ANSELMO. *Maria . . .*
MARIA. *Who was that, uncle?*
ANSELMO. *It was da police—dey want you to go to Scotland Yard. Dey want to t'ank you for what you did last night.*
MARIA. *What I did?*
ANSELMO. *Dey say you were very brave. Dere was a man hurt, a detective. You help to save him. Dey are very kind. You will see.*
MARIA stares vaguely at ANSELMO.
MARIA. *Do something for me, uncle?*

ANSELMO. *Any mortal t'ing, child.*
MARIA smiles sadly.
MARIA. *Ring up Louis. I must see him.*
ANSELMO. *You t'ink Louis can 'elp you—you don' trust me any more?*
MARIA (with a sad smile). *Take care of Nora. Get her off to her class, will you? She's best out of the way.*

E.5 INT. LOBBY OF LOUIS' LONDON LODGINGS. DAY (STUDIO)
LOUIS is letting MARIA into the house.
LOUIS. *The committee only want to talk to you before you go to Scotland Yard. You needn't be frightened.*
MARIA. *I'm not frightened.*
LOUIS. *But, remember—they don't know you. Don't give a wrong impression, Maria.*
MARIA. *Upstairs?*
LOUIS. *Yes.*
They go upstairs.

E.6 INT. CORRIDOR OUTSIDE LOUIS' LONDON LODGINGS. DAY (STUDIO)
There is a light in the curtained corridor as they come upstairs.
MARIA. *What do you mean—a wrong impression?*
LOUIS. *That you're ratting.*
MARIA (pointing to door). *Here?*
LOUIS (nodding). *Go in.*
LOUIS knocks on the door of the room where they had spent the previous evening.
MARIA. *Aren't you coming?*
LOUIS. *I'll be there.*
BILL opens the door and nods to MARIA, who momentarily shows alarm on recognising him. LOUIS lights a cigarette.
BILL. *Miss Brent?*

E.7 INT. LOUIS' LONDON LODGINGS. DAY (STUDIO)
BILL guides MARIA by torch into the dark room—points torch at couch.
BILL. *Will you sit there?*
The door closes.
A powerful light suddenly shines on Maria's face—it should be strong enough and so shaded as to black out everything on the screen for the audience, who only see Maria's head outlined against a glare. Trains rattle by.
DEEP BASS VOICE OF BENTLEY. *Miss Brent?*
MARIA. *Yes.*
MARIA shows distress at the lighting.
BENTLEY'S VOICE (conciliatory). *I'm sorry, it'll be better for you not to know us by sight just at present. We want to welcome you. You acted very efficiently last evening.*
MARIA (pausing for strength). *Doesn't it matter who is killed?*

E.8 GROUP SHOT (STUDIO)
Another view, showing Maria's face in the top left corner, takes the glare off the audience's eyes and shows three pairs of legs at the right hand side of the picture. One pair on the left is in thick tweed trousers with boots. One in the middle a woman's legs in silk stockings and low-heeled shoes, and on the right, in well-cut trousers and well-polished shoes. These are Bill's. There are other legs in the background.
BILL. *No one can blame you for what happened.*
MARIA. *But the whole plan. When I saw that girl dying, I knew how wicked it was.*
BENTLEY. *Do you mean unlawful? I must point out that people like Galbern*

are outside the law. They acknowledge no limits on their powers. General Galbern is an outlaw.

MARIA. *Galbern is evil—but that little waitress—*

WOMAN. *That was an accident.*

MARIA. *I should have known other people might be killed. But I'd never seen people dead by violence. Ordinary people.*

While MARIA speaks, BENTLEY has extended his tweed legs and shows his nailed boots.

BENTLEY. *We all have to take risks for the sake of the cause.*

MARIA. *Risk our lives—but not innocent lives.*

WOMAN (impatient). *Innocent people—women and children—are killed every day all over the world.*

Bill's feet have been jerking impatiently for some time.

MARIA. *By accident.*

BILL. *By governments, by dictatorships, by men like Galbern, who serve the dictators.*

Bentley's legs cross each other as though the owner were leaning back in his seat.

BENTLEY. *Miss Brent, I think I know how you feel. All of us have had feelings like that. But in our service we agree to take a very special risk, don't we? We agree to devote even more than our lives—our conscience as well.*

E.9 LOUIS (STUDIO)

Louis' face lights faintly as he draws at his cigarette. He is standing leaning against the wall near the door.

WOMAN'S VOICE (coldly). *It is not a question of our personal feelings, Miss Brent. We must set them aside.*

E.10 MARIA (STUDIO)

MARIA. *But what have we got to go on but our own feelings?*

E.11 LOUIS, BILL, MARIA (STUDIO)

LOUIS is leaning against the wall near the door (as in E.9). MARIA, silhouetted, is in the foreground. Bill's feet have been jerking furiously for some time.

BILL. *Let's get to the point, Miss Brent. I believe you uttered a certain threat.*

Louis' face lights in the background.

E.12 MARIA (STUDIO)

MARIA. *A threat? I?*

LOUIS. *I have to report, Maria. It's my duty.*

BENTLEY. *You said 'I won't have any more killing.'*

MARIA is becoming more tense.

WOMAN. *That's sheer sentimentality.*

BENTLEY. *You understand that we can't pass over that kind of thing? It would make the whole of our operations impossible. We must have discipline.*

MARIA. *I'm nothing to do with you.*

E.13 GROUP SHOT (STUDIO)

CAMERA SHOOTING across room taking into shot MARIA, surrounded by the Committee, including LOUIS, and door.

WOMAN. *You undertook the work of your own free will.*

MARIA glances at LOUIS.

WOMAN. *You can't back out of your responsibilities.*

BENTLEY. *Gregor tells us a certain Marco was a friend of yours.*

MARIA (bewildered). *Marco?*

LOUIS. *We are going to tell you the truth about him now, Maria.*

WOMAN. *As a warning.*

LOUIS. *As a lesson.*

BENTLEY. *Do you know how he died?*

MARIA. *No.*
LOUIS. *We killed him.*
MARIA. You *killed him?*
LOUIS. *We knew he was fond of good living. He found our life difficult. Then he went just too far. He didn't get drunk. It just oiled his tongue. . . The police arrested one of us. We didn't know who had given him away. But there was a big job coming off. Several of us were going to be working together in the same place. We couldn't take the risk of leaving Marco free.*

E.14 MARIA (STUDIO)
MARIA makes a speechless, shocked movement

E.15 GROUP SHOT (STUDIO)
Louis' face lights in the glow of his cigarette. Footsteps are heard on the stairs. The door is opened quickly. The silhouette of STEENIE enters. LOUIS moves quickly towards him. The presence of the two together tell MARIA (and the audience) the facts of Marco's death.

E.16 MARIA (STUDIO)
MARIA recognises STEENIE.

E.17 LOUIS, STEENIE (STUDIO)
STEENIE by the door. Louis' cigarette glows beside him as LOUIS reaches the door. STEENIE whispering into Louis' ear.

E.18 MARIA (STUDIO)
MARIA looking towards STEENIE and LOUIS.
BENTLEY'S VOICE. *Just a moment, Miss Brent.*
She turns and there is a bright flash. Someone has taken a flashlight photograph of MARIA in the dark.
MARIA. *Yes, but—*

E.19 MARIA, LOUIS (STUDIO)
BENTLEY'S VOICE (off). *That was a photograph for our records. You can go now.*
The door is opened, the spotlight goes out in the room and LOUIS is seen guiding MARIA into the passage. The door is closed behind them.

E.20 INT. CORRIDOR OUTSIDE LOUIS' LONDON LODGINGS. DAY (STUDIO)
MARIA, staggering against the wall, covers her eyes with her hands. LOUIS reaches for his cigarettes. He keeps his eyes on MARIA, sympathetically but alertly.
LOUIS. *You'll get over it in time.*
MARIA, dropping her hands, just stares at him. She can't even answer.
LOUIS. *But when you go to Scotland Yard—watch your tongue.*
MARIA (with an effort). *Shall I have to go?*
LOUIS. *They'd pull you in if you didn't. Be careful, that's all. I'm vouching for you to the organisation. But you've not made it easy for me. If the police show any signs of acting on information—I can't answer for your safety. You understand that?*
LOUIS takes out two cigarettes, offers one to MARIA. MARIA, tortured, shakes her head, and goes without speaking. LOUIS opens the door to the room. The committee are seen burning a mound of papers in the fireplace. STEENIE is just inside the room and turns quickly. He sees the front door shut behind MARIA.
STEENIE (joining Louis). *You think she'll give us away?*
LOUIS (confidently). *No.*
STEENIE (not so sure). *Come away, Louis!*
LOUIS. *Rodd is standing by. He'll fly you out.*
STEENIE. *I'm staying with you.*
LOUIS. *It's risky.*

N

STEENIE. *But, Louis, you were ordered not to take risks. You got to keep out of trouble.*

LOUIS. *This is my job.* (calling into the room) *Charlie!*

CHARLIE comes up to the door.

E.21 EXT. SCOTLAND YARD. DAY (LOCATION)

Outside Scotland Yard, CHARLIE is keeping watch.

E.22 INT. ENTRANCE HALL OF SCOTLAND YARD. DAY (LOCATION)

A MESSENGER approaches MARIA and ANSELMO, who is scarcely able to conceal his intense agitation. They are occupying two of a row of chairs.

MESSENGER *Miss Brent? This way, please.*

MARIA follows him, leaving ANSELMO sitting there, a picture of mental anguish.

E.23 INT. CORRIDOR. SCOTLAND YARD. DAY (STUDIO)

In the long corridor, the MESSENGER knocks on the door of an interview room, MARIA behind him.

INSPECTOR ELIOT'S VOICE. *Come in!*

E.24 INT. INTERVIEW ROOM, SCOTLAND YARD. DAY (STUDIO)

CAMERA SHOOTING from corridor as MARIA and MESSENGER enter the room. The MESSENGER announces:

MESSENGER. *Miss Brent, sir.*

CAMERA TRACKS forward past MESSENGER, who goes into Interview Room where INSPECTOR ELIOT is seated at the desk. Thirty-five years old, athletic and intelligent. Seated near him is MISS JACKSON, a policewoman in her early thirties. Both are wearing quiet civilian clothes. ELIOT touches a button on his desk as he rises.

ELIOT. *Glad to see you, Miss Brent. My name's Eliot. This is Miss Jackson.*

MISS JACKSON comes forward, very friendly, and shakes hands with MARIA.

MISS JACKSON. *How do you do?*

MARIA (to both). *How d'you do?*

ELIOT. *Do sit down. We wanted to thank you for what you did last night at Sandy House.*

E.25 REVERSE SHOT (STUDIO)

MISS JACKSON. *Your first aid saved a man's life—one of our men.*

MARIA can scarcely stand the strain.

MARIA. *I'm glad.*

ELIOT (glancing at a file). *Your name was formerly Brentano?*

At a table behind MARIA, MISS JACKSON is pouring tea. One cup is on a small tray with a milk jug and sugar bowl.

MARIA. *Yes.*

MISS JACKSON. *You'd like a cup of tea, wouldn't you?*

MARIA. *Thank you.*

She appears confused, pauses and looks nervously about her. SERGEANT NEWCOME enters carrying something in a small box. He, too, is in civilian clothes and is rather older than ELIOT.

ELIOT. *This is Sergeant Newcome.* (Maria nods to him) *You were standing quite near at the time of the explosion?*

MARIA. *Yes.*

MISS JACKSON offers MARIA the cup of tea on the small tray, which she puts down on the desk by MARIA.

MISS JACKSON. *Help yourself to milk.*

The police are studying MARIA.

MARIA (helping herself). *Thank you.*

ELIOT. *You didn't notice anything suspicious?*

178

E.26 INSERT OF BOX AND CONTENTS (STUDIO)
Newcome's hand holds out a box containing some small object.

NEWCOME'S VOICE (off). *We picked this up, miss—it looks like part of a vanity case.*

E.27 MARIA, MISS JACKSON (STUDIO)
CAMERA SHOOTING from low angle towards MARIA, with MISS JACKSON in background.

MARIA (with an effort). *It's a cigarette case—it was mine.*

Maria's voice becomes dry and hoarse. She drinks some tea. MISS JACKSON eyes the cup and saucer which MARIA holds in foreground.

E.28 ELIOT (STUDIO)
CAMERA SHOOTING from low angle on to ELIOT.

ELIOT. *You mean your case was destroyed by the explosion?*

E.29 GROUP SHOT (STUDIO)
CAMERA SHOOTING group in low angle. MARIA looks round the group as if in terror.

MARIA. *I want to explain . . .*

ELIOT (trying to keep her calm). *You think you can tell us something about the people who did it?*

MARIA. *Yes. I was one of them—we went to kill General Galbern.*

MARIA puts the cup and saucer down on the small tray.

ELIOT. *You realise what you're saying, Miss Brent?*

MISS JACKSON removes the tray and takes it to the tea table near the door, where she exchanges a quick look with the SERGEANT.

MARIA. *I do.*

MISS JACKSON (kindly). *Of course, Miss Brent, you understand we get people coming in here and confessing to all sorts of crimes.*

The INSPECTOR scribbles a note, which he passes to the SERGEANT, who goes out of the room, taking with him the small box containing the fragments of the cigarette case and the tray with Maria's cup and saucer. CAMERA TRACKS with the Sergeant's movements.

E.30 GROUP SHOT (STUDIO)
CAMERA SHOOTING group at Eliot's desk.

ELIOT. *You say you went to kill Galbern? Why?*

MARIA. *He killed my father.*

ELIOT. *Pietro Brentano?*

MARIA. *Yes.*

The SERGEANT returns and nods slightly to the INSPECTOR. ELIOT looks at the file.

ELIOT. *But you couldn't have placed the bomb? You were nowhere near.*

MARIA. *I carried it in. Someone else placed it.*

ELIOT. *Who?*

MARIA. *I don't know. There was a password.*

E.31 GROUP SHOT (STUDIO)
ELIOT glances incredulously at MISS JACKSON, who nods reassuringly.

MISS JACKSON. *D'you want to make a statement, Miss Brent?*

MARIA is silent.

ELIOT. *If your evidence can help us, Miss Brent, you might—earn a pardon. I suppose you realise that?*

MARIA is utterly weary. MISS JACKSON goes to the tea-tray.

MARIA. *I haven't come here to sell my friends.*

ELIOT. *Will you identify them to us?*

MARIA. *No.*

ELIOT. *But you believe they're planning another attempt on Galbern?*

MARIA. *No, I don't know.*

MISS JACKSON hands MARIA a second cup of tea.

MISS JACKSON (kindly). *Just you drink this, Miss Brent.*
ELIOT. *Excuse me, Miss Brent, but we'll want a little more than that—we'll have to make some enquiries.*
MARIA. *Don't you believe me?*

E.32 GROUP SHOT (STUDIO)

CAMERA SHOOTING from new angle revealing second door.
ELIOT (indicating a door nearby). *If you'd just come in here and answer a few questions. You can bring that with you.*
MARIA (with cup). *Thank you.*
He opens the second door and they go towards the other room.

E.33 INT. SECOND INTERVIEW ROOM. DAY (STUDIO)

CAMERA SHOOTING through doorway to 2nd Interview Room to a C.U. of RODD, who is sitting there. The tea-cup rattles on its saucer.

E.34 INT. FIRST INTERVIEW ROOM. DAY (STUDIO)

CAMERA NOW SHOOTING ON MARIA, who almost drops the cup in her amazement upon seeing RODD.

E.35 ELIOT, MARIA, MISS JACKSON (STUDIO)

The INSPECTOR rescues the cup and MISS JACKSON steps alongside MARIA.
ELIOT. *You know each other?*

E.36 INT. SECOND & FIRST INTERVIEW ROOMS. DAY (STUDIO)

CAMERA SHOOTING through doorway connecting the two Interview Rooms as RODD speaks.
RODD (huffed). *No. Who is she, anyway?*
The police watch. MISS JACKSON takes Maria's arm and leads her back, CAMERA TRACKING, through the doorway. ELIOT closes the door.
ELIOT. *Thank you, Miss Brent.*
MARIA looks round wildly. ELIOT offers her the cup of tea, which she refuses with a gesture.
MARIA. *He's just a child—they'll use a child. I had no idea he's in it, too.*
ELIOT. *It's a pretty big organisation. Spread all over the world. They use all sorts of people.*
MARIA (steadying herself against the desk). *Oh, my God!* (N.B. Alternative exclamation required for American version.)
ELIOT. *Have you been in it long?*
MARIA (shakes her head). *I had nothing to do with it till yesterday. My father was not one of them.*
MARIA looks around on sound of door opening.

E.37 MESSENGER AND GROUP. (STUDIO)

A MESSENGER enters and hands MISS JACKSON a note. She reads it and passes it to ELIOT. The MESSENGER leaves.

E.38 INSERT OF NOTE (STUDIO)

The handwritten message reads:
'Finger-prints on saucer identical with one of those found on bomb fragment.'

E.39 ELIOT, MISS JACKSON, MARIA (STUDIO)

After reading the note, ELIOT turns to MARIA.
ELIOT. *Now, Miss Brent, you're in our charge. You'll have our protection from now on.*
MARIA. *I don't want any favours from the police.*
ELIOT. *You won't notice it until you need it. Miss Jackson?*
MISS JACKSON comes forward to help MARIA to the door.

E.40 EXT. SCOTLAND YARD. WHITEHALL. DAY (LOCATION)

MARIA and ANSELMO enter a bus and drive away, watched by CHARLIE.

E.41 OUT:

E.42 INT. INTERVIEW ROOM. DAY (STUDIO)

ELIOT and NEWCOME are preparing to leave.

ELIOT. *They wouldn't dare do anything to her in the café. They're too clever . . . If we see her leave with anyone, we'll pull 'em in for questioning.*

MISS JACKSON. *She's our only link with them. We mustn't let her get herself arrested or she'll shut up like a clam.*

ELIOT. *Don't worry. We'll handle her with kid gloves.*

NEWCOME. *That's more than her friends will do . . .*

E.43 OUT:

E.44 EXT. EDGWARE ROAD. DAY (LOCATION)

The police car turns out of the Edgware Road into a side street and stops. ELIOT, NEWCOME and two other plainclothes men get out of the car. NUMBER ONE plainclothes man stops and buys an evening paper, loitering behind. NUMBER TWO strolls over into Morton Street towards Anselmo's café.

E.45 EXT. MORTON STREET. DAY (LOCATION)

ELIOT and NEWCOME walk along Morton Street and look unobtrusively at the house opposite Anselmo's café. The ground floor is Daly's chemist shop. Beside the chemist's doorway is the open door to the stairs which lead up to the converted flats above. STEENIE is lounging on the opposite pavement.

NEWCOME. *I know this street, sir. There's a young woman in the first floor flat.*

ELIOT. *Will she play ball?*

NEWCOME (airily). *Oh, yes, sir. She's got plenty on her plate.*

They enter the doorway and climb the stairs.

E.46 INT. FIRST FLOOR LANDING OVER DALY'S. DAY (STUDIO)

There is no bell on the door of the flat. NEWCOME knocks. After a moment or two:

FLOOZIE'S VOICE. *Just a minute.*

Another moment. The door is opened from within. The FLOOZIE is in a wrapper and none too tidy. She recognises NEWCOME.

FLOOZIE. *What's it this time?* (notices Eliot). *Scared to come alone?*

ELIOT produces his pass, in a leather case with a celluloid panel.

ELIOT. *We were just wondering if you would give us a bit of help.*

FLOOZIE. *But I don't know anything about anything, do I?*

ELIOT. *It's like this—could we have your front window for a day or two?*

FLOOZIE. *A day or two! Want me to cook for you?*

NEWCOME. *That's quite an idea. You ought to be good at cooking things.*

FLOOZIE. *Just a minute, dear. My 'usband's just off to business.*

The FLOOZIE goes back into the room. A man's voice murmurs something. ELIOT and NEWCOME turn away and look over the stairs. Suddenly, a LITTLE MAN in a raincoat bolts past them down the stairs, keeping his head down and jamming on his bowler hat. ELIOT and NEWCOME remain passive.

ELIOT. *Well, he won't give us away.*

The FLOOZIE emerges.

FLOOZIE. *Well, what a room—you'll think I'm a regular slummock.*

NEWCOME. *All between friends.*

They enter the flat.

E.47 EXT. HOUSE ENTRANCE BY DALY'S SHOP. DAY (LOCATION)

The house door is open. The LITTLE MAN slows up at the foot of the stairs and pulls himself together. He buttons up his waistcoat. When he looks up, there is NUMBER ONE on the pavement, newspaper under arm, watching him. The LITTLE MAN grows agitated and hurries away up the street, CAMERA PANNING. NUMBER ONE turns, looks at the café, then strolls into Daly's shop, CAMERA TRACKING FORWARD.

E.48 & 48a EXT./INT. DALY'S SHOP WITH STREET OUTSIDE. DAY (LOCATION OR STUDIO)

CAMERA SHOOTING from back of Daly's shop towards street, where, across the road, NUMBER TWO is on the watch.
In the shop, DALY steps forward to NUMBER ONE.
DALY. *Yes, sir?*
NUMBER ONE. *Can you give me something for a headache?*
Number One's eyes are always watching the café.
DALY. *Certainly, sir. Cinema type or hangover?*
NUMBER ONE. *Hangover.*
PENNY *hurries into the shop.*
PENNY. *Morning, Mr. Daly. Bottle of aspirin, please.*
DALY. *Hangover, too?*
PENNY. *No such luck. Had a rotten night, though. So did Maria. Gave her the last of mine this morning. There she is now. Oh, dear! Ninepence. Good-bye, ducks.*

E.49 INT./EXT. DALY'S SHOP AND ANSELMO'S CAFE. DAY (LOCATION)

CAMERA SHOOTING from back of Daly's shop towards street as PENNY hurries out and across the road. ANSELMO and MARIA approach and enter the café.

E.50 EXT./INT. DALY'S SHOP. DAY (LOCATION OR STUDIO)

CAMERA SHOOTING from viewpoint of street into Daly's shop, as DALY hands the draught to NUMBER ONE, whose eyes are on the café all the time.
DALY (to Number One). *Chatty little woman. That'll be fourpence, sir. Perhaps that's why she never quite got married.*

E.51 OUT:

E.52 INT. ANSELMO'S CAFE. FIRST FLOOR LANDING. DAY (STUDIO)

MARIA is at the telephone. She is finishing dialling a number.

E.53 INT. LOUIS' LONDON LODGINGS. DAY (STUDIO)

The Foley Street room has been left in disorder. Police are searching. One takes off the receiver and listens . . .

E.54 INT. ANSELMO'S CAFE. FIRST FLOOR LANDING. DAY (STUDIO)

CAMERA STARTS on C.S. of MARIA as, still by the telephone on the café landing, and realising that someone is at the other end of the line, she says:
MARIA. *Hullo. Is that you, Louis?*
LOUIS' VOICE. *Hullo.*
MARIA whirls round, CAMERA TRACKING to M.S. LOUIS is standing behind her. He takes the receiver from her and replaces it.
LOUIS. *Come inside.*

E.55 INT. ANSELMO'S LIVING-ROOM. (DAY (STUDIO)

CAMERA STARTS on door of living-room as MARIA and LOUIS enter the living-room.
LOUIS (controlled). *How did it go?*
MARIA. *They've caught Rodd. I saw him.*
LOUIS. *So that's where he is. What else?*
MARIA. *I . . . I didn't tell them about anyone except myself. They showed me some pieces of the silver case.*
LOUIS. *Go on.*
MARIA. *You must go away, Louis.*
LOUIS. *Rodd was going to fly us out—you and me. It won't be so easy now.*
MARIA. *I'm not coming.*

182

LOUIS. *What?*
MARIA. *I identified the case. I told them I carried it.*
LOUIS. *Maria! Are you mad?*
MARIA. *I'm not with you, Louis.*
LOUIS goes to the window.

E.56 INT/EXT. ANSELMO'S LIVING-ROOM AND STREET. DAY (LOCATION)

LOUIS peers out of the window as far as the curtains will allow. He sees STEENIE below on the pavement. LOUIS turns into the room.
LOUIS (hard). *You are coming with us, Maria.*

E.57 INT. ANSELMO'S LIVING-ROOM. DAY (STUDIO)

MARIA. *No, Louis.*

E.58 INT./EXT. STREET AND LIVING-ROOM. DAY (LOCATION)

LOUIS, in a cold fury, throws his cigarette out of the open window to fall at Steenie's feet . . .

E.59 EXT. ANSELMO'S CAFE. DAY (LOCATION OR STUDIO)

STEENIE becomes alert, begins peering up and down the street.

E.60 INT/EXT. FLOOZIE'S WINDOW ABOVE DALY'S SHOP. DAY (STUDIO)

CAMERA SHOOTING from the street towards Floozie's window above Daly's shop. ELIOT and NEWCOME watch.

E.61 EXT. ANSELMO'S CAFE. DAY (LOCATION)

CAMERA SHOOTING from viewpoint of Floozie's window as STEENIE strolls into the café.

E.62 INT. ANSELMO'S CAFE. DAY (STUDIO)

STEENIE enters the café and strolls through and upstairs. NUMBER ONE is sitting at the counter, lighting a cigarette.
ANSELMO. *Wot 'e doing?*
PENNY (pouring out coffee for Number One). *Gone up to Mr. Louis, I suppose.*
ANSELMO (agitated). *Louis upstairs?*
PENNY (nodding). *He went up to wait for Maria.*
ANSELMO can scarcely control his feelings.

E.63 INT. ANSELMO'S LIVING-ROOM. DAY (STUDIO)

STEENIE enters the living-room without knocking. MARIA watches him.
LOUIS. *Anything?*
STEENIE. *Not so far. Has she got any news?*
LOUIS. *I think they're on to us.*
STEENIE. *Bill's got the car down the street. She coming?*
LOUIS. *We'll be down.*
STEENIE goes.

E.64 INT. ANSELMO'S CAFE. DAY (STUDIO)

CAMERA SHOOTING from viewpoint of window. ANSELMO and PENNY are behind the counter. She places a cup of coffee in front of NUMBER ONE, who hears someone on the stairs.
PENNY (cheerfully). *Anything to eat?*
NUMBER ONE. *Doughnut.*
FRACK enters and pauses in front of ANSELMO.
FRACK. *How did Nora's act go last night?*
ANSELMO (not in the mood). *Dey liked it, I t'ink.*
FRACK takes a newspaper out of his pocket and points at a stop press headline.
FRACK (reading). *'Waitress killed at Country House. Mysterious explosion.'* (he turns to Anselmo) *Wasn't the party they went to, by any chance?*
ANSELMO. *Wot you say? Can't you see I'm busy?*

183

FRACK remains at the counter. STEENIE, meanwhile, has come quietly downstairs and walks out of the side door into the alley, ignoring the customers.

E.65 EXT. MORTON STREET. ANSELMO'S CAFE. DAY (LOCATION)

CAMERA SHOOTING across to Anselmo's café, taking in front of café and alley at side, including side door. STEENIE leaves side door and walks along the alley towards the main street. He turns into the main street, but just fails to stop BILL from entering the café by the front door. STEENIE follows him and lounges in the front doorway.

E.66 INT. ANSELMO'S CAFE. DAY (STUDIO)

BILL stops at the counter.

BILL. *Morning, all.*

ANSELMO. *Coffee, sir?*

BILL nods. STEENIE looks up and down the street.

E.67 EXT. MORTON STREET. DAY (LOCATION)

CAMERA SHOOTING UPWARDS from Morton Street towards the Floozie's window, taking into shot NUMBER TWO as the curtain of the first floor window moves slightly. NUMBER TWO is looking up at it.

E.68 INT. ANSELMO'S CAFE. DAY (STUDIO)

CAMERA SHOOTING from viewpoint of counter as FRACK, further down the counter, gets up.

PENNY (sharply, holding out her hand). *What about that tuppence, Mr. Frack?*

FRACK. *Now, I had some coppers somewhere.*

PENNY. *You're lucky. They're never around when we need them.*

ANSELMO places coffee before BILL.

LITTLE OLD MAN (at counter). *Speakin' of coppers—*

He wags his head towards the plain clothes man (NUMBER ONE). STEENIE, at the entrance, looks sharply round at the plain-clothes man and notices his regular looks and neat appearance, more suited to the city than to Paddington. STEENIE strolls in and pulls Bill's coat tails. Both go upstairs, casually, BILL carrying his coffee cup.

NUMBER ONE. *Excuse me, Mr. Anselmo—what's upstairs—a club room?*

ANSELMO (startled). *No—it's all private.*

PENNY holds out her hand to FRACK, who is still fumbling and laughing nervously. NUMBER ONE looks dubiously towards the staircase.

E.69 INT. ANSELMO'S LIVING-ROOM. DAY (STUDIO)

CAMERA SHOOTING towards door as BILL and STEENIE enter living-room where LOUIS is standing. CAMERA PANS to show MARIA sitting with bent head in the corner.

STEENIE (fidgeting). *There's a bloke downstairs that looks like a plain clothes man and some funny blokes in the street, too. I shouldn't wonder if they're all around us.*

BILL. *I passed a radio police car further down the street.*

LOUIS. *Go and have a look down the alley. Best place is the back bedroom.*

MARIA shows contempt for Louis' lack of consideration.

BILL. *O.K.*

BILL goes towards Maria's bedroom.

STEENIE (hopping around room). *It's that nark, Frack.*

LOUIS (glancing at Maria). *No—I don't think so. They must have followed her.*

STEENIE jumps up and tiptoes to her with his hands in his pockets. BILL has halted in the bedroom doorway.

STEENIE. *You? What did you say to them at Scotland Yard?*

MARIA. *Ask Louis—I warned him. You want to shoot me?*

STEENIE. *And bring the whole lot down on us?*

His eyes tell LOUIS and BILL to leave the room. LOUIS steps between them.

LOUIS. *That's my job. We're leaving now. Go and watch from the roof, Steenie. If you see anything happen to us, warn the Committee at once. Remember*

there's a way out through the cellar.
STEENIE. *You're not going to let her go?*
BILL (gravely). *If she did give us away, I think she ought to be dealt with* now.
BILL goes into the bedroom. STEENIE hesitates.
LOUIS (threatening). *Go and watch from the roof.*
He opens the door and turns STEENIE out of the room.

E.70 EXT. ANSELMO'S CAFE. WINDOW OF BEDROOM. DAY (LOCATION)
CAMERA SHOOTING UPWARDS from alley to Maria's bedroom, where BILL is looking out through the bedroom window.

E.71 EXT. ANSELMO'S CAFE. WINDOW IN ROOF. DAY (LOCATION)
CAMERA SHOOTING up to top window in the roof of the café building as STEENIE cautiously opens the window and looks out. Noticing nothing, he leans out over the coping, looking along the roof both ways and down into the street.

E.72 EXT. MORTON STREET. DAY (LOCATION)
CAMERA SHOOTING from Steenie's viewpoint on roof down on to Morton Street. The police car is still there. Nothing conspicuous about the room over the chemist's shop. Another car drives up the street and stops near the café. No one gets out.

E.73 EXT. FIRST FLOOR WINDOW OVER DALY'S SHOP. DAY (LOCATION OR STUDIO)
A CLOSE SHOT looking into the closed windows of the upstairs room above the chemist's shop, shows ELIOT and NEWCOME. They seem to recognise the car.

E.74 EXT. MORTON STREET. DAY (LOCATION)
CAMERA SHOOTING DOWNWARDS from Floozie's window on to car near Anselmo's café. It is another police car.

E.74a RESUME ELIOT AND NEWCOME (AS E.73)
They look up.

E.75 INT./EXT. FIRST FLOOR WINDOW OVER DALY'S SHOP. DAY (LOCATION)
CAMERA SHOOTING from first floor window UPWARDS on to roof of Anselmo's café from Eliot's and Newcome's viewpoint. They see STEENIE at the roof window.

E.76 RESUME ELIOT AND NEWCOME. (AS E.73 AND E.74a)
ELIOT goes back into the room from window towards the door.

E.77 INT. ANSELMO'S LIVING-ROOM. DAY (STUDIO)
LOUIS, coming back from bedroom, finds MARIA sitting in a chair, half collapsed. He seizes her roughly by the arm and pulls her upright.
LOUIS. *Come, Maria.*
MARIA. *It's no use, Louis.*
LOUIS. *I've got a job to finish. You're coming with me.*
LOUIS leads her to the door.

E.78 INT. ANSELMO'S CAFE. FIRST FLOOR LANDING. DAY (STUDIO)
LOUIS takes her out and looks down over the banisters.
LOUIS. *You wouldn't want anything to happen to Nora, would you?*
MARIA reacts and follows more willingly.
LOUIS. *Make straight across the café into the alley. If people look, just behave naturally.*

E.79 INT./EXT. MARIA'S BEDROOM. DAY (LOCATION)
CAMERA SHOOTING out of Maria's bedroom on to the mews, showing BILL at the window. He sees a THIRD PLAIN CLOTHES MAN in the mews at the back of the café. (N.B. FROM THIS POINT TO END OF SEQUENCE, EVERY SHOT WHICH DOES NOT INCLUDE MARIA, IS TAKEN FROM MARIA'S VIEWPOINT)

185

E.80 INT. ANSELMO'S CAFE. DAY (STUDIO)

CAMERA HOLDS MARIA in CLOSE SHOT as she speaks.

MARIA. *What about the others?*

CAMERA PANS to include LOUIS as he turns to answer.

LOUIS. *My orders are—to save myself.* (jerking her round) *And I obey orders.*

MARIA nods acceptance. She is in the first big C.U. of this sequence. From now on the CAMERA shares her point of view and no one else's.

MARIA. *I shan't run away.*

LOUIS (thrusting her towards the head of the stairs). *Go on, hurry up.*

BILL appears from the bedroom.

BILL. *Cops are everywhere.*

CAMERA LOOKS DOWN into the café. ANSELMO and PENNY are serving, the one behind the counter, the other over by the tables.

NUMBER ONE is moving to the foot of the stairs, where he looks up curiously at MARIA, who appears on the landing followed by LOUIS and BILL. NUMBER ONE looks quickly in the direction of the side door to the alley.

E.81 MARIA, ANSELMO, PENNY, NUMBER ONE. DAY (STUDIO)

CAMERA SHOOTING towards café as CAMERA CRANES DOWN the stairs as MARIA descends. MARIA looks towards ANSELMO as she goes downstairs followed by LOUIS and BILL. Below them, NUMBER ONE redirects his glance from the side door to MARIA.

E.82 M.S. MARIA, LOUIS, BILL, NUMBER ONE, THIRD PLAIN CLOTHES MAN. (STUDIO)

CAMERA SHOOTING from centre of café in M.S. towards stairs as LOUIS, MARIA reach ground level. LOUIS hesitates with MARIA, suspicious of Number One's glance to the side door. From where they are now, MARIA and LOUIS can see the THIRD PLAIN CLOTHES MAN just outside it in the alleyway. LOUIS hesitates again, then makes for the cellar door under the stairs.

As BILL follows, NUMBER ONE steps behind him and pats his pockets. BILL hits him on the jaw and knocks him down.

MARIA begins to sense the violence to which her actions of the night before are inevitably leading. She sees LOUIS dash down the cellar steps calling to BILL, who is following him to the cellar door.

E.83 INT. ANSELMO'S CAFE. CELLAR DOOR UNDER STAIRS. DAY (STUDIO)

Maria's viewpoint.

CAMERA, SHOOTING from Maria's viewpoint, shows LOUIS calling to BILL.

LOUIS. *Bring Maria.*

CAMERA PANS ROUND as, panicking, FRACK runs towards the front street door of the café.

FRACK. *Help! Police! Help!*

E.84 INT. ANSELMO'S CAFE. DAY (STUDIO)

CAMERA SHOOTING UPWARDS, part of stairs and landing, past MARIA in bottom foreground, who sees STEENIE run down stairs from the top of the house and draw his revolver. Without hesitation he fires at FRACK.

E.85 INT. ANSELMO'S CAFE. CAFE DOORWAY. DAY (STUDIO OR LOCATION)

Maria's viewpoint.

FRACK, with a surprised grin, falls into the arms of NUMBER TWO just outside the front door of the café.

E.86 INT. ANSELMO'S CAFE. DAY (STUDIO)

CAMERA SHOOTING UPWARDS past MARIA, on to landing where STEENIE is bending down again, aiming through the banister. There is a sound of boxes being overturned in the cellar.

STEENIE. *Stay where you are, everybody.*

E.87 INT. ANSELMO'S CAFE. DAY (STUDIO)

MARIA shrinks back, out of sight of STEENIE, against the wooden partition below the stairs and between the cellar and kitchen doors.

E.88 INT. ANSELMO'S CAFE. DAY (STUDIO)

Maria's viewpoint.

CAMERA SHOOTING in M.S. from Maria's viewpoint towards ANSELMO behind the counter, who opens the safety valves of the two hot water urns, releasing the vapour in clouds and obscuring the café and blotting out STEENIE and his field of vision.

E.89 INT. ANSELMO'S CAFE. ENTRANCE TO CELLAR. DAY (STUDIO)

MARIA hears STEENIE run down the stairs behind her and sees him dash past her down into the cellar. Then MARIA looks towards the main door of the café.

E.90 INT. ANSELMO'S CAFE. DAY (STUDIO)

Maria's viewpoint.

CAMERA SHOOTING from Maria's viewpoint towards main door of café as ELIOT gropes his way from the main door through the fog vapour towards MARIA.

There is now the sound from below of crates being overturned and someone battering on the door at the farther end of the cellar.

LOUIS' VOICE. *Get Maria!*

MARIA, now in shot, follows ELIOT into the doorway to the cellar steps. Below them, they see BILL pull a small object from his pocket, adjust it and throw it towards ELIOT.

E.91 INT. ANSELMO'S CAFE. ENTRANCE TO CELLAR. DAY (STUDIO)

Maria's viewpoint.

CAMERA, SHOOTING in CLOSE SHOT, PANS with bomb as it flies past ELIOT on the staircase at entrance to cellar and rolls across the café floor. It is similar to the bomb MARIA used at the garden party. NUMBER TWO, entering the café, kicks the bomb back into the cellar.

E.92 INT. ANSELMO'S CAFE. ENTRANCE TO CELLAR. DAY (STUDIO)

MARIA struggles forward from Anselmo's grasp and goes to the cellar door.

MARIA (three steps down). *Come back! It's a bomb!*

E.92a C.U. ANSELMO

He reacts in terror.

E.93 INT. ANSELMO'S CAFE. DAY (STUDIO)

CAMERA SHOOTING through cellar door as ELIOT runs back up the stairs. MARIA, facing downstairs, holds out her hand to pull him up, just as there is an explosion below in the cellar. There is smoke followed by a glare of flame.

E.94 INT. ANSELMO'S CAFE. CELLAR DOORWAY. DAY (STUDIO)

Smoke and flames in foreground as CAMERA is in CLOSE UP of MARIA.

E.95 INT. ANSELMO'S CAFE. STAIRS AND CELLAR. DAY (STUDIO)

Maria's viewpoint.

The EXPLOSION. The CAMERA FALLS through the doorway and down the steps into the confusion in the cellar below.

ANSELMO'S VOICE. *Maria!* . . .

BLUR OUT:

(END OF SEQUENCE 'E')

N.B. Anselmo's Voice calling 'Maria!' is carried through the Dissolve as an echo and merges into the first mention of 'Lena' in Scene F.1.

SEQUENCE 'F'

BLUR IN:

F.1 INT. PRIVATE ROOM IN HOSPITAL DAY/NIGHT (STUDIO)

Maria's viewpoint. The IMAGES are seen from the disordered viewpoint of a very sick patient lying in bed.

The IMAGES are blurred and pulse in and out of focus, though at first none of the focus is at all sharp. The IMAGES are linked by an effect as of an oily ripple passing across the screen, the first IMAGES appear only momentarily and the whole effect slows down while the focus becomes more distinct. The IMAGES are faces which are not always occupied with business on screen.

A list of IMAGES follows:

1. A NURSING SISTER.
2. THREE NURSES.
A. A YOUNG DOCTOR.
4. A MIDDLE-AGED SURGEON.
5. A HOSPITAL MATRON.
6. TWO HOSPITAL ORDERLIES.
7. SURGEON AND GROUP DRESSED FOR OPERATING THEATRE.
8. NURSING SISTER.
9. THE SURGEON, DOCTOR AND SISTER.
10. THE NURSES.
11. MISS JACKSON.
12. SISTER AND ELIOT.
13. ELIOT.

Overscene voices are heard, as follows, saying, 'Lena Collins.'

1. WOMAN'S VOICE.
2. MAN'S VOICE.
3. GENERAL VOICES.
4. 2ND WOMAN'S VOICE.
5. 2ND MAN'S VOICE.
6. MISS JACKSON'S VOICE.
7. ELIOT'S VOICE.

And interspersed with these voices, is that of MARIA, saying 'Who is Lena Collins?' —at first mistily, then quite clearly, then drowsily again.

F.2 INT. PRIVATE ROOM. DAY (STUDIO)

In the last and clearest image, a NURSING SISTER is holding a patient's progress chart, and the CAMERA PANS for the first time as the SISTER sets the chart down on the bedside table and leaves it to go to the door of what is obviously a private room in a hospital. The CAMERA RISES and looks down at the chart alongside the bed. The patient's name is 'Lena Collins.'

F.3 MARIA (STUDIO)

CAMERA HOLDS C.U. of MARIA in bed. She is very weak but has managed to raise herself on one arm to look at the chart.

MARIA. *Who is Lena Collins?*

F.4 SISTER AND MAN (STUDIO)

Maria's viewpoint. The SISTER turns in the doorway. There is a MAN outside seated across the passage—he is in fact NUMBER TWO Plain Clothes Man from E.43. The SISTER closes the door again.

SISTER. *We've told you. But you always forget again.*

F.5 MARIA (STUDIO)

MARIA (anxiously). *My head gets so misty. But I really feel different to-day. Explain to me. My name's Maria Brentano.* (she corrects herself) *Maria Brent.*

188

F.6 SISTER (STUDIO)

CAMERA SHOOTING from Maria's viewpoint as SISTER approaches.

SISTER (speaking kindly). *You do look—different—to-day.*

MARIA. *And Nora? Tell me about Nora. And Anselmo?*

SISTER. *You know, you are better! I think I'll get someone to come and have a chat with you.*

MARIA. *Nora?*

SISTER. *No, you must be patient. But you remember Miss Jackson? At Scotland Yard?*

She hands MARIA a dose of medicine in a glass, and goes out of the room to telephone.

F.7 MARIA (STUDIO)

CAMERA SHOOTING in C.U. Maria's head lying on her pillow.

MARIA (beginning to remember). *Miss Jackson—*

BLUR OUT:

F.8 INT. PRIVATE ROOM. HOSPITAL. DAY (STUDIO)

Maria's viewpoint. CAMERA SHOOTING to side of bed where MISS JACKSON is looking at the 'camera-patient.' She smiles and nods.

MISS JACKSON. *Well, I hear you've really turned the corner. Look what I've brought you . . .*

She brings into view a bunch of chrysanthemums. She is wearing wool for a chilly day.

F.9 MARIA (STUDIO)

MARIA. *Chrysanthemums. Thank you.*

Maria's smile changes to bewilderment.

MARIA. *But, is it . . . ?*

F.10 MISS JACKSON AND SISTER (STUDIO)

Maria's viewpoint.

The SISTER takes the flowers and puts them in a vase.

MISS JACKSON. *It's October now. You've been ill a long time.*

F.11 MARIA AND MISS JACKSON (STUDIO)

CAMERA STARTS on C.U. of MARIA.

MARIA. *Is Nora all right?*

MISS JACKSON sits down into CAMERA and leans forward close to MARIA.

MISS JACKSON. *Yes, and she's doing very well.*

MARIA. *And my uncle? Was he injured?*

MISS JACKSON. *Only a few scratches. The café was a mess but they're rebuilding it. How much do you remember?*

MARIA. *I remember there was this terrible explosion. Then nothing till this moment. Have you been here with me?*

MISS JACKSON. *Yes, lots of times. You've forgotten. You've been very ill.*

MARIA. *Please explain to me once more—why do they keep calling me Lena Collins? That isn't my name.*

MISS JACKSON. *Well, you see—just to be on the safe side, we made up a name for you. It wasn't safe to use your own name any more.*

MARIA (sadly and thoughtfully). *I see. I understand . . . Can I see my sister soon?*

F.12 MISS JACKSON (STUDIO)

MISS JACKSON (evading the question). *You'd better ask Inspector Eliot. He'll be here to-morrow.*

BLUR DISSOLVE:

F.13 INT. PRIVATE ROOM. DAY (STUDIO)

CAMERA STARTS on C.U. of MARIA lying propped up in bed, a little stronger. CAMERA TRACKS BACK to show ELIOT is sitting by her, reading to her from a typewritten statement. The SISTER is watching MARIA. MISS JACKSON is also present. CAMERA PANS to a C.U. of ELIOT and PULLS BACK to show MARIA in profile.

> ELIOT (reading). *I saw three men go down into the cellar. First Bill, the car driver. Next, Louis Balan. Steenie followed. No one else went down before the bomb exploded.*

ELIOT stops reading and speaks to MARIA.

> ELIOT. *That's right, isn't it?*
> MARIA (tired now). *Yes. That's all I remember.*

MISS JACKSON helps MARIA to sit up and sign the document. Then MARIA sinks back, tired, on to her pillows.

> ELIOT (to Miss Jackson). *That should satisfy the coroner.*

F.14 ELIOT. (STUDIO)

ELIOT opens a small box he has had with him.

> ELIOT. *I wonder if you can identify any of these things . . .*

F.15 INSERT. CONTENTS OF BOX (STUDIO)

> ELIOT'S VOICE. *. . . They were found in the remains of a jacket in the cellar.*

F.16 CLOSE GROUP SHOT (STUDIO)

CAMERA FAVOURS MARIA as she turns towards ELIOT and gives her attention to the contents of the box.

> MARIA. *That's Louis' cigarette case. These I don't know. Oh—this is my father's pen. I gave it to Louis.*
> ELIOT. *You're sure?*
> MARIA. *Oh, yes!*

She shows him the initials on the pen.

> ELIOT. *And Louis had it in his possession?*
> MARIA. *Yes.* (a pause) *Inspector Eliot—is Louis dead?*
> ELIOT. *We don't know. He and Steenie are missing.*
> MISS JACKSON. *That's what we call it when we're not sure.*
> ELIOT. *Would you like to keep the pen? I'm afraid it's rather battered.*
> MARIA. *It's all I have left of my father's. Thank you.*
> ELIOT. *I'll go now. We mustn't tire you.*
> MARIA. *But first—can I see my sister soon?*
> ELIOT. *We'll think about that to-morrow. When you're stronger.*

Over her head, ELIOT and MISS JACKSON exchange a look. They move away from the bed.

> SISTER. *It won't be long now. Settle down and rest.*

BLUR DISSOLVE:

F.17 to F.19 INT. PRIVATE ROOM. DAY (STUDIO)

MARIA is considerably better. She is sitting up in an easy chair, wrapped in shawls. MARIA is handing a letter, addressed to NORA, to MISS JACKSON.

> MARIA (LENA). *I've written to Nora. It won't be opened? It's private.*
> MISS JACKSON. *Because you've signed yourself Maria?*

MARIA (LENA) shrugs. She takes back the letter.

> MISS JACKSON. *Listen, Lena. We call you Lena Collins for your own safety.*
> MARIA (LENA). *Not—for always?*
> MISS JACKSON. *Yes.*
> MARIA (LENA). *But not for Nora? Not for Anselmo?*
> MISS JACKSON. *No one must know that Maria Brent is alive. No one.*
> MARIA (LENA). *They believe I'm dead?*
> MISS JACKSON. *Lena, it had to be so. You yourself told us you could never be*

safe again. You see—we had a lot of trouble over that Galbern business; it created a very delicate situation. We can't afford to give the organisation another chance. It's not just you—it really is an international problem. We can't afford to let them strike again.

MARIA (LENA). *So Nora and Anselmo must believe I'm dead?*

MISS JACKSON. *I told them you were dead, Lena.*

MARIA (LENA). *You told them?*

MISS JACKSON. *We couldn't let them learn it from the papers.*

MARIA tears up the letter. It is a surrender.

MARIA (LENA). *I suppose I deserve it. But my brain is not dead. My body is going to get well. What am I going to do with all the years? Where can I go now?*

MISS JACKSON. *Lena—*

MARIA (LENA). *You're going to put me in prison?*

MISS JACKSON. *No. Not if you become Lena Collins. Now, mind, Lena, I'm going to trust you. Will you give me your word not to let me down?*

MARIA (LENA). *I can't promise what I don't know.*

MISS JACKSON. *No, of course not. But if you don't accept what we're going to offer you, will you promise not to talk about it to anyone?*

MARIA (LENA). *Oh, yes. I promise that.*

MISS JACKSON. *Good. And remember that Inspector Eliot and I are vouching for you.*

MISS JACKSON stands up.

MARIA (LENA). *Where are you going?*

MISS JACKSON. *Inspector Eliot should be here by now. He'll tell you.*

MARIA (LENA). *You won't leave me?*

MISS JACKSON (holding Maria's hand reassuringly). *I'll be here, Lena.*

MISS JACKSON opens the door.

MISS JACKSON. *Come in, Inspector.*

INSPECTOR ELIOT enters.

ELIOT. *Good-morning. And how is Lena?*

MARIA (LENA). *'Lena' is better.*

ELIOT. *Thank you. Now—we've got a scheme to put to you.*

MISS JACKSON. *She's going to be very helpful.*

ELIOT. *Good. You know, Lena, we've been studying you all this time. We don't want to keep you cooped up somewhere all your life. That would be a waste of a real person like you. But you can't live as Maria Brent, as you know. How would you like to be the real Lena Collins?*

MARIA (LENA). *You mean—pretend to be someone else for the rest of my life?*

ELIOT. *More than that. Be another person.*

MARIA (LENA). *But—they'd recognise me.*

ELIOT. *We can take care of that. You can dye your hair.*

MISS JACKSON. *You have a high forehead. A fringe would suit you.*

MARIA (LENA). *Is that all?*

ELIOT. *No. We would need to alter the shape of your face slightly.*

MISS JACKSON. *It's done in beauty treatment every day.*

ELIOT. *Plastic surgery.*

MARIA (LENA). *No—I couldn't.*

MISS JACKSON. *Lena, dear. You've been very brave. You've had surgical treatment already.*

MARIA (LENA) (panic). *You wouldn't do it against my will? You wouldn't do it without telling me?*

ELIOT. *Of course not.*

MISS JACKSON. *Don't be frightened, Lena. We want to give you a fresh start. You could even see Nora again.*

MARIA (LENA). *I could——*

191

ELIOT. *Not to talk to—we can't alter your voice. But you could see her dance. Look at this sketch.*

F.20 INSERT OF SKETCH (STUDIO)

ELIOT (continuing). *Not bad looking. That's the surgeon's idea of Lena Collins.*
MARIA (LENA) (looking at sketch). *I could see Nora again.*

F.21 GROUP SHOT (STUDIO)

MISS JACKSON has been looking through a copy of "The Dancing Times" (or other appropriate magazine). She hands her the magazine opened at a photograph.
MISS JACKSON. *Here's something to cheer you up. Nora's coming on very well. D'you know her partner? He looks charming.*

F.22 INSERT OF MAGAZINE (STUDIO)

F.23 MARIA (STUDIO)

MARIA begins to look at the article and photographs which indicate NORA as one of the coming dancers.

F.24 ELIOT. MISS JACKSON (STUDIO)

MISS JACKSON and ELIOT are happy to note Maria's contented reaction.

F.25 INSERT MAGAZINE AND SKETCHES (STUDIO)

When the CAMERA has taken stock of Nora's prospects, it shifts its point of view to include the plastic surgeon's sketches which are lying on Maria's knee.
ELIOT'S VOICE. *Think it over. You can take your time.*

F.26 INT. CAR. DAY (B.P.)

CAMERA on C.U. of insert of label, stuck on a small case, the case resting on someone's knee in a car. Label: 'WANTED ON VOYAGE.' CAMERA PANS SLIGHTLY to show a second label (a tie-on): 'MISS LENA COLLINS, Passenger to Cork via Dublin.' CAMERA PANS FULLY UP past the hands to the strange new face of LENA COLLINS. The skin is almost too smooth. The hair is a different colour. Only the eyes are Maria's. LENA COLLINS is an attractive-looking woman. The CAMERA reveals MISS JACKSON sitting next to her.
MISS JACKSON (to say something at a difficult moment). *You won't recognise the café!*

F.27 INT. CAR. DAY (B.P.)

It is a summer's day as, from inside the car, the CAMERA turns into the street where Anselmo's café stands.
MARIA watches quietly as the car slowly threads its way through the traffic. The new café is about to re-open. ANSELMO and PENNY are there. MARIA says nothing until the street is left behind them.

F.28 INT. CAR. DAY (B.P.)

MARIA. *You live in a street for years, and it is nothing. Just a street. And now I've remembered every single thing . . . And Nora . . . in and out to her classes . . . All part of London.*
MISS JACKSON (matter-of-fact, but friendly, to break any tension). *You'll be seeing her dance to-morrow—I'm longing to see her myself.*
CAMERA PANS DOWN to the word 'Dublin' on the label of a piece of luggage.

DISSOLVE:

NOTE: Re the Gaiety Theatre, Dublin, MISS JACKSON and MARIA (LENA COLLINS) are seated in a box, which is one of a row of boxes behind the side of the dress circle. Only the one box and partof two rows of seats in front need be built. The view from this box includes the orchestra pit and one side of the proscenium arch (with the

boxes contiguous) and most of the floor of the stage. There is no need to build any other part of the auditorium, nor the top of the proscenium arch.
The dress circle bar is a few feet from the door of the box.
A passage runs from the door of the bar behind the entrance doors to the boxes and finishes at an iron door which leads backstage. The door carries an appropriate notice and is locked during performances. In the actual passage are certain doorways which can be omitted for clarity of action.

F.29 INSERT THEATRE PROGRAMME (STUDIO)

A theatre programme headed 'The Gaiety Theatre, Dublin.' A minor English ballet company is giving two ballets. NORA BRENT and FEDOR LUKI are appearing as guest artistes in the second ballet.

F.30 to F.34 INT. GAIETY THEATRE, DUBLIN. BOX AND STAGE. NIGHT (STUDIO)

CAMERA SHOOTING PAST MARIA (LENA COLLINS) and MISS JACKSON sitting in the theatre box during the performance. The programme is in Miss Jackson's hands, in the darkened box behind the Dress Circle. MARIA (LENA COLLINS) occupies the next seat. A flourish from the orchestra heralds Nora's appearance. Here follows the first section of the ballet.

F.35 INT. THEATRE BOX. NIGHT (STUDIO)

MISS JACKSON turns to MARIA (LENA COLLINS).
   MISS JACKSON. *She's very, very good.*
   MARIA. *She's just eighteen. I wonder if she's happy?*
MISS JACKSON makes a friendly gesture.
   MARIA (to Miss Jackson). *It is possible she's happy.*

F.36 to F.40 INT. GAIETY THEATRE. STAGE. NIGHT (STUDIO)

Here follows the Main Section and climax of the ballet. Nora's performance is impressive. Her partner, FEDOR, is virile and sympathetic, with an interesting, irregular face. Together, they make an attractive pair.
The dance ends with NORA and FEDOR in command of the stage. There is strong applause. NORA receives the ovation with the calm and assurance of a ripened artiste. She gives FEDOR a happy smile. The curtains close.

F.41 INT. THEATRE BOX. DUBLIN. NIGHT (STUDIO)

MARIA (LENA COLLINS) sits on, lost to the bustle of the audience around her. MISS JACKSON looks at her sympathetically and touches her arm.
   MISS JACKSON. *We both need a drink!*

F.42 INT. GAIETY THEATRE, DUBLIN. DRESS CIRCLE BAR. NIGHT (STUDIO)

MISS JACKSON and MARIA (LENA COLLINS) are standing in the Dress Circle Bar, each holding a glass. Maria's (Lena Collins) thoughts are entirely of Nora.
   MISS JACKSON (studying the programme). *This next scene—it's something to do with the wine harvest.*
   MARIA (pushing her glass forward). *Have another?*
   MISS JACKSON. *I'm supposed to be on duty.*
   MARIA (charmingly). *For me. We'll drink to my new life. Two more, please.*
Their glasses filled once more, they raise them to their lips. Then they hear a voice.
   BENTLEY'S BOOMING BASS VOICE. *I say, miss, I've asked you for a double whisky. Don't you ever come over this side of the bar?*
   IRISH BARMAID. *I'm being as quick as I can. Curtain won't be up for another five minutes. Everyone'll get served.*
MARIA (LENA COLLINS) has turned round, her eyes searching for the man with the bass voice. He can only be the big, burly fellow at the other end of the bar to their right?
   MISS JACKSON. *What's the matter, Lena?*

193

o

MARIA (LENA COLLINS) concentrates on BENTLEY, who knocks back his double whisky and flings a coin on to the counter.

MISS JACKSON. *What is it?*

MARIA (LENA COLLINS). *That man . . . with the deep voice.*

BENTLEY, walking away from the bar, passes close. MARIA (LENA COLLINS) stares at the unmistakable shape and pattern of his thick, tweed trousers and boots, and at the WOMAN he joins, whose low-heeled shoes and characteristic legs she also recognises.

MARIA (LENA COLLINS). *I must be right—I could never forget a single one of those voices, the committee in the dark room—only their legs and shoes—and that woman.*

MISS JACKSON. *Where did they go?*

MARIA (LENA COLLINS). *Along there. Quickly.*

F.43 INT. GAIETY THEATRE, DUBLIN. CORRIDOR, NIGHT (STUDIO)

CAMERA SHOOTING towards her as they leave and turn left into the passage. It ends in a door, which they open. CAMERA TRACKS with them as they enter another passage which leads to a door at the end marked: 'BACKSTAGE, NO ADMITTANCE.'

MISS JACKSON (agitated). *Are you sure? They didn't go back to the auditorium?*

MARIA. *Yes. I'm sure.*

They move further along the passage, a terrible thought in both their minds, looking left and right for a possible way to somewhere else. But there is only the one door, and it is marked 'BACKSTAGE.' MARIA (LENA COLLINS) tries the door, but it is locked.

MARIA (controlling her fear). *He couldn't have gone to see Nora—why should I think that. He has gone to see her.*

MISS JACKSON. *It's possible. We'd better go round to the stage door.*

MARIA (tortured). *Nora——*

MISS JACKSON. *There may be nothing in it.*

They begin to return the way they came.

DISSOLVE:

F.44 EXT. DUBLIN CASTLE. NIGHT (LOCATION)

The Irish Police Headquarters. The street lights are already lit. A number of police cars and motor cyclists drive out of the courtyard and disperse in all directions. Only a few windows in the building still show light. A PLAIN-CLOTHES MAN steps into a police car and drives off. Uniformed police are in the background.

F.45 INT. OFFICE IN DUBLIN CASTLE. NIGHT (STUDIO)

In a room inside the castle, MARIA (LENA COLLINS) and MISS JACKSON are in the company of TWO IRISH POLICE OFFICERS, an IRISH INSPECTOR and a SERGEANT, both in plain clothes. The INSPECTOR is speaking into a telephone.

The IRISH INSPECTOR rings off and speaks to MISS JACKSON.

IRISH INSPECTOR. *Security are getting through to Inspector Eliot in London on the direct line.*

MARIA (LENA COLLINS) (really desperate). *What can he do? If we wait for him, it'll be too late.*

MISS JACKSON. *That's all right. It's only to keep in touch. We shall act without him, of course.*

SERGEANT. *Don't be exciting yourself, Miss Collins. Nora Brent's only a messenger, probably. A go-between. But she might lead us to some bigger fish.*

MARIA (LENA COLLINS). *She mustn't come to any harm. If only I could do something.*

IRISH INSPECTOR (to Miss Jackson). *Would you ask Eliot to let Miss Collins help us? She might identify someone and give a signal.*

One of the telephones rings. The IRISH INSPECTOR answers it.

IRISH INSPECTOR. *Is that you, Eliot? . . . You have? . . . Have they got a line on it . . .?* (strongly) *Early next week*¯ . . . *I should say so! Just a minute, Miss Jackson's with me.*

He hands the receiver to MISS JACKSON, who begins talking to ELIOT.

IRISH INSPECTOR (to Sergeant). *You know what? That new air attaché due next week. He's the son of General Galbern.*

SERGEANT. *General Galbern!*

MARIA (LENA COLLINS). *Oh, God!* . . . (N.B. Alternative exclamation required for American version.)

F.46 INT. GAIETY THEATRE, DUBLIN. STAGE. NIGHT (STUDIO)

The orchestra at the theatre breaks into the main theme of the last act, the dance of the wine festival, which is Anselmo's favourite tune.

F.47 INT. GAIETY THEATRE, DUBLIN. BACKSTAGE PASSAGE. NIGHT (STUDIO)

The PLAIN CLOTHES MAN (from F.44) picks up the receiver of a public telephone and dials a number. The music is still loud overscene.

F.48 INT. OFFICE IN DUBLIN CASTLE. NIGHT (STUDIO)

The Irish C.I.D. INSPECTOR lifts the receiver and the faint distorted sound of the orchestra catches Maria's (Lena Collins) attention. She hears nothing of the conversation, for the music absorbs her imagination. The IRISH INSPECTOR puts down the receiver and both he and MISS JACKSON turn to speak to MARIA (LENA COLLINS). And still she hears nothing but music. Then MISS JACKSON shakes her arm.

IRISH INSPECTOR. *Miss Collins, we're talking to you.*

MARIA (LENA COLLINS). *I'm sorry. Nora's dancing. I'm ready.*

IRISH INSPECTOR. *Now, you remember what we've told you?*

MARIA (LENA COLLINS). *Yes.*

MISS JACKSON. *As soon as you recognise anyone, drop your handkerchief and clear out of the way. If you have to speak, say as little as possible.*

MARIA (LENA COLLINS). *I understand.*

F.49 EXT. GAIETY THEATRE, DUBLIN. NIGHT (LOCATION)

The stage door of the Gaiety Theatre, Dublin, is in the front of the building by the main entrance. The DANCERS are emerging, some signing autographs for members of the crowd. An ELDERLY WOMAN is selling flowers. CAMERA PANS and shows that across the road a taxi is standing, and near it, against the wall, a WOMAN is watching the stage door—MARIA (LENA COLLINS). To her comes the IRISH INSPECTOR. He nods and strolls along the pavement to a station wagon.

F.50 NORA, FEDOR, DOORKEEPER, CROWD (LOCATION OR STUDIO)

NORA, dressed for the street, comes to the entrance, followed by FEDOR.
The STAGE DOORKEEPER nods to her.

NORA. *Good-night, Gerry.*

DOORKEEPER. *Good-night, Miss. Good-night, sir.*

FEDOR. *Good-night.* (to Nora) *Come and eat.*

NORA. *No. Sorry.*

FEDOR. *Can I see you to your digs?*

NORA signs her name a few times.

NORA. *Not to-night, Fedor. I'm meeting someone.*

They make their way through the crowd until they are on their own. NORA pauses for FEDOR to leave her.

FEDOR. *You know what Anselmo said about being home late.*

NORA (pursuing her argument). *It's strictly business.*

FEDOR (imitating Anselmo). *Run along, child, an' don' be late.* (Then in his own voice). *Early call in the morning, you know.*

NORA. *Oh, dear. Good-night, Fedor.*
FEDOR (fond of her). *Good-night, Nora.*
FEDOR walks away past the main entrance and towards St. Stephen's Green.

F.51 NORA, MARIA (LENA COLLINS) LOCATION
NORA watches him go, liking him. Then she turns and goes off in the opposite direction.
Along the street, in a doorway, a match is struck. NORA checks herself and then saunters slowly along towards the burning match. MARIA (LENA COLLINS) enters shot from behind CAMERA and close to the wall; walks after NORA, who enters a waiting car followed by a MAN (double for STEENIE). The car drives off. At once, the taxi starts up and drives to MARIA (LENA COLLINS), who jumps in. The taxi follows the car at a discreet distance. The station wagon takes up the chase.

F.52 EXT. PHŒNIX PARK. ENTRANCE GATES. NIGHT (LOCATION)
Phœnix Park Gates. The three cars enter the park. There is other traffic on the road.

F.53 EXT. PHŒNIX PARK. MAIN ROAD. NIGHT (LOCATION)
CAMERA PANNING. In the lower foreground is a signpost pointing to Dublin. The three cars travelling from Dublin, come out of a side turning and, passing an equestrian statue, drive away along the main road through the park, the CAMERA PANNING with the taxi.

F.54 INT. LENA'S TAXI. NIGHT (B.P.)
MARIA (LENA COLLINS) watching anxiously ahead.

F.55 EXT. PHŒNIX PARK. MAIN ROAD. NIGHT (LOCATION)
Nora's car turns off the main road along a turning to the left. The taxi slows down.

F.56 EXT. PHŒNIX PARK. SIDE ROAD. NIGHT (LOCATION)
Nora's car stops and NORA and her ESCORT (STEENIE) alight. The car drives on.

F.57 EXT. PHŒNIX PARK. SIDE ROAD. NIGHT (LOCATION)
MARIA (LENA COLLINS) and the DRIVER watching ahead from the stationary taxi.

F.58 EXT. PHŒNIX PARK. PATHWAY. NIGHT (LOCATION)
TWO PASSERS-BY pass NORA and her ESCORT, who use a torch to light the ground. NORA and her ESCORT turn right and walk away from the road, apparently over the grass.

F.59 EXT. PHŒNIX PARK. SIDE ROAD. NIGHT (LOCATION)
The TWO PASSERS-BY pass the taxi with a friendly "Good-night." The station wagon comes up behind the taxi with lights extinguished. MARIA (LENA COLLINS) alights. The IRISH INSPECTOR and MISS JACKSON joining her.
IRISH INSPECTOR (nodding towards Nora). *They're following a path. You'll have to signal us with your torch. We'll be close behind you.*
MARIA (LENA COLLINS) hurries on. The IRISH INSPECTOR returns to the station wagon.
IRISH INSPECTOR. *Sergeant, Miss Jackson and I will follow Miss Collins. You wait here for the second car and bring the men after us. The rest of you, drive round to the other side of this patch of ground and approach from the rear. Send the car back the minute you get there. We'll see the headlights as she turns.*

F.60 EXT. PHŒNIX PARK. PATHWAY. NIGHT (LOCATION)
MARIA (LENA COLLINS) turns off the road and follows the path, CAMERA TRACKING. Ahead of her, she sees the ESCORT with the torch walking back towards her. He shines the torch up into her face for a moment. MARIA (LENA COLLINS) retaliates with her torch. The man is STEENIE.

STEENIE. *Beg pardon, Miss.*

He walks on.

F.61 MARIA (LENA COLLINS), LOUIS, NORA (LOCATION)

MARIA (LENA COLLINS) is appalled at the sight of STEENIE. She controls herself and walks on. She hears a murmur of voices. NORA and a man are seated side by side on a log near the path. The man lights two cigarettes in his mouth. It is LOUIS. He gives a cigarette to NORA, who accepts it as customary.

F.62 MARIA (LENA COLLINS) (LOCATION)

CAMERA in C.U. of MARIA (LENA COLLINS). Her worst fears are confirmed.

F.63 MARIA (LENA COLLINS), LOUIS, NORA (LOCATION)

CAMERA FAVOURS LOUIS and MARIA. LOUIS looks up at MARIA (LENA COLLINS), curious at her shock on seeing him.

NORA. *Do you want anything?*

MARIA. *Yes.*

LOUIS stiffens. His eyes are fixed firmly on hers. Then he looks at her hands.

NORA. *Are you looking for someone?*

F.64 MARIA (LENA COLLINS) (LOCATION)

MARIA. *I was looking for you, Nora.*

F.65 LOUIS, NORA, MARIA (LENA COLLINS) (LOCATION)

The impact of the voice on NORA is terrifying. To LOUIS, it is a confirmation. He rises, CAMERA PULLING BACK to include all three.

LOUIS. *You had the advantage of me for a moment, Maria.*

NORA. Maria?

She looks in astonishment at MARIA (LENA COLLINS).

F.66 MARIA (LENA COLLINS), NORA (LOCATION)

An impulsive affectionate gesture from MARIA (LENA COLLINS) towards NORA. CAMERA TRACKS IN CLOSE.

NORA. *You're not Maria. Maria's dead.*

MARIA. *I've been in hospital, Nora* (with a gesture to her face). *They had to change me.*

NORA takes hold of MARIA.

NORA. *Why didn't we know?*

F.67 LOUIS, NORA AND MARIA (LENA COLLINS) (LOCATION)

CAMERA FAVOURS LOUIS and MARIA (LENA COLLINS).

LOUIS. *Police orders. The oldest trick of all.*

MARIA (LENA COLLINS) (to Nora). *To save my life.* (To Louis, bitterly). *I thought you were dead, too. We're both ghosts in the same world.*

LOUIS. *The betrayer and the betrayed.*

All this time NORA is clinging to MARIA (LENA COLLINS).

NORA. *To save your life? What do you mean? Louis talks of you as a saint. You were together.*

MARIA. *To-night I saw you dance, Nora. I came just to see you. Before I go away.*

LOUIS. *You're lying. You're working for the police. Nothing else could bring you here.*

NORA turns into profile towards LOUIS.

NORA. *Louis—you loved each other!*

A moment of awful silence. A distant sound. The headlights of the station wagon flash behind them as it turns on the road beyond.

F.68 STEENIE (LOCATION)

STEENIE, caught in the lights, turns back on the path, apprehensive.

F.69 LOUIS, NORA, MARIA (LENA COLLINS) (LOCATION)

CAMERA SHOOTING towards LOUIS and NORA, MARIA (LENA COLLINS) is back to CAMERA.
NORA. *You didn't give Louis away to the police!*
LOUIS. *Don't expect the truth from her. Come, Nora.*

F.70 LOUIS, NORA, MARIA (LENA COLLINS), STEENIE, PASSERS-BY (LOCATION)

CAMERA SHOOTING in THREE-SHOT, favouring MARIA (LENA COLLINS). STEENIE (in background) walks with deliberation towards the three, watching this strange meeting with a third person he does not know.
MARIA (LENA COLLINS). *Nora, my darling, listen. They lied to make you work for them. They don't think I'm a saint. There's nothing but horror for you with Louis' people. Your dancing, my darling, stick to your dancing—don't throw yourself away.*
LOUIS, in profile in foreground, has been looking around for other signs of danger.
TWO PEOPLE go by along the path, one of them laughing.
LOUIS. *Just talk, Maria. Nora's grown up. She's her own mistress.*
MARIA (LENA COLLINS). *You never loved anyone, Louis.*
STEENIE is coming close.
LOUIS. *I trust Nora.*
STEENIE (warningly). *Louis!*
MARIA (LENA COLLINS). *You mean you use her. You only use people because they let themselves be used by men like you.*
LOUIS. *So much the better if they're useful fighters.*
MARIA (LENA COLLINS). *Your fight's gone rotten. You've let it drag you down to Steenie's level. You must believe me, Nora.*
STEENIE, who has been standing thunderstruck at what he hears, moves swiftly up to MARIA (LENA COLLINS) as she mentions his name, gazing at her with fanatical hatred and complete confidence. NORA is horrified.
STEENIE (urgently). *Get going, Louis.*
STEENIE draws a knife and stabs MARIA (LENA COLLINS).
As MARIA sinks to the ground supported only by Nora's arms. STEENIE plucks at Louis' arm.
STEENIE. *Come on!*
LOUIS throws STEENIE off. STEENIE runs away into the darkness.

F.71 LOUIS, MARIA (LENA COLLINS), NORA (LOCATION)

LOUIS stands, looking down at MARIA (LENA COLLINS). There is the sound of feet approaching at a run over the turf—a scuffle—a cry from STEENIE. A hand grasps Louis' shoulder, but he does not move or resist in any way.

F.72 MARIA (LENA COLLINS), NORA, LOUIS (LOCATION)

NORA is bent over Maria's body, Maria's (Lena Collins) hand is lying on the ground by the spilt contents of her handbag; Pietro Brentano's gleaming fountain pen is prominent.

F.73 MARIA (LENA COLLINS), NORA, LOUIS (LOCATION)

NORA listens close to Maria's moving lips.
MARIA (LENA COLLINS). *Nora—understand—believe.*

F.74 MARIA (LENA COLLINS), NORA, LOUIS (LOCATION)

MARIA'S (LENA COLLINS) hand becomes inert beside the pen.

F.75 MARIA (LENA COLLINS), NORA, MISS JACKSON, LOUIS (LOCATION)

NORA (whispering). *Maria!*
NORA looks up from Maria's body.
NORA. *But the blood—it won't stop . . .*
She is in exactly the same position as was MARIA when the waitress died in her

198

arms, and the look on Nora's face is the same. MISS JACKSON enters shot. Two Policemen (out of shot) are lifting away MARIA'S (LENA COLLINS) body. MISS JACKSON lifts
NORA from her kneeling position and into shot.

F.76 LOUIS, NORA, MISS JACKSON, NIGHT (LOCATION)
LOUIS looks at NORA.

F.77 LOUIS, NORA, MISS JACKSON. NIGHT (LOCATION)
NORA looks at LOUIS, then away.

F.78 LOUIS, NORA, MISS JACKSON, POLICEMEN. NIGHT (LOCATION)
LOUIS is led away by two POLICEMEN.

F.79 NORA, MISS JACKSON. NIGHT (LOCATION)
NORA, supported by MISS JACKSON, gains strength as she looks up and away to the
sky.
Music begins the prinicipal dance theme of the ballet.

FADE OUT:
                        END OF PICTURE

Appendices

★

AUTHOR'S NOTE: As the introduction explains, the design of this book precluded an entirely comprehensive account of the progress of *Secret People* from conception to (literally) screen. So that the appearance of each might be simultaneous, the book was in fact in the press while final trims or additions were being made to the film, and while music and sound effects were being added. Not wishing to vary the chosen approach by deserting the particular for the general, I have not provided any factual outline of these techniques; readers whose curiosity is stirred can find them adequately described in any of a number of reputable handbooks. Amongst this miscellaneous assortment of appendices, however, are two in particular which should give some idea of the stages through which a film passes after coming off the floor: Section II covers the period of editing, and Section III lists the further steps leading up to the picture's first public showing.

I should like to have finished the story with one of those three-line notices in which reviewers in the national Press are liable to dispatch the fruit of months, or years, of serious endeavour with the names of the leading players, a couple of wide epithets, and an attempt at an epigram. But this is one omission which the early reader, if he so desires, will doubtless be able to rectify for himself.

I—Treatment into Shooting Script

Two pages of the full treatment as expanded for the shooting script.

The cafe landing. MARIA is at the telephone. She is finishing dialling a number.

    MARIA: (in a low voice) Hullo.
                  Is that you, Louis?

Shot of Foley Street room - empty and left in disorder.
Police are searching. One takes off the receiver and listens...

Maria by the telephone on the cafe landing and realising that someone is at the other end of the line, repeats:

    MARIA: Is that you Louis?

    LOUIS: Hullo.

MARIA whirls round and LOUIS is standing behind her. He takes the receiver from her and replaces it.

    LOUIS: Come inside. We can't talk here.

They enter the living room.

    MARIA: They've got Rodd. He's at
                  Scotland Yard.

    LOUIS: So that's why he failed to
                  contact us. What did they ask you?

    MARIA: They showed me some pieces of
                  the silver case.

    LOUIS: Go on.

TREATMENT I
A page of the full treatment of
Secret People
(continued on page 204)

E.52   INT. ANSELMO'S CAFE. FIRST FLOOR LANDING. DAY (STUDIO)

MARIA is at the telephone. She is finishing dialling
a number.

E.53   INT. LOUIS' LONDON LODGINGS. DAY (STUDIO)

The Foley Street room has been left in disorder. Police
are searching. One takes off the receiver and listens...

E.54   INT. ANSELMO'S CAFE. FIRST FLOOR LANDING. DAY (STUDIO)

CAMERA STARTS on C.S. of MARIA as, still by the telephone
on the café landing, and realising that someone is at the
other end of the line, she says:

                    MARIA
               Hullo. Is that you, Louis?

                    LOUIS' VOICE
               Hullo.

MARIA whirls round, CAMERA TRACKING to M.S. LOUIS is
standing behind her. He takes the receiver from her and
replaces it.

                    LOUIS
               Come inside.

E.55   INT. ANSELMO'S LIVING-ROOM. DAY (STUDIO)

CAMERA STARTS on door of living-room as MARIA and LOUIS
enter the living-room.

                    LOUIS (controlled)
               How did it go?

                    MARIA
               They've caught Rodd. I saw him.

                    LOUIS
               So that's where he is. What else?

                    MARIA
               I...I didn't tell them about anyone
               except myself. They showed me some
               pieces of the silver case.

                    LOUIS
               Go on.

SHOOTING SCRIPT I
The equivalent page of shooting script
(continued on page 205)

From page 202

> MARIA: You must go away, Louis.
>
> LOUIS: Rodd was standing by to
> take us. It won't be so
> easy for us, now.
>
> MARIA: I'm not coming.
>
> LOUIS: What?
>
> MARIA: I identified the case.
> I told them I carried it.
> I said I'd give you all away.
>
> LOUIS: Maria! Are you mad?
>
> MARIA: I'm not with you, Louis.

LOUIS peers out of the window as far as the curtains will allow.
He sees STEENIE below.

> LOUIS: (hard) You are coming with us,
> Maria.
>
> MARIA: No, Louis.

LOUIS in a cold fury, throws his cigarette out of the window to
fall at STEENIE'S feet....

STEENIE becomes alert, begins peering up and down the street.
ELIOT and NEWCOME watch the scene.

STEENIE enters the cafe and strolls through and upstairs.

> ANSELMO: Wot 'e doing?

          MARIA
              You must go away, Louis.

          LOUIS
              Rodd was going to fly us out - you
              and me. It won't be so easy now.

          MARIA
              I'm not coming.

          LOUIS
              What?

          MARIA
              I identified the case. I told them
              I carried it.

          LOUIS
              Maria! Are you mad?

          MARIA
              I'm not with you, Louis.

      LOUIS goes to the window.

E.56   INT./EXT. ANSELMO'S LIVING-ROOM AND STREET. DAY (LOCATION)

       LOUIS peers out of the window as far as the curtains will
       allow. He sees STEENIE below on the pavement.
       LOUIS turns into the room.

          LOUIS (hard)
              You are coming with us, Maria.

E.57   INT. ANSELMO'S LIVING-ROOM. DAY (STUDIO)

          MARIA
              No, Louis.

E.58   INT./EXT. STREET AND LIVING-ROOM. DAY (LOCATION)

       LOUIS, in a cold fury, throws his cigarette out of the
       open window to fall at STEENIE'S feet...

E.59   EXT. ANSELMO'S CAFE. DAY (LOCATION OR STUDIO)

       STEENIE becomes alert, begins peering up and down the
       street.

E.60   INT./EXT. FLOOZIE'S WINDOW ABOVE DALY'S SHOP. DAY (STUDIO)

       CAMERA SHOOTING from the street towards Floozie's window
       above Daly's shop. ELIOT and NEWCOME watch.

E.61   EXT. ANSELMO'S CAFE. DAY (LOCATION)

       CAMERA SHOOTING from viewpoint of Floozie's window as
       STEENIE strolls into the cafe.

E.62   INT. ANSELMO'S CAFE. DAY (STUDIO)

       STEENIE enters the café and strolls through and upstairs.
       NUMBER ONE is sitting at the counter, lighting a cigarette.

          ANSELMO
              Wot 'e doing?

SHOOTING SCRIPT II

II—Script into Film

Although there are film-makers who maintain that the script's the thing, there is in fact no limit to the changes and developments which a film is liable to undergo after the ratification of the shooting-script. These may be divided into two classes: modifications made during shooting, and those decided on during editing. Directors vary in their belief as to the degree and rigidity of pre-planning advisable, as well as in their authority to make changes in dialogue and action on the floor. In general *Secret People* followed its script faithfully but without pedantry: where the actors unwittingly substituted phrases of their own, or for one reason or another suggested alternative lines, the director rarely insisted on adherence to the original. As far as the *découpage* went (the splitting of the action into shots and angles) he himself may be said to have used the script as a life-line—to be grasped and realised literally when conditions got rough, time pressed, or temperatures were soaring; to be varied, expanded, departed from when things were going smoothly and imagination was suggestive.

The editor's is more the bird's eye view. Both as the film is coming together while it is still on the floor, and as it is being finally shaped and trimmed after shooting, considerations of balance and accent become clear which were perhaps not apparent from a reading of the script. It may well be decided (as it was here) that a certain sequence is not going to be necessary and need not be shot at all; that another is not right and must be re-written and shot again; that an extra shot is required here, an added emphasis there. Though shots may still be added or retaken after the picture has come off the floor, it then becomes a question chiefly of refining away, judging the exact position and length of each set-up so that it will both carry the maximum single impact, and contribute most to the shape and flow of the whole. This is the time when faces are apt to be left on the cutting-room floor, even whole scenes discarded —not because they are necessarily faulty in themselves, but because the architecture of a film frequently turns out to differ from the architecture of its script. Incalculables, unforseeables have been added. A film—there is no denying it—is alive in a way that a script is not.

On its first assembly, or rough cut, *Secret People* ran one hour and fifty-four minutes. This, it was felt, was too long. The excision of a whole scene, together with wholesale paring throughout the film, got the length down by fifteen minutes; but, on re-assessment, it was decided that the cuts were too savage, shifting the emphasis too much from character to incident, and in some places obscuring the story's development. Replacements gave the film a final approximate length of one hour and forty minutes.

The notes that follow do not pretend to detail every change made in the script during shooting and editing. They include the principal cuts and modifications, together with any other points which seemed of likely interest. For generous help in their preparation I am grateful to Peter Tanner and his assistants, Alastair McIntyre and Roy Baker.

SEQUENCE "A"

A.1 Instead of starting on a close-up of the parcel, for instance, the film fades in to the postman in full length advancing down Morton Street. This obviates the "pull back" and the camera movement is reduced to a simple pan.

A.3 Taken from inside the café. No pan to Penny was necessary: Daly's shop becomes visible on the opposite side of the street as the parcel is removed from close-shot and focus is rapidly pulled.

A.4, 5 Telescoped into one set-up, shot on location, from precisely the opposite angle specified for A.5—shooting from the interior of the shop to include the street in the background.

A.7 Visual cut to A.8 after Daly's "Penny girl"—the rest of the dialogue being played over Penny putting the parcel on the kitchen shelf. *Dissolve* on Daly's "new government", cutting the last three exchanges.

A.10 Shot in two set-ups: first from the foot of the bed, then (for Penny's entrance) on the reverse angle, over Anselmo's shoulder. This was the first shot taken.
After shooting, Pietro's letter was adjusted to include the line: *An English poet has written "We must love one another or die"* . . . —the words which Pietro's voice repeats over the end of the film.

A.22 Dialogue and "business" with the gramophone omitted during shooting. Anselmo calls *Nora!* Camera pans to her as she falls.

A.23/4 Cut in editing.

A.25/33 Not shot. Scheduled for second-unit shooting, designs for these were in hand when it was decided that such a sequence at this juncture would weigh more than it would be worth.

A.36/7 Cut in editing. A.35 dissolves (from a close-up shot of Maria) into A.38.

A.42 Discussion on the floor changed Anselmo's reaction in this shot—he now suspects nothing until the parcel is opened. (The book title of *Mahatma Gandhi* was chosen as one which would have clear significance regardless of language.)

A.43 This shot, when viewed in sequence, seemed to call for an insert of Maria's hands continuing to examine the contents of the parcel. This was taken (using Valentina Cortesa's stand-in) during the last week of shooting, and cut in under Maria's words: *He hated violence and destruction.*

A.44 Cut to A.45 on Anselmo's: *You no longer come to my café.* The general trimming of this sequence was designed to emphasise its character as a prologue to the story proper.

A.45 The somewhat complicated set-up indicated in the script was simplified on the floor into a forceful triangular composition (Nora asleep—Maria at the door—Louis' photograph), with the camera static but for a slight track back as Maria closes the door. (Still on Plate IX.)

SEQUENCE "B"

B.2 Maria's last remark not used.

B.6 The only one of the café shots to be taken on a wide-angle lens—to include the required spread.

B.7 Split into two set-ups, dividing at Maria's: *He didn't mean me to do this all my life* . . .

B.8/11 Not shot: cut straight to stock shots of fireworks bursting, etc.

B.21 Not shot.

B.22 Anselmo merely mutters *Foreigners!* as Steenie moves away.

B.23 Split into a number of set-ups, to echo the rhythm of the sequence generally. The manager's *Blimey!* disappeared in editing.

B.36 An incident abstracted between first draft and final shooting scripts—Steenie, jostled in the crowd just below Anselmo and the girls, drops his revolver on the ground and hastily recovers it. When the picture was being edited, it was decided that the point was a useful one to make, so Geoffrey Hibbert was recalled and the incident was shot, in two close set-ups which avoided set-building or hire of crowd.

B.37 Anselmo and Nora are lost at the beginning of the shot. Maria is swept into the crowd by herself and carried along until Louis' hand reached into frame and grasps her by the arm.

B.40 Another close-up of Louis (from the tail-end of B.38) is cut in to the end of this dialogue.

B.50/3 This series of shots provides an interesting example of the way a sequence may develop, and of the variety of influences that may bear upon it. (The illustrations referred to, covering each set-up, are on Plate VIII.)

B.50 Shot as scripted, with the addition of another kiss at the end of the dialogue. Before the shot a few seconds of the back-projection plate (the view from the back of a car driving through a Paris street) are cut in to establish the location. During the dialogue the camera tracks in from mid-shot to a close-up as Maria and Louis kiss (Illustration 1). Straight cut to

B.51 This was first of all shot as scripted, in a long, continuous take. Starting with Louis and Maria in mid-close shot (Louis at the kitchen stove, Maria making herself up in the mirror beyond it), the camera tracked back as Louis came forward from kitchen to living-room to answer the telephone, panned and tracked over to the table for the remainder of the scene. On viewing, this gave a number of dissatisfactions. Without close-ups the scene was felt to lack intimacy; the actors were not particularly enthusiastic about their performances; Sir Michael felt that the angle from which the latter half of the scene was covered showed the exterior backing of sky and Paris roofs to disadvantage. A week later the scene was reshot, using four new set-ups. These were cut together with a relatively small portion of the original take, to produce the final continuity:

1. Close-shot of prawns frying in wire basket on the gas stove (Illustration 2). This provides a much easier transition from B.50 (without an optical) than the shot with which the scene originally opened.
   Pan up to Louis in close-up, with Maria behind in medium close-up. The telephone rings (Illustration 3).
   MARIA. *There's your 'phone call. Listen—* cut to

2. MARIA. *Tell him you're busy all day, will you?*
   Medium shot outside kitchen door; camera tracking back as Louis comes forward to the telephone: holds this angle for his conversation (Illustration 4). This is all that remains of the original take.
   On Louis' *Goodbye,* cut to

3. Long shot over the table (set-up as in Illustration 5). Maria comes forward from the kitchen with the dish of prawns; Louis enters from the left, camera easing over slightly with him.
   MARIA. *Bring the salad, please . . . Tell me, how long is it—*
   Cut, as Louis sits, to

4. Close-shot Louis (Illustration 6)
   MARIA. *—since anyone called you Louis?*
   LOUIS. *Not since the last time we mixed a salad.*
   (The business of tasting the salad was omitted.)
   Cut back to

5. Medium-shot over table.

MARIA. *Yes, I remember, with Marco interfering all the time. Dear Marco, what a wonderful charming person he was. Do you still see him?*

LOUIS. *No, I don't.*

MARIA. *I wondered how he would fit in with your hard life.*

Cut to

6. Close-shot Louis.

LOUIS. *He didn't fit in. He's dead.*

Cut to

7. Close-shot Maria (Illustration 7). Her line is omitted.

LOUIS. *Don't let's talk about that life, Maria* . .

Cut to

8 Close-shot Louis. (An extra cut which was introduced at a fairly late stage, when it was felt that Louis' first appearances in the picture should be strengthened.)

LOUIS. *. . . we have such a short time.* (Pause.)

9. Medium shot over the table, as Maria starts to cut bread (Illustration 5).

MARIA. *I am thinking . . . I might stay in Paris a little longer, you know?*

LOUIS. *I have to leave Paris to-morrow. That's what the telephone call was about.*

MARIA. *Maybe sometime you can come to London?*

LOUIS. *I don't know. Let's enjoy to-day. We must have a wonderful time.*

As he leans forward to kiss Maria, cut to

10. Close-shot Maria. Camera eases left as her cheek rubs against Louis (Illustration 8).

Quick dissolve to

B.53 *Vieux Chapeau*: dance music and crowd noise. Louis and Maria dance into frame in medium close-shot (Illustration 9. The frontispiece gives a further idea of this scene, before and behind the camera).

B.57 As filmed, this is a shot on Steenie rather than Louis: a long tracking shot up the side of the dance floor, covering Steenie as he makes his way through the dancers, the crane rising at the end of the shot as he mounts the steps to the exit.

B.59 Cut in editing.

B.61 Shot from the reverse angle to that specified—from in front of the bar, with Louis, Anselmo and his girl reflected in the mirror behind it.

B.63/8 Re-shot during editing, on a Thames-side location.

B.69 Woman's first sentence edited out.

B.70/2 Shot with considerable latitude. Nora's informal "exhibition" dance (in B70) was changed to a general carnival atmosphere in the club, with comic hats worn all round: the band playing faster and faster, exhausted couples dropping out until only Nora and Rodd are left on the floor, to win the prize of a bottle of champagne. This idea (which came to the director in his bath on the morning of shooting) gave rise to an ironic touch as Louis re-enters the club—the hat-check girl planting a straw hat on his head and taking him for a moment by surprise as she does so. Also inserted was an extra shot to "plant" the idea of the flashlight photograph: Anselmo giving instructions to the photographer to snap Maria and Louis at their table.

B.73/4 An extra scene, included in the first draft shooting script but dropped to save length, was re-inserted here by the director and shot on the same afternoon as B.51. The last frame of B72 is "frozen", and dissolves to the still photograph

lying on the table in Louis' lodgings: Louis' hand comes into frame and stubs out a cigarette in an ashtray full of ends. Cut to
Medium shot: Louis at the table. Rodd asleep on the bed behind. The alarm clock goes off; Rodd wakes and sits up.

RODD. *What's wrong? Are you ill or something?*

LOUIS. *No. I couldn't sleep.*

RODD (gets up and goes into kitchen). *Well, we'd better get going. Oh—Nora's going to get a bit of a shock when she sees us to-night.*

LOUIS gets up, walks to kitchen doorway, leans against the jamb. Camera tracks with him). *Listen Rodd. I don't want you to see Nora or Anselmo or Maria.*

RODD. *Not see her? But you nearly handed Nora to me on a plate last night.*

LOUIS. *Sorry. Those are orders.*

Fade-out.

SEQUENCE "C"

C.1 Fade-in to the photograph lying on the top of clothes, etc., in an open suitcase. Maria is unpacking, helped by Penny, in the bedroom; Anselmo watches. Maria's *He nearly jumped out of his skin* omitted; Penny's *What a shame!* becomes *Oh, he's shy!*

C.3 Penny's reaction at end of shot is changed to a laugh.

C.5 Shot as a continuation of C.4, camera on Penny and Frack, till Penny's *keeping 'em for the stew*, when cut to Louis and Maria in the kitchen.

C.21 Nora's "Pantorello the clown" re-dubbed as "Cairoli" and scene shortened (Illustration on Plate IX).

C.23 In two angles, one favouring Louis, one Anselmo, and all dialogue eliminated.

C.25 Sonia's *You'll have to lead the way*, etc., omitted.

C.35 The shot ends as Burnett calls into the room *It's in the bag, girls.* Through the door we see Nora and Maria hug each other in jubilation.

C.36/7 The beginning of this scene divides into three angles: close-shot of Louis emerging from the pub and looking down the street; long-shot of Maria waving Nora off in her taxi; medium-shot as Louis and Maria come together. This last shot continues, tracking before the artistes as they walk down the street, to the end of the scene (still on Plate X). Dissolve to C.38.

C.39 On the screen the room is both less dark and less bare than the script indicates. An extra set-up, covering the dialogue down to Maria's *A home of you own . . .* was taken on location, with Maria and Louis together at the window; a train passes as they speak. (Plate XI.)

C.40 Originally shot as written. When viewed in context (about half-way through shooting, when most of the first half of the script had been covered), it was decided that the dialogue was too concerned with principles and argument: something more emotional was needed. The scene was therefore re-written, and shot again during the last week of shooting.

MARIA. *How many times I've worried over you, Louis. And always afraid you were in danger.*

LOUIS. *You wouldn't want me to give it up?*

MARIA. *Oh no, of course not. Oh Louis, do you remember the old days, all our dreams? Do you still love me?*

LOUIS. *Yes, Maria. When I'm away from you, I think I forget how much I love you. Yes, I remember.*

MARIA. *Do you remember the first time you kissed me?*

LOUIS. *Yes.*

MARIA. *I was seven years old . . . And the first time you told me you loved me.*

210

LOUIS. *Up in the mountains.*

MARIA. *Yes, and all the time the donkey was eating your straw hat. But you didn't mind.*

LOUIS. *Maria!*

(They embrace.)

During editing, the latter half of this dialogue was cut, the scene ending on an embrace after Louis' *Yes, I remember.* An additional shot from the window is cut in here, as another train passes.

C.43 Rewritten before shooting. Starting on a close shot of the door from the inside, Louis' hand comes into frame, opens the door. He and Maria go out; as they reach the step, a clock strikes eleven. Louis looks at his watch.

LOUIS. *Eleven o'clock. Forgive me, Maria. I'd forgotten everything.*

MARIA. *Oh I can go home by myself, darling.*

LOUIS. *To-morrow I'll come to see you off—in your dress.*

MARIA. *All right. Before we part, Louis . . . Father's pen. I want you to have it now. His sword, remember?*

LOUIS. *A relic from another world. Forgive me. I must go. You'll be all right, Maria?*

MARIA. *Of course, darling. Goodnight.*

LOUIS. *To-morrow.*

C.44 After this shot, the scene-order of the rest of the sequence was rearranged in editing. C.45 was cut out, and C.44 dissolved directly into C.50. After the committee scene (shot with extra close-ups, establishing Charlie and Bill), we cut to C.49, eliminating C.46, 47 and 48.

C.49 Fade-out on Nora's *I'm much too excited.*

SEQUENCE "D"

D.4 Shot in two angles, with interpolated close-shots of Louis, somewhat mystified. Editing cuts include from the Scarf saleswoman's *Good afternoon* to the entry of the hairdresser; and from the hairdresser's *Let's have a nice cuppa* to the end of the shot.

D.7 Covered in four set-ups, as illustrated on Plate XII.

D.9/10 Not shot.

D.15 At this point, during editing, a sizeable portion of script was cut. This scene was finally replaced, but the following scene remained out; D.15 dissolving to the end of D.19, as Anselmo switches off the café lights and the girls return.

D.22 Covered in four set-ups. Long-shot of the girls by the window; medium close-shot; mid-shot of Louis; close-up of Maria.

D.24 "Location" directions for this sequence did not apply: it was shot in the studio. Although the script can give the dramatic shape of a scene such as this, and its main path of development, its exact construction is bound to depend on the appearance of the material when shot. Nora's dance, for instance, and (even more importantly) the clowns' routine were unknown when the script was prepared. It was to this sequence, dependent almost entirely on juxtaposition and cumulative impact of images and sounds, that the director was referring when he remarked how, in all his pictures, he liked to have one sequence at least of pure and unmistakeable "cinema".

D.30 An inspiration on the floor considerably eased this tricky moment—that Bill should slip the bomb into a cigarette carton.

D.48/51 See Plate XIII.

The remainder of the sequence is shot with the camera tipped off the horizontal.

E.18 Illustration on Plate XV.

E.21 Camera pans away from Charlie, and tilts up on to an exterior view of Scotland Yard.

E.22 Cut.

E.24 A close-up of Miss Jackson is interpolated as she shakes hands with Maria: the friendly but searching glance of the professional police officer.

E.25 In fact Sergeant Newcome, as cast, is much younger than Inspector Eliot.

E.27 As played, Maria is drinking from her cup as she is shown the case, and almost upsets it in her emotion.

E.29 Close-shot on Miss Jackson for her line.

E.36 Illustration on Plate XIV. Maria's last line omitted.

E.48 Cut after Eliot's *Well he won't give us away.*

E.57 Maria's *I'm not with you, Louis* became *No, I'm not.*

E.69 Cut to E70 after Louis' *Best place is the back bedroom.*

E.90 Extra close-shot cut in, of Bill throwing the bomb.

E.91 Extra close-shot, on floor level, as Number Two kicks the bomb back into the cellar.

SEQUENCE "F"

F.1 These images, as they blur in and out of focus, are accompanied by the heavily magnified soundtrack of a heart beating.

F.4 The Sister alone is seen. Sister's line is changed to *That's your name now.*

F.5/7 Omitted in shooting.

F.8 MISS JACKSON. *Well, I hear you're really better now . . .*

F.11 Rewritten before shooting. Maria asks Miss Jackson: *Why do they keep calling me Lena Collins?* Miss Jackson: *I've told you already, but you keep forgetting. How much do you remember?* Maria starts hesitantly, then the screen blurs. Maria's *It's all so strange and misty* cut.

F.12 Omitted.

F.17/19 Rewritten before shooting and much contracted. Shot with a general set-up favouring Maria, and two others favouring Miss Jackson and Inspector Eliot.
Eliot's last line omitted.

F/20a Omitted, but Miss Jackson's line kept

F.23 Fade-out on this shot.

F.26 Miss Jackson's line changed (for obvious reasons) to *The café's hardly changed.*

F.27 Not Back Projection. Taken from a car driving past the café, Anselmo and Penny cleaning outside—from Maria's viewpoint, but she is not in the shot.

F.28 Illustration on Plate XIV. Maria starts: *Dear Anselmo . . . Strange—you live in a street for years . . .* etc.

F.29 Name of the theatre changed to "Doric Theatre"—the result of deciding, for economy and convenience, to shoot the ballet at the Bedford, Camden Town, instead of attempting a reconstruction of the Gaiety, Dublin.

The ballet programme with which the sequence starts is not Maria's; lowered, it reveals the stage from the back of the circle as the dancers appear on the stage. In editing, the length of the ballet was reduced by about a half—bringing the focus more consistently on to Nora.

F.35 Omitted; replaced by two silent close-shots of Maria and Miss Jackson watching the dance. (Shot in the studio.)

F.40 Illustration on Plate III.

F.50 Rewritten to conform with an ending, for some time discussed, which would bring Nora back to the theatre for a second house.

Nora, dressed for the street but in stage make-up, comes to the stage-door . . .

NORA (signing autographs). *How's business, Gerry?*

DOORKEEPER. *Business is it, Miss? You'd better go round the front and see them pouring in. It's worse than the Galway Races.*

NORA. *That's wonderful* (To the fans) *I'm sorry, I must go. Goodbye.*

FEDOR (joining Nora). *Hey! My Guinness. It's on you to-night.*

NORA. *To-morrow, Fedor. Sorry. I'm meeting someone.*

FEDOR. *You know what Anselmo said.*

NORA. *Strictly business.*

FEDOR. *You haven't much time.*

DOORKEEPER. *Only forty-five minutes, Miss.*

NORA. *Shan't be long, Gerry.* (To Fedor) *Buy you a Guinness to-morrow.*

FEDOR. *O.K. Nora.*

F.59 Irish Inspector's second speech cut to: *Sergeant, Miss Jackson and I will follow Miss Collins. When the second car comes, send it round to the other side of that patch of ground.*

F.64/5 This moment of recognition is strengthened by two extra close-shots, taken in the studio. First, on Maria's hands, then camera tilting up to her face and in to a huge close-up of her eyes. Second, close-up of Louis, out of which he rises into

F.65 as shot on location.

F.66 and following. Script divisions in a scene such as this are not intended to be rigorously followed in editing. In this case the editor has at his disposal four set-ups, covering most of the dialogue up to Steenie's intrusion. The scene as screened represents his assembly (based on the dramatic rhythm of performance as well as the indications of the script) of these four viewpoints: a close-shot on Maria; a two-shot on Louis and Nora; a three-shot favouring Maria; and a three-shot favouring Louis and Nora.

F.70 Maria's speech rewritten. *Nora, my darling—Nora—listen to me. They don't think I'm a saint. They lied to make you work for them. They lied to me too. They don't fight with clean hands. They just kill. They don't mind who they kill. Nora, there's nothing but horror for you with Louis' people. Don't throw yourself away.* A close-shot of the knife open in Steenie's hand was added in the studio.

F.71 Here again the film differs, or rather develops considerably from the script. In close-shot we see Maria in Nora's arms, murmuring incoherently: *Nora . . . Nora . . . try to understand . . . believe . . .* Then a shot of Louis; he calls to Nora as the police approach. From his viewpoint we see Nora look round: *I'm not with you, Louis.* (Maria's line from scene E.57, omitted when that scene was shot and transferred to Nora by the director on the night location.) The police break in and the Inspector grips Louis by the shoulder; he makes no attempt to escape; his cigarette falls from his fingers (Illustration on Plate XV). A brief shot (taken in the studio) covers Steenie's arrest by the police. The camera shoots down on to Nora: she looks up to the Inspector: *The blood . . . it won't stop.* Close-up of Louis. Back to Nora as she is helped to her feet by Miss Jackson. For a moment she clings to her, weeping; then allows herself to be led away, the camera tracking before them. This brings us to the end of the script, but not to the end of the film as eventually agreed on. As described in the Diary, a first alternative ending dissolved back to the theatre, to show Nora dancing again in her ballet, watched by Miss Jackson. This was in fact shot, but not liked. The clue to the ending finally adopted was given by F.72—Brentano's fountain pen fallen from Maria's handbag. It was decided to end with this, the symbol of the values for which Maria had died, and to super-impose over it some fitting words in Brentano's voice. A quotation from a poem by Auden was chosen (in conscious defiance of chronology) and this was worked into Brentano's letter to Anselmo (A.10/1). The end of the film thus cuts from Nora being led away by Miss Jackson, to a shot of the ground at Maria's feet, littered with the spilled contents of her handbag. The camera tracks in to a close-up of Pietro Brentano's battered fountain pen.

Brentano's voice: *We must love one another or die.*

III—Music

There is no incidental music in the film, the only music is natural to the demands of the story. This necessary music is intrinsic to the story and reinforces its emotional development.

There are two principal themes. One is composed as a folk tune of the country from which the principal characters come. The other is the theme of the two lovers, Maria and Louis, and is also meant to be native to their country of origin.

Theme A is first stated on a barrel organ at the beginning of the main titles; after a few bars a full orchestral version of theme B takes over. Theme A returns on the barrel organ at the opening of the film. It reappears as a gramophone recording in a popular version played by a small orchestra: at appropriate moments theme B is introduced on the same record, particularly at Maria's first appearance in Anselmo's café.

Again at the Paris Exhibition this arrangement is played by a military band, with theme B accompanying the first meeting of Maria and Louis.

In the Vieux Chapeau night-club theme B is played as a tango with a lyric in French (written by Marcel le Bon).

Towards the end of the film Nora dances in a ballet first with the corps de ballet and then in a pas de deux. Theme A is used for the first dance and theme B for the pas de deux. Theme B is used also to accompany the cast list at the end of the film.

IV—Steps After Shooting

POST SHOOTING PERIOD DATES

"SECRET PEOPLE"

TO: SIR MICHAEL BALCON

FROM: HAL MASON

No. 1 Issue—16th July, 1951

	INCIDENT	REMARKS	DATE
1.	1st Rough Cut for viewing by Sir Michael Balcon	...	5th July, 1951
2.	Viewing by Composer and Sound Cutting Dept.	...	15th July, 1951
3.	Final cut for viewing by Sir Michael Balcon	...	Fri, 27th July, 1951, 2.15 p.m.
4.	Music Session	To be completed by 21st Sept, 1951	...
5.	Post-Synchronising	To be completed by 20th July, 1951	...
6.	Title Cards	In hand by 20th July, 1951	...
7.	Dubbing	...	Completed by 7th Sept, 1951
8.	Negative Cutting	To be in hand by dubbing time	25th Sept.—9th Oct., 1951
9.	First Synchronised Print	...	16th October, 1951
10.	(a) Preview(s)	To be arranged	...
	Synchronised copy delivered to G.F.D.		
11.	(a) Neg. Mute and Sound delivered to G.F.D.		
	(b) Fine Grain Print delivered to G.F.D.		30th October, 1951
	(c) Separate Sound Neg. delivered to Denham Labs		
12.	Trailer	To be viewed by N.S.S. 31st July, 1951	To be completed by 25th Sept, 1951
13.	Censor	Double head showing	7th August, 1951
14.	Trade Show (London)	...	...
15.	Trade Show (Provinces)	...	...
16.	Press Show	...	...
17.	West End Première	...	...
18.	General Release	...	...

V—Studio Plan

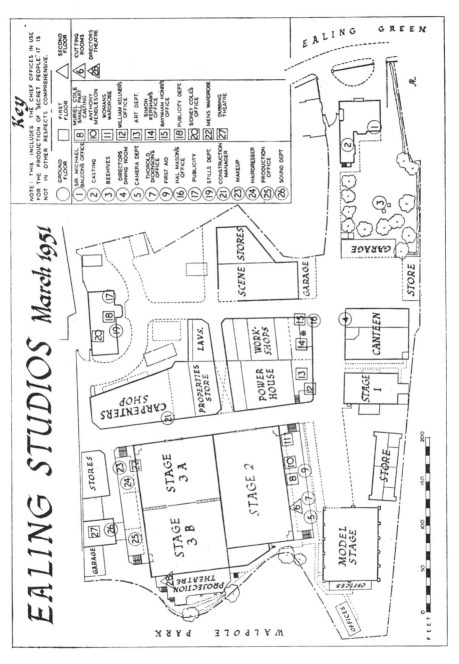

EALING STUDIOS March 1951

Key

NOTE: THIS INCLUDES THE CHIEF OFFICES IN USE FOR THE PRODUCTION OF 'SECRET PEOPLE'. IT IS NOT IN OTHER RESPECTS COMPREHENSIVE.

○ GROUND FLOOR

□ FIRST FLOOR

△ SECOND FLOOR

① SIR MICHAEL BALCON'S OFFICE
② CASTING
③ BEEHIVES
④ DIRECTORS DINING ROOM
⑤ CAMERA DEPT
⑦ THOROLD DICKINSON'S OFFICE
⑨ FIRST AID
⑯ HAL MASON'S OFFICE
⑰ STILLS DEPT.
⑲ CONSTRUCTION MANAGER
㉑
㉓ MAKEUP
㉔ HAIRDRESSER
㉕ PRODUCTION OFFICE
㉖ SOUND DEPT

⑧ MURIEL COLE SMALL PART CASTING
⑩ ANTHONY MENDLESON
⑪ WOMANS WARDROBE
⑫ WILLIAM KELLNER'S OFFICE
⑬ ART DEPT.
⑭ SIMON KERSHAW'S OFFICE
⑮ BAYNHAM HONRI'S OFFICE
⑱ PUBLICITY DEPT.
⑳ SIDNEY COLE'S OFFICE
㉒ MENS WARDROBE
㉗ DUBBING THEATRE

⑥ CUTTING ROOMS
㉘ DIRECTORS THEATRE

EALING GREEN

WALPOLE PARK

SCENE STORES

GARAGE

CARPENTERS SHOP

PROPERTIES STORE

LAVS.

POWER HOUSE

WORK-SHOPS

STORES

STAGE 3 B

STAGE 3 A

STAGE 2

PROJECTION THEATRE

CANTEEN

STAGE 1

MODEL STAGE

OFFICES

OFFICES

STORE

GARAGE

STORE

FEET 0 50 100 150 200

217

VI—SECRET PEOPLE : *Full Credit Titles*

The following are the full credits for Secret People *as they appear on the screen.*

Fade in the J. Arthur Rank Organisation Presents title
Dissolve to:

1

An Ealing Studios Production

Released through General Film Distributors Limited (small)

* (Make also three versions for (1) Canada and Western
Hemisphere [excluding U.K.])

(2) Australia

(3) U.S.A.

*1. Delete "Released through General Film Distributors Limited".

2. Substitute "British Empire Films" for "General Film Distributors Limited".

3. Substitute "A Universal-International Release" for "Released through General Film Distributors Limited".

2.

VALENTINA CORTESA   SERGE REGGIANI

with AUDREY HEPBURN

in

---

3.   Thorold Dickinson's

SECRET PEOPLE

from his original story

(with acknowledgments to Joyce Cary)

M.P.A.A.15342   G.B.-Kalee   R.C.A.
and Seal   (Emblem)   (Emblem)
                      Sound System   Sound System

Copyright MCMLI by Ealing Studios Limited

4

with

CHARLES GOLDNER

MEGS JENKINS

IRENE WORTH

REGINALD TATE

MICHAEL SHEPLEY

ATHENE SEYLER

5.

and
SYDNEY TAFLER
GEOFFREY HIBBERT
JOHN RUDDOCK
MICHAEL ALLAN
JOHN FIELD
CHARLIE CAIROLI AND PAUL

The events and characters portrayed in this film
are fictitious and any similarity to any incident,
name or individual is coincidental.

6.

Screenplay by
THOROLD DICKINSON
WOLFGANG WILHELM

Additional Dialogue by Christianna Brand

7

Production Supervisor
HAL MASON (½ total screen)
Director of Photography
GORDON DINES, A.R.P.S.
Editor
PETER TANNER

8.

Unit Production Manager	RALPH D. HOGG
Sound Supervisor	STEPHEN DALBY
Camera Operator	CHIC WATERSON
Assistant Director	SPIKE PRIGGEN
Recordist	ARTHUR BRADBURN
Continuity	PHYLLIS CROCKER
Costume Designer	ANTHONY MENDLESON
Special Effects	SYDNEY PEARSON
Make-up	ERNEST TAYLOR AND H. WILTON
Hairstyles	BARBARA BARNARD

Art Director
WILLIAM KELLNER

9.

Music by
ROBERTO GERHARD
played by the
PHILHARMONIA ORCHESTRA   (all names on this
card to be same
conducted by   size)
ERNEST IRVING
choreography by
ANDREE HOWARD

219

Produced by
SIDNEY COLE

Directed by
THOROLD DICKINSON

Ealing Studios Trade Mark

Roll-up Cast List

Maria	VALENTINA CORTESA
Louis	SERGE REGGIANI
Anselmo	CHARLES GOLDNER
Nora	AUDREY HEPBURN
Nora (as a child)	ANGELA FOULDES
Penny	MEGS JENKINS
Miss Jackson	IRENE WORTH
Inspector Eliot	REGINALD TATE
Sergeant Newcombe	NORMAN WILLIAMS
Manager of the British Pavilion	MICHAEL SHEPLEY
Mrs. Reginald Kellick	ATHENE SEYLER
Syd Burnett	SYDNEY TAFLER
Steenie	GEOFFREY HIBBERT
Daly	JOHN RUDDOCK
Rodd	MICHAEL ALLAN
Fedor Luki	JOHN FIELD
Charlie Cairoli and Paul	THEMSELVES
General Galbern	HUGO SCHUSTER
Frack	LIONEL HARRIS
Bentley	ROLLO GAMBLE
Bill	JOHN PENROSE
John	JOHN CHANDOS
Charlie	MICHAEL RIPPER
Woman on London Committee	YVONNE COULETTE
Members of Paris Committee {	JOHN MANSI / JOHN GABRIEL / OLGA LANDIAK
Galbern's Bodyguard {	FREDERICK SCHILLER / PHAEDROS ANTONIO
Queval	GASTON RICHTER
Plain Clothes Men {	DEREK ELPHINSTONE / EDWARD EVANS
Postman	JACK MCNAUGHTON
Shoe Shop Girl	INGEBORG WELLS
Hairdresser	BOB MONKHOUSE

220

Scarf Woman	HELEN FORD
Manicurist	ANN LANCASTER
Floozie	GRACE DRAPER
Little Man	BERTRAM SHUTTLEWORTH
Waitress	PAMELA HARRINGTON
The Valet	JOHN ALLEN
Nursing Sister	BAY WHITE
Irish Police Inspector	JOE LINNANE
Irish Police Sergeant	SAM KYDD

Made at Ealing Studios, London, England

VII—Biographical Notes

THOROLD DICKINSON. Director and Screenwriter. Born London, 1903. Educated Clifton and Keble College, Oxford. Entered films in 1926, working for George Pearson in Paris. Worked as editor in most British studios in the thirties; finally supervising the cutting rooms for Basil Dean at Ealing. Directed his first film at Ealing in 1937: *The High Command*. In Spain 1938, where he made *Spanish A.B.C.* and *Behind The Spanish Lines* with Sidney Cole. Since directed: *The Arsenal Stadium Mystery* (1939); *Gaslight* (1940); *The Next of Kin* (1941). From 1942 organised production of Military Training films. 1943-5: directed and collaborated on the screenplay of *Men of Two Worlds*. 1948-9: *The Queen of Spades*.

SIDNEY COLE. Producer. Born London, 1908. Educated Westminster City School and London University. Started at Stoll Studios, 1930. Then with various studios, including G.P.O. Film Unit. At Ealing graduated to position of supervising editor, where he edited the first films of both Thorold Dickinson (*The High Command*) and Carol Reed (*Mr. Midshipman Easy*). Co-directed *Spanish A.B.C.* and *Behind the Spanish Lines* with Thorold Dickinson in Spain, 1938. Amongst pictures edited: *Gaslight, Pimpernel Smith, Nine Men, San Demetrio, London*. 1944 appointed Associate Producer, Ealing Studios. Amongst his films: *Dead of Night, Against the Wind, Scott of the Antarctic*. 1949, co-director on *Train of Events*. Associate Producer *Man in the White Suit* (1950-1).

WOLFGANG WILHELM. Screenwriter. Born Austria, 1906. Entered films in Berlin, 1926; script department U.F.A., 1928. Came to Britain 1933. Worked on screenplay *Farewell Again* (London Films); *This Man Reuter* (Warners). 1940: collaborated on *Freedom Radio*. 1941: *Pimpernel Smith*. 1942: *Squadron Leader X*. 1944: *Great Day, Land of Promise*. 1945: *I See a Dark Stranger*. 1947-8: Collaborated on screenplays *Captain Boycott, The End of the River*. 1949-50: Screenplay, with Thorold Dickinson, for *The Mayor of Casterbridge*.

GORDON DINES. Cinematographer. Born London, June, 1911. Entered films 1926 as camera assistant at Elstree. Worked on *Blackmail, The Informer, The Constant Nymph, Rome Express*, etc. Joined A.T.P. Studios at Ealing as camera operator, then director of photography on Gracie Fields, George Formby pictures. 1940-6 served in Royal Navy. Rejoined Ealing as head of camera department. Director of photography on: *Nicholas Nickleby, Train of Events* (coll.), *The Blue Lamp, Pool of London*.

PETER TANNER. Editor. Born Surrey, 1914. Educated Westminster. Entered films 1933 in cutting rooms—Ealing, Elstree, Isleworth. 1936 appointed editor, Fox Films, for whom he worked in London and Hollywood. 1939 returned to Britain, edited *Sabotage at Sea, Lady from Lisbon* (British National). Joined Verity Films as supervising editor. Amongst pictures: *Steel, We Serve, Land of Ulster, Out of Chaos, Five Towns*. Joined Ealing to work on *Scott of the Antarctic*. Since: *Kind Hearts and Coronets, The Blue Lamp, Pool of London, One Sinner*.

WILLIAM KELLNER. Art Director. Born 1905. Took university degree (Architecture) in Vienna; built there, then in Berlin, Paris and London. Naturalised British subject. Joined film industry 1942, part-time working at Denham on *Cæsar and Cleopatra*. To Ealing in 1947 as art director on *Saraband for Dead Lovers*. Pictures since: *The Queen of Spades* (from Oliver Messel's designs), *Kind Hearts and Coronets*, *A Run for Your Money*, *The Wooden Horse*, *The Lavender Hill Mob*.

VALENTINA CORTESA. Actress. Born Milan, 1924. Studied first as an art student in Rome, then at the Rome Academy of Dramatic Art. Started film career in 1941, making many pictures simultaneously with frequent stage appearances. Amongst her films: *Americano in Vacanza, I Miserabili, Il Notte Porta Consilio*. Played in English in the American *Cagliostro (Black Magic)*, and the British *Glass Mountain* and *Shadow of the Eagle*. To Hollywood in 1949 for: *East of the Rising Sun, Thieves' Highway, The House on Telegraph Hill*. In Europe, 1950, made *Donne Senza Nome*.

SERGE REGGIANI. Actor. Born Reggio-Emilia (N. Italy). 1922. Family emigrated to Paris. Started acting as a film extra; enrolled at the Paris Conservatoire; made his debut in the theatre in 1940. Varied experience as dancer, singer, straight actor. Plays included *Britannicus, Les Parents Terribles, Emily Brontë* (as Branwell), *Les Justes*. First featured film appearance in *Carrefour des Enfants Perdus* (1943). His many films include: *Les Portes de la Nuit*, the unfinished Carne-Prévert *La Fleur de l'Age, Manon, Les Amants de Verone, La Ronde, Anita Garibaldi* (in Italy), *Casque d'Or*.

AUDREY HEPBURN. Dancer and Actress Born Brussels, Belgium, 4th May, 1929. Father, British. Mother, Dutch. Studied dancing at Arnhem (where she lived throughout the war) and made first appearance at illegal concerts in aid of Dutch resistance movement. After liberation studied ballet in Amsterdam and London. Danced in chorus of *High Button Shoes* and *Sauce Tartare* in London, followed by solo appearance in *Sauce Piquante*, cabaret and television work and first film role in *Laughter in Paradise*. Other films: *One Wild Oat, The Lavender Hill Mob, Young Wives' Tale, Nous Irons à Monte Carlo* (in France). Title role in *Gigi*, New York stage production from the novel by Colette.

CHARLES GOLDNER. Actor and producer. Born Vienna, Austria, 7th December, 1900. Studied at the Academy of Dramatic Art, Vienna. First stage appearance, at age of 18, at the Lustspiel Theatre, Vienna; later worked for Max Reinhardt in Vienna and Berlin; producer and actor in Zurich and Milan until 1938. In London since 1941 appearing at the 'Q' Theatre in *The Velvet Touch*. Scored a success in *Watch on the Rhine* on the stage. Films include *One Night With You, Black Magic, The Shadow of the Eagle, Give Us This Day, I'll Get You For This*.

GEORGE ALLEN & UNWIN LTD
LONDON: 40 MUSEUM STREET, W.C.1
CAPE TOWN: 58–60 LONG STREET
SYDNEY, N.S.W.: 55 YORK STREET
TORONTO: 91 WELLINGTON STREET WEST
CALCUTTA: 17 CENTRAL AVE., P.O. DHARAMTALA
BOMBAY: 15 GRAHAM ROAD, BALLARD ESTATE
WELLINGTON, N.Z.: 8 KINGS CRESCENT, LOWER HUTT